THE WAY IT WAS

THE WAY IT WAS

A History of Gigha

Catherine Czerkawska

BIRLINN

This edition published in 2016
by Birlinn Limited
West Newington House
10 Newington Road
Edinburgh
EH9 1QS

www.birlinn.co.uk

First published as
God's Islanders: A History of the People of Gigha in 2006

ISBN 978 178027 385 3

British Library Cataloguing-in-Publication Data
A catalogue record for this book is available from the British Library

Typeset by Initial Typesetting Services, Edinburgh
Printed and bound by Grafica Veneta
www.graficaveneta.com

There's such a lot that needs to be done. We have a million pounds to return to the Land Fund. It's a lot of money. But we're out here in the Western Isles where hardy men survive and I think we'll do it. There is no doubt in my mind at all that each and every person here will do their very best to see that it is paid back, because a Highlander is always known for his straightness and honesty. We're helped by a lot of professionals. Many a thing I've done in sixty-six year, but I've never bought an island.

Willie McSporran MBE, discussing the state of Gigha and repayment of the £1 million loan that helped the islanders to buy their home in 2002

★

Contents

Appendices

List of Illustrations

Acknowledgements

Thanks are due to:

The Isle of Gigha Heritage Trust

Willie and Ann McSporran, for many years of friendship, for so much invaluable information and for lending me their photographs

John Martin, for showing me the great well and the holy stone and for lots of other information besides

Rona Allan, for answering all my questions with kindness and patience

Lorna and Archie McAlister, for their help and hospitality (and for the tows, twice in thirty years isn't bad!)

The late Angus McAlister, whose presence is much missed

The late Vie Tulloch, for her enthusiasm and knowledge

Kenny and Malcolm McNeill and the late Betty McNeill

Kenny and Betty Robison of Springbank

Freddy and Val Gillies

Russell and Caroline Town

Andy and Viv Oliver

And everyone else from the island who has shown us so much kindness over the years

Also to:

Angus and Kenneth Allan for the loan of photographs, and for all the detailed accompanying information about them

Seamus McSporran of Gigha and Ardrishaig (the man of the fourteen hats)

Glasgow University Hunterian Museum, Paisley University Library, the National Library of Scotland and *The Scots Magazine*

Angus Martin and the Kintyre Antiquarian and Natural History Society for their excellent online resource, the *Kintyremag*, which so often lead me back to primary sources

The Scottish Arts Council for the bursary that made this project possible and which came at exactly the right time; to the Authors' foundation, for their invaluable help towards initial research; and to the Royal Literary Fund

Finally, as always, thanks to my husband Alan and son Charles as well as family and friends for their help and support

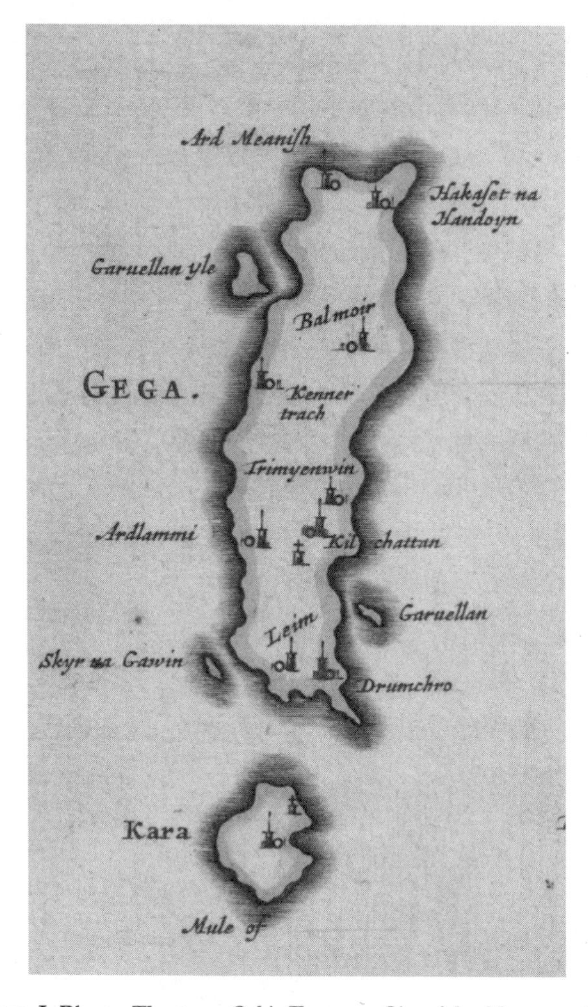

From J. Blaeu, *Theatrum Orbis Terrarum Sive Atlas Novus, vol. 5.*
Reproduced by permission of the Trustees of the National Library of Scotland.

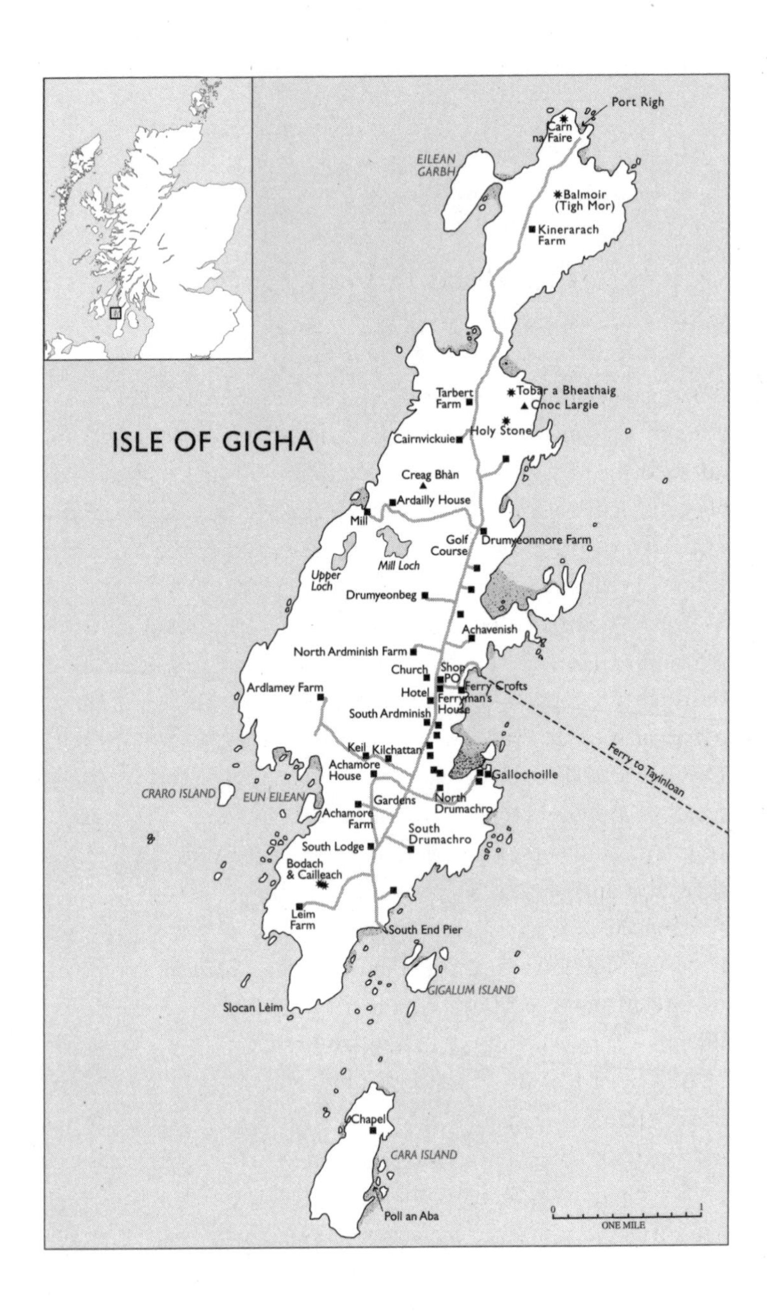

ISLE OF GIGHA
Port Righ
Carn na Faire
EILEAN GARBH
Balmoir (Tigh Mor)
Kinerarach Farm
Tobar a Bheathaig
Cnoc Largie
Tarbert Farm
Holy Stone
Cairnvickuie
Creag Bhàn
Ardailly House
Mill
Golf Course
Drumyeonmore Farm
Mill Loch
Upper Loch
Drumyeonbeg
Achavenish
North Ardminish Farm
Church
Shop
PO
Ferry Crofts
Ardlamey Farm
Hotel
Ferryman's House
South Ardminish
Keil
Kilchattan
Achamore House
Gallochoille
Ferry to Tayinloan
CRARO ISLAND
EUN EILEAN
Gardens
North Drumachro
Achamore Farm
South Drumachro
South Lodge
Bodach & Cailleach
Leim Farm
South End Pier
GIGALUM ISLAND
Slocan Lèim
Chapel
CARA ISLAND
Poll an Aba
0
1
ONE MILE

1

The Road to Gallochoille

There is an old saying that when the gorse is in bloom, kissing's in season, the reason being that there is some kind of gorse, or *whin* as it is called in Scotland, in bloom, just about all year long. Even midwinter sees a scattering of yellow flowers, but in spring, on the Isle of Gigha, a glittering surfeit of yellow dazzles your eyes to the point of pain.

At the heart of the island, across from the main gates of Achamore House, you will find the road to Gallochoille, a narrow rutted track, leading towards the sheltered east coast, a typical Gigha track, with gorse flowering on either side. Driving or walking, the effect of these high banks is uncomfortably intense. On a sunny day, and the island has many sunny days, when clouds leap over this sliver of land to shed their rain on Kintyre, the scent is an intense coconut. I always find myself wondering what people equated it with before they had ever smelled coconut oil and whether anyone, travelling to foreign parts, exclaimed that the coconut smelled exactly like the whins back home in Scotland.

At the end of the road to Gallochoille is a sheltered harbour, one of so many, where old creels lie heaped together, incongruous splashes of blue and orange twine on the grass. A pair of big grey mullet are often to be seen, winding their way sinuously along the sandy bottom. These fish are practically uncatchable. They will come up and nose at the bait but never take it if there is a hook attached. Like the wise fish of Celtic legend, they seem to have some sixth sense that protects them. Up on the rise, to the right of the harbour, are the remains of an old dun, or hill fort.

Between the jetty, home to a few small boats, and the dun, a couple of houses lie huddled away from the worst of the weather. These buildings are some 200 years old, but there is evidence that Gallochoille was once the site of a much older laird's house, although I have never seen anything to indicate its location.

The smaller of the cottages at Gallochoille used to be the home of the late and much missed Vie Tulloch, until she moved to one of the newly built houses in Ardminish village. She lived with a whippet called Jazz, as slender, elegant and full of character as she was herself. The unrenovated cottage was simply furnished, homely, comfortable and crammed with books and paintings. Down there, Vie created many beautiful woodcarvings, usually working to commission and often using found woods from the shores of the island, with wildlife as her inspiration.

Long before we were married, my husband and his brother-in-law were running their own small diving business in Scottish waters. They were fishing for clams in the perilous Sound of Gigha when the engine of *Striker*, their small boat, broke down. Some local fishermen came to their rescue, among whom was a certain Willie McSporran and a very young Archie McAlister, but as well as towing ropes, they threw a six-pack of beer aboard which greatly impressed the weary divers. Alan and David spent some time on Gigha while the engine was being repaired, mostly with spare parts, cannibalised from an elderly vehicle, by that same Willie McSporran.

Cue forward some years to the birth of our son in 1986. My husband had been talking about Gigha for as long as I had known him. It was his talisman, an iconic place, which had somehow lodged itself in his mind. Whenever it was in the news, usually because the whole island was on the market yet again, like a house where nobody can quite settle, he would say 'One day I'll take you to Gigha.' Sometimes he would vary it with, 'If I was a multi-millionaire, I'd buy Gigha.'

By that time, he was working as a yacht skipper, for a small Clyde-based company, so – although there was little chance of him ever becoming a millionaire – the island was a regular stopping-off place for him, the first port of call after a yacht rounded the Mull of Kintyre, on its way north and west. But I had never been there, although I had heard plenty about it.

When our son was old enough to appreciate beaches and paddling and fishing, the time suddenly seemed ripe and we booked a holiday, staying in the post office, which also houses the island's only shop, and which was then run by Seamus and Margaret McSporran, brother and sister-in-law of the redoubtable Willie. Seamus, incidentally, was the legendary man with all the jobs. Various newspapers would photograph him, wearing his many hats: shopkeeper, hotelier, taxi driver, undertaker, part-time policeman, sub-postmaster, fireman, ambulance driver. He had a total of fourteen different occupations at one time, and I've often wondered if the Dennis Lawson role in *Local Hero* – charming hotelier, accountant, general Mr Fix-it – wasn't modelled to some extent on Seamus.

I found myself enchanted by Gigha. It is hard to analyse why such a small place should be so magical. Partly it is the landscape itself, which is varied and peculiarly pleasing: an island some seven miles long by a mile and a half broad, and yet with twenty-five miles of coastline. There are white sandy beaches and bays, rocks and islets in plenty. Moreover, the interior of the island is as complex as the coastline, full of hidden valleys and large numbers of archaeological remains, testament to a long history as a place of human habitation. Partly it is the people, who are friendly and welcoming. And partly it is something else, some quality that is still hard for me to define.

Like Prospero's Isle, Gigha seems to me to be an enchanted place, one which contains within a relatively small area hundreds of reminders of the past. It is a peculiarly resonant place, where many layers of history and tradition are overlain, one on top of another. Nothing is lost, and everything, in some sense, remains. It is a place where the islanders walk a tightrope between history and hope for the future, and so far seem to be doing it with a great deal of grace. Over successive visits, I found myself fascinated by the relationship between the complex landscape of the island and the equally complicated history of the islanders. Then, some years ago, I was commissioned to write this new history of the people of the island.

Several excellent books have already been written by Gigha devotees and it was to these, as well as to primary sources, that I turned for my first overview of island history. Anderson's *The Antiquities of Gigha*, first published in 1939, is a detailed account of the archaeology of the island as precisely observed and recorded by the Revd R.S.G. Anderson. Most of Anderson's archaeological work was concerned with Galloway, which seems to have been where he was based, but he made an exception for Gigha. His descriptions of the archaeology of the island are most valuable because he made accurate observations and measurements at a time when the landscape had changed very little and his book, small enough to slide into a pocket, accompanied me on many an island foray.

Kathleen Philip's paperback, *The Story of Gigha: The Flourishing Island*, published by the author, in Ayrshire, in 1979, is an astute piece of research into island history, particularly that of the McNeills. *Life on God's Island* by Freddy Gillies is a highly readable account of everyday life on the island within living memory. Freddy also writes about the fishing industry of Kintyre from direct personal experience, while Vie Tulloch researched and wrote about the flora and fauna of the island over many years.[1] Social historian Angus Martin has written extensively about the folk history of Kintyre itself and the fishing industry in Argyll and the islands, with plenty of references to Gigha, and his recent book *Kintyre Country Life* has been a helpful resource for me. There are also several accounts of the island from travellers in preceding centuries, not least an early mention from Martin Martin in his *Description of the Western Isles of Scotland Circa 1695* as well as Captain T.P. White's *Archaeological Sketches in Scotland*, which has a whole chapter devoted to Gigha in the nineteenth century, with particular references to the carved stones at Kilchattan.

What emerged very clearly from all these texts was that those who write about the island do so with the affection that seems to strike everyone who visits or who lives there. However, I still felt that there was a great deal that I would like to explore, and so much that could be deduced about the history of the island, not just from documentary evidence, but from the landscape itself. I researched my book over a period of years, but work was slow and the demands of earning a living kept intervening. Then a grant from the Authors' Foundation, and a generous bursary from the Scottish Arts Council allowed me to devote much more time to writing the book. *The Way it Was* is the result.

This is an account of the island and the people who inhabited it, broadly covering the years from prehistoric times to the present day and organised as much by place as by chronology. I hope that it covers some territory not addressed before, as well as analysing certain factors of island history in a new way. With a Master's in Folk Life Studies from Leeds University, I have always had an interest in place names and their origins, and even in my plays and my fiction, I have found myself turning to social history and prehistory for my themes and stories. Consequently, this is very much a personal exploration, a writer's account of a much-loved place, as well.

I set out to explore the history of Gigha through the people who lived there and the places where they lived. Not unexpectedly, I found that the changing settlement patterns of the island, where and how people lived, reflected the changes in the nature of the successive people who had made Gigha their home. As well as drawing on the work of others, I have made my own investigations, and have compared events on Gigha with happenings in the wider Scottish world. But invariably, I have gone back to the island, time and time again, because it is there, among the islanders now, and among the remnants in stone of those who have gone before, that I have found the most convincing answers to some of my questions. Gradually a picture has emerged that involves the fascinating warp and weft of a small community evolving and changing over the many hundreds of years of human occupation, a community moreover that seems to me like a microcosm for developments within a wider Scotland.

Gigha has always had a certain strategic importance. When, during the first millennium, Gaelic-speaking émigrés from Ireland established their kingdom of Dalriada, with Dunadd, near Lochgilphead, at its heart, the Kintyre peninsula was a significant area of settlement, and Gigha, with its excellent, sheltered harbours, was seen as a pearl of great price for more than one group of warrior-bearing ships. This geographical accident has been its blessing and its curse throughout its long history and this is still, to some extent, true, although for different reasons. For much of the second half of the twentieth century, the island was perceived to be 'unspoiled', a remote and beautiful paradise island for a string of more or less suitable owners. Then, with the new millennium came another profound change. Over the past few years, for better or for worse, Gigha has often been in the news as the place where the islanders have at last contrived to buy their own island. We have seen Gigha, along with a handful of small Scottish communities, leading the way, showing us just how our perceptions of land use and community ownership in Scotland might develop, so that our small, vulnerable settlements can remain not just viable, but thriving monuments to co-operative living. None of this has been easy, and there have been teething troubles. But it seems to me that it is better than the alternative.

This book is dedicated to so many people who have been helpful to me over all this time, and they are named and credited in the acknowledgements. But some of them deserve a more special mention. The first is the late Vie Tulloch herself, who on one of our sporadic visits to the cottage at

Gallochoille, showed my son the wings of the birds of Gigha. By that time my husband was also working as woodcarver, so visits to Vie were full of conversations about the properties of different woods and the advantages or otherwise of power carving tools. On one memorable afternoon in her sheltered garden, within tantalising sound of the sea, she brought out a plastic bag and shook it onto her table. We were astonished to see that it contained dozens of wings, of many species, some of them feathered, most of them tiny configurations of bones, and a few avian skulls as well. She told our fascinated son that she had picked most of them up on the beach. The birds were long dead, and had been washed ashore. As a sculptor she needed to know exactly 'what lay beneath' and how it all worked. It struck me then that, as a writer of fiction, I too needed to know what lay beneath. In researching and writing this book about Gigha, I think that the same desire applies. It is an attempt to find out what lies beneath, how it is constructed, the pattern of it, and how it all fits together, how it all works.

My second invaluable helper was a man I met late in the day, but I had seen him on television, talking about the island at the time of the community buyout. John Martin had been the estate joiner and carpenter on Gigha for many years and consequently is familiar with every inch of the place. I found him to be a man after my own heart in his appreciation of the landscape and history, his sense of what is precious about the island and his vision for its future.

'When the idea that we could buy the place ourselves was first mooted,' he says, 'some were for it, and some were not. There were those who were afraid. It was rocking the boat in a big way. But I thought why not? What could possibly be worse than what we have now, with all its uncertainty? We have to go for it.' John Martin showed me parts of the island that I would never otherwise have discovered, and for that I am extremely grateful. Besides these, Rona Allan, who worked for the Gigha Heritage Trust has answered my many email questions with kindness and patience and has always done her best to answer them as fully as possible.

Finally, profound thanks must go to Willie McSporran MBE and his wife Ann. Without Willie's invaluable input and help, so much would simply not have been possible. I feel privileged to count him among my friends. If Gigha is sometimes called God's Island, Willie is certainly one of God's islanders and of him it can truly be said that – like his island – when God made him, he threw the mould away.

2

Sailing to an Island

For all that the little island of Gigha lies only a few miles west of the Scottish mainland, for all that it lies slightly to the south of the city of Glasgow, there is a sense of otherness about it, a truly Hebridean air. A ferry trip of some twenty minutes will carry you from Tayinloan on the mainland to Ardminish on Gigha, but that mainland is the Kintyre peninsula, which in itself has many of the qualities of an island. In the late eleventh century, Norse king Magnus Barelegs, so called because he dressed in the Scottish way, agreed with King Malcolm of the Scots that he could have sovereignty over all the islands around which he could sail. Magnus ordered his men to carry his longship across the isthmus at Tarbert so that he could lay claim to it. As Magnus's own saga says 'the king himself sat in the boat and took control of the helm and so he got possession of all the coasts'.

The perception of the casual visitor is that Gigha is a remote place. Scotland's geography constantly cheats the unwary. Distances that look easy on a map, turn out to be difficult in reality, even given the benefit of new and better roads. A surprisingly large number of Scots may have heard of the island, but have no idea where it is, and many of them don't even equate the spelling with the pronunciation of the name itself.[1]

Even from the central belt of Scotland, the journey to Argyll entails a long drive, always heading north and west. The long haul of busy Loch Lomondside and the aptly named Rest and Be Thankful can be circumvented by taking the car ferry from Gourock to Dunoon and driving up the side of Loch Eck, but even so it is a long way. In the process, you will pass a succession of sea lochs, with picturesque shorefront roads switchbacking past snug, white or grey stone cottages, most with Gaelic names and well-tended hillside gardens. There are guesthouses and craft shops selling small souvenirs of Scotland. It is a picturesque drive on a fine day, and a *dreich* one when the clouds tumble down the hills and envelop the view in drizzle.

Inverary is pretty, but faintly anomalous, in its worn elegance. Perhaps because it was such a stronghold of the much-favoured Clan Campbell, the town has a self-possessed and prosperous air, although nowadays that prosperity is due to the fact that it is awash with tourists visiting its museums and the castle. For many years Gigha was strategically important because it was poised between Argyll and the rest of the Isles, and was torn between Campbell and Macdonald interests, with the McNeills of the island struggling to maintain their own position between two more powerful neighbours, always an unenviable position.

Tarbert is the last real stopping-off place of any size on the way to Gigha, a busy, bracing little port that clambers up a hill, with a handful of fishing boats still doggedly pursuing the diminishing resources of these waters and Italian fish and chip shops where the young man behind the counter is as likely to be a visiting cousin from Naples as a local lad. The Traditional Boat Festival attracts many visitors.

Tarbert is where you suddenly scent the western sea, and know that you are within striking distance of Gigha. Tarbert is the place where (as well as Campbeltown) the farmers of Gigha used to bring their animals to be sold at market. It is also the occasional resort of those islanders and visitors alike who miss the last ferry to the island, or who are stranded on the mainland on those occasions when the ferry is storm-bound.

Beyond Tarbert the road negotiates the exhilarating switch-back of the Kintyre peninsula until at last it begins to offer you tantalising glimpses of Gigha, long and low on the horizon, 'like some mysterious hump-backed animal' as I wrote in my novel. The island is small and on all but the clearest of days is a mysterious and misty smudge that somehow belies its comparative closeness to the mainland.

At Tayinloan there is a right turn, down to the ferry, past several newly built houses, one knock-on effect of the recent community buyout on Gigha. The way is long and straight, and the lozenge of the Gigha ferry, with its bright CalMac colours, can be seen all the way across, as it heads for the terminal, its progress slightly erratic, as the skipper avoids the submerged rocks beneath. At the terminal is the Ferry Farm B & B and a welcome tearoom. The roll-on roll-off ferry *Lochranza* was built at Hessle near Hull in 1987 and is a flat-bottomed Loch Class boat, specially designed for these short crossings. Gigha is only some three miles from the Kintyre mainland but all the same, the Loch Class isn't a particularly easy craft to manage in the high winds or powerful tides that beset these waters and just occasionally sailings have to be cancelled.

Freddy Gillies, writing about Gigha as seen from the inside, describes the potential problems. 'Sometimes, on the weather shore, conditions appear to be fine, with the wind blowing off the land, and little in the way of motion to be seen. However, it can be so very different, three miles across the Sound, on the lee shore.'[2]

Ferries (for at one time there were several serving the island) have always been very important to the economy and sustainability of Gigha, as they have been for all our Scottish islands. As far back as the eighteenth century, small ferries (wooden rowing boats or clinker-built sailing boats or a combination of both) ran from the mainland to *Caolas Gigalum*, the sheltered strait running between Gigha itself and the tiny islet of Gigalum at the south end of the island, though not, of course, on the Sabbath. Old records tell us that occasionally the rules were broken, much to the chagrin of the church authorities, but they were still slow to blame the ferryman himself, being content to censure those who had persuaded him to take out his boat on a Sunday, for whatever reason. It is hard to decide whether this was in recognition of the difficulty of his position, or because antagonising somebody so important to the smooth running of the community might be inadvisable, even for the elders of the kirk.[3]

The first ferries on Gigha must have been purely for the practical use of the islanders in their interactions with the mainland and with the neighbouring islands of Jura and Islay. Visitors would not have been of much importance, although a handful would have toured for map-making purposes, or purely out of personal interest. Among them was one Martin Martin, who styled himself a 'gentleman'. A native of Skye, he spent his later years in London, but visited the Western Isles, including Gigha, in 1695 and wrote a fascinating account of them.[4] His book 'a very imperfect performance' according to a scathing Boswell, was nevertheless one of the inspirations behind Dr Johnson's 1773 tour of the Hebrides.

The Reverend James Curdie, minister of Gigha for some fifty years, gives us an inkling of affairs with regard to ferries, in his account of the state of his parish, written in the 1840s. 'Between Gigalum and Gigha, there is a sound which affords good anchorage for large vessels and is frequented by Her Majesty's Cutters and by vessels going to and from England and Ireland. There is a ferry from each of the properties to Tayinloan on the mainland.' Two ferrymen, one from each major estate on the island, plied their boats between the island and the mainland, one from Gallochoille, and one from Achnaha, which was the name of the old Ferry House and Croft, *Achadh na h-Atha*, the field of the kiln.[5] He continues, 'A steamer which plies between West Loch Tarbert and Islay passes the north end of Gigha thrice a week in the summer and once a week in winter and a boat attends for the purpose of landing passengers.'[6]

Curdie, for all that he is describing a time some 150 years distant, still manages to conjure up a picture of an island in the thick of things, a busy place, with good harbours and useful anchorages. The Gigha of history was just such a place. Even so, these craft were generally visiting the island for practical purposes and the islanders had little thought of encouraging visitors, who might be coming purely for pleasure, or of taking economic advantage of them if they did venture across the sound. The concept of mass tourism was one which would arrive not just with the industrialisation of the central belt of Scotland, but only when people had the financial resources to make such excursions feasible. It was in the late 1800s and throughout the 1900s, that Clyde steamers began to call at the island, bringing with them, as to the whole of the Clyde, an influx of tourists.

The little 1812 *Comet* – to be seen in Port Glasgow to this very day, albeit sadly grounded in the town centre – ushered in the age of steam and steamers to the Clyde, soon to be followed by the spring and summer exodus 'doon the watter' for working people anxious to escape the confines of the city, in search of a breath of clean sea air. The first steamer that we know for sure called at Gigha was MacBrayne's *Lochiel*, in 1877. The *Glencoe* swiftly succeeded her, and the paddle steamer *Pioneer* began visiting the island in 1905. In 1895 the pier at *Caolas Gigalum* was reconstructed, so there must have been enough maritime traffic by this time to make this a feasible proposition.

Kathleen Philip, writing about the island in 1979, gives us an account of Willie Orr, who became official ferryman to the island in 1871.[7] She describes an oil painting dated 1880, which shows the large open boat which Willie was accustomed to row, 'with its huge oars, and a dozen or so passengers, wet, windblown and anxious at the prospect of scrambling up onto a larger vessel, or at the equally alarming prospect of clambering ashore over slippery, weed-glazed rocks on Gigha.' William Orr died in 1895 at the age of sixty-six and is buried in the old graveyard at Kilchattan on the island.

Then, in 1885, island owner Captain W.J. Scarlett appointed one John Wotherspoon as ferryman. His duties were onerous, or they seem so to us today. He was to carry 'the proprietor and his family, friends and servants, and such tradesmen and others that may be employed on the proprietor's affairs.'[8] At certain times of the year, he had, as well as having to work on his own croft (a fairly full-time job in itself), to be available to work on the estate if his services were needed. If he went any further from the island than Tayinloan, on the mainland side, he had to provide a substitute ferryman out of his own pocket. He was responsible, moreover, for 'such boats as Captain Scarlett may happen to have on Gigha at any one time, whether for fishing or any other purpose', so he must have had shipwrighting skills. He had to give a month's notice if he wished to leave his position, but for his part, the more fortunate Captain Scarlett could dismiss him out of hand, if he chose to do so.

John Wotherspoon's remuneration for all this was the tenancy of the Ferry Croft, a house that lies down on the shore at Ardminish Bay and which is now a self-catering holiday house, in the ownership of the Gigha Heritage Trust. At the time Wotherspoon was allocated the tenancy of the croft 'except that piece surrounding the house of Mrs McNeill, which she rents' and the 'ferry dues'.

The Ferry Crofts, incidentally, sit atop a rather interesting mound, opposite the site of the old kilns (probably used for kelp burning) to which the old place name *Achadh na h-Atha* refers. Here, in the spring of the year, before the vegetation has grown too high, it is possible to see the distinct remains of an old causeway leading up from the shore and straight onto the flattish top of the hillock on which the two houses stand. It is well away from the present entrance to the site, although whether this was for the purposes of dragging a small boat within the precincts of the croft, or an even older entrance to some dun that may have been sited here, it would be impossible to say without excavation.

The ferry dues, which John Wotherspoon collected, probably made the whole enterprise worthwhile, and they are set out in some detail in Curdie's account. They make fascinating reading, not just for the wealth of detail, but in the pictures they conjure up of the actual journeys that must have been undertaken. One passenger travelling alone would be charged two shillings, but where more than six passengers voyaged together, the trip cost them only sixpence each. It was therefore better to go in a group, if possible and this is exactly what must have happened on many occasions. A horse cost a fairly hefty four shillings – there would have been a great many horses on the island at this time – with every additional horse costing two shillings, although one wonders exactly how many horses the ferry could have transported at any one time. A cow cost only two shillings with every additional cow costing a shilling but it is pretty certain these were the small, hardy, native cattle of Kintyre, and not the larger beasts of today. Sheep were much less expensive at threepence per head, whereas a pig cost two shillings. If there were more than four pigs, John Wotherspoon could only charge four pence each.

One wonders whether fellow travellers might have been wise to avoid the pig days altogether, particularly in view of the fact that these same animals are perceived to be notoriously unlucky at sea, to the extent that, even nowadays, a fisherman is reluctant to name them on board a boat. To embark with them must have seemed a peculiarly risky business to an islander born and bred. Bulls and stallions, which (perhaps fortunately) only occasionally had to be transported, cost double fare. The problems of transporting bulls to and from the island continued over many years, as we shall hear in a later chapter.[9] Two one-year-old stirks[10] were equal in price to one cow. Barley was sixpence a quarter to transport and a telegram, which usually brought bad news, and was therefore a permissible expense, even in days when every penny counted, cost two shillings. John Wotherspoon must have been a hard-working and obliging man, because he was employed as ferryman for Captain Scarlett for many years, until the outbreak of the First World War, when a man named Archibald McCougan took over.

Kathleen Philip observes that the people of Gigha could readily access the 'labour hungry mainland and the Clyde estuary' as well as having the means to travel much further afield in search of a new life.[11] Although we perceive the island to be remote, for the islanders themselves, of course, this has never been the case and there has always been interaction, not just with the mainland and with neighbouring islands, but with Ireland too.

Particularly during and after the famine years, 1845–8, there was a great demand in Ireland for seed potatoes, and we know that Gigha was a source of excellent potatoes, grown in the sandy fields beside the shore. We know too that Irish merchants came specifically to buy them. Stories are told that these merchants would occasionally use the good Gigha crop to place on the top of sacks of potatoes of inferior quality, to attract buyers.

There seems to have been a fairly regular trade between Ireland and Gigha, on the part of potato merchants and fishermen, and there are intriguing stories of the visiting Irish quite deliberately setting out to make pilgrimages to various ancient sites on the island. These Irish, whose relationship with the West of Scotland was of ancient standing, seem to have had specific knowledge of the sacred sites of Gigha, persisting well into more modern times.

As Anderson points out 'The Irish who visited Gigha in great numbers for trade up to the last century . . . seem to have had a much deeper interest in the tales and folklore of the island than the islanders themselves'.[12]

As we shall see, the relationship between the old religion and Celtic Christianity was a curiously tolerant one, and remained so in Ireland, long after religious changes in Scotland, with a concomitant stern impulse to sweep away 'superstition', resulted in the destruction at worst, and the desertion at best, of many ancient sites and their related customs and beliefs, not to mention a wealth of songs and stories.

We can deduce therefore, that there was a constant to-ing and fro-ing between Gigha and the mainland, between Gigha and the nearer Scottish islands, between Gigha and Ireland. In the twentieth century, puffers, like the *Vital Spark*[13] of literary and later television fame, came to and from the island, bringing coal, gravel, fertilisers, animal feedstuffs and various other supplies for the use of the islanders. Besides this, islanders would have travelled to and from the great herring fisheries of Loch Fyne, the Clyde and Kilbrannan Sound, as well as further afield, but the 'silver darlings' that came to these waters in such profusion are long gone and will never come again.

In addition to this day-to-day traffic, larger ferries plied the Islay and Jura route and called at Gigha on the way. Freddy Gillies mentions a paddle steamer called *The Pioneer*, which visited the island from 1905 until 1939. Then came the *Lochiel* and another *Pioneer*, which visited the island in the 1970s. Before the reconstruction of the pier at *Caolas Gigalum*, visitors would have been intrepidly transferred from ship to shore in rowing boats, and one wonders not just what they made of Gigha, but what Gigha made of them.

The story of the dedicated Gigha ferries themselves, as opposed to sporadic visiting vessels, is one of gradually increasing size. A nineteen-foot sailing boat called the *Broad Arrow* gave place to the slightly bigger *Village Belle* and *Jamie Boy*, both with that splendid and reliable Kelvin petrol paraffin engine beloved of all West Coast fishermen, and much preferred by them to the East Coast Gardner. Later came the *Shuna*, and the *Cara Lass*, and then in 1979 Caledonian MacBrayne began to run a car ferry from Gigha to Kennacraig, using the Island Class ferry the *Bruernish*. Before the slipways were constructed vehicles had to be craned ('worryingly', somebody told me 'especially when you loved your car') on and off the *Bruernish* at the south end of the island.

Nowadays, the ferry brings the bin lorry, various forms of fuel including oil, the daily papers, deliveries for the shop, and the tourists, including coach parties, who come in large numbers to visit the famous gardens at Achamore. Islanders go on shopping trips to Campbeltown, Oban or Glasgow. The island fire engine goes to the mainland, for maintenance. The ferry also brings the children to and from school each day. Some years ago, the secondary school children spent their weeks in Campbeltown and only came home at weekends. There was no ferry early enough to get them to school on time. This meant that they had to stay with friends and relatives or, less satisfactorily, in mainland hostels, and – so islanders said – mentally, they had already left the island by the time they had left school.

This situation was perceived by many as a deterrent to families wishing to settle on Gigha, because so many parents were wary of sending their children away from home at such a young age, particularly where incoming families had no convenient mainland relatives to provide accommodation and support. Now, however, there is an extra, early morning ferry during term time, courtesy of the Scottish Executive, a gift to mark the community buyout by the islanders, back in 2002. Cynics might wonder if the ever-increasing risks and costs associated with keeping children away from home for weeks at a time, in an ever more litigious age, might have outweighed the costs of laying on an extra ferry, but whatever the truth of the matter, the ferry has given another much-needed boost to the island's younger population.

Travelling to Gigha is always an exciting business. No matter how many times I visit this island, I always feel the same thrill of anticipation on boarding. The ferry takes its slightly erratic path across the Sound of Gigha, avoiding the many submerged rocks, and docks at the tiny terminal, at one arm of Ardminish Bay. From there, the road skirts the seashore and then slopes gently up towards Ardminish village with its shop and its hotel. In my mind's eye, I always associate Gigha with a certain vivid palette of spring and summer colours, by no means as subtle as might be expected. Autumn and winter are darker, and bleaker and more bracing, although the spring comes early to Gigha, here on the western edge of the country.

Sailing to the island, as so many have done before me, as so many will do after me, never fails to excite me. There is something about the white sand that worms its way into every crevice of your life and you know instinctively that those Irish fishermen and merchants were right in their determination to visit and revisit the ancient holy sites of this place. In quiet moments, the island is a small, insistent presence at the back of your mind and you think that this was how it was for them, too. They would come to work, and stay to worship, or simply to commemorate a long-standing relationship.

Few places are as you expect them to be. But I still remember my first sight of Gigha, that magical moment when the island resolved itself from a nebulous, misty mass on the horizon to a real landscape. And yes, it felt familiar. It was as though I had seen the place before. Disembarking from the ferry felt like a homecoming. All these years later, sailing to this island still feels like coming home.

3

The Lost Language of Stones

The prehistory of Argyll in general, and Gigha in particular, is a pattern of migration and consequent interaction between indigenous people and incomers, all contained within a small geographical area. Although Argyll itself was once – and for a very long time remained – a place of political significance for the rest of Scotland, it is now an area that tends to be dismissed as marginal. This may be due in part to its complicated geography – an intricate network of sea lochs, peninsulas and islands – but it means that there has been relatively little formal exploration of the prehistory of this place, and the research that has been done seems to throw up many disagreements and anomalies.

The island of Gigha had its own part to play, perhaps because it was so perfectly poised between the mainland and the more remote isles. It was a place of sheltered and accessible harbours and anchorages, a fertile island where successive invaders or peaceful settlers – from mainland Scotland, from Ireland or from Scandinavia (what the Gaels, in ancient song and story used to call the Kingdom of Lochlin) – might pause, draw breath, take sustenance and occasionally think again.

It may be useful, at this point, to summarise the prehistory of this area with Gigha at its heart. Some five or six thousand years ago, when the Mesopotamians were inventing the written word, Kintyre and its nearby islands, including Gigha, were inhabited by a Mesolithic, or Middle Stone Age, people about whom very little is known, except that they were hunter-gatherers who moved from place to place with the changing seasons. Scattered archaeological finds paint a picture of self-sufficient communities that nevertheless traded in raw materials such as flint (hard to come by in Scotland, except for the occasional piece washed ashore by wind and tide), which they needed for making tools and beautifully crafted arrow-heads. Arrow and axe heads have been discovered by farmers throughout Gigha, and are probably preserved in many an old farmhouse kitchen or dresser drawer. From discoveries elsewhere, we know that the dug-out canoe was used throughout prehistory and we can assume with some confidence that such boats were in use on islands such as Gigha which were, after all, well within sight of the mainland, and other islands such as Jura and Islay. The plentiful fish and shellfish of these waters would have been the dietary mainstay of these communities.

The time spans are so great that we can't say with any certainty when people began to congregate in more settled communities or whether – as seems likely – this process had begun even before the introduction of agriculture as a way of life. Characteristic of various West Coast settlements are the 'huge accumulated middens of discarded shells of over two dozen species of mollusc' described by Stuart Piggott.[1] These shell middens seem to have been deliberately allowed to build up around the dwellings, and, however unpleasant in modern terms, when our sense of smell is, if not keener, then more discriminating, would have provided a certain amount of insulation from wintry weather. These people were not so very different from us in their need for shelter, warmth and a place to call home.

People hunted with bows and arrows, spears and harpoons. They fished and they made basketwork lobster pots. They slept on beds of heather, possibly with skin canopies, to keep out the rain, which must have dripped from inadequate roofs. They would have constructed recognisable 'dressers' from wood or stone, as storage for food, and also as places where treasured pieces of pottery might be displayed. They built (and almost certainly maintained, day and night) fires in the middle of their huts and, like the inhabitants of these islands (Gigha included) at a much later date, would have simply allowed the smoke to find its way out as best it could. Piggott goes on to observe, however, that the agriculture, which had brought a more settled way of life, had come about not as an intrinsic development, but because of 'actual immigration of farming communities who brought with them . . . the practical means of setting up a farm in new territory.'

Little remains on Gigha of the settlements of these earliest Scottish farmers. They would have come in small numbers, by boat, from the mainland, bringing sheep, cattle, perhaps goats as well, with them. The progression may well have been from Ayrshire to Arran, from Arran to Kintyre, and from Kintyre to the near western islands, including Islay, Jura and Gigha. Certainly it would have been a short hop from mainland Kintyre to Gigha, which would have been an enticement on the horizon to these early settlers, and a fertile discovery when first they pulled their canoes onto its white sands.

We know that they buried their dead in chambered tombs, circular or oblong (long chambered tombs seem to have been favoured in the Western Isles) collective graves, built above ground, with stone-roofed passages and a covering mound. Often, however, these burial sites were used over long periods of time, and by later peoples, who treated their dead differently, so the sites themselves can be confusing. There is some evidence that, in general, they constructed their houses in timber where possible, but for religious or ceremonial purposes, they would build in stone: tombs, individual standing stones, pairs or circles of stone.

The language of these stones is lost to us and although all kinds of meanings, from repositories of hidden energies, to Stone Age observatories, have been posited for them, we have no real key to deciphering them. We know these people by their monuments, but very little about their domestic lives. One possible reason for this may be that present-day settlements, villages, houses have overlain all evidence of past habitations. What suits a settled and agricultural people now may well have suited a reasonably settled and agricultural people all those years ago, in the form of the availability of fresh water, fertile land and a sheltered setting. It is quite likely that some of the current Gigha farmhouses are situated on top of much older settlements.

One thing we can say with any certainty is that the northern part of the island was as important as the south, if not more so. There are burial cairns, standing stones, cists and cup-and-ring-marked stones in plenty, beyond the bays at Tarbert, where the island narrows to a small isthmus, a natural boundary, and it seems no accident that the settlement of this northern part of the island was continued into historic times, so that Pont's early map of the island, published by Blaeu in 1654, finds the largest dwelling or settlement on the island situated up there: *Balmoir*, meaning the large town or *Tigh Mor*, as Willie McSporran describes it, meaning the large croft. Just after the community buyout, when some of the older houses on the island were undergoing renovation, a curious carved stone was discovered, being used as the lintel stone of a fireplace in an old cottage up at the north end. A few years ago it was still on the island, under cover in joiner John Martin's workshop, a broad, flattish stone with such a miscellany of carvings that it seems well-nigh impossible to place it to any one period. There are very ancient symbols: a sun wheel, a cup-and-ring mark; there is what looks like a quatrefoil cross, and something that echoes another symbol found elsewhere on the island, at the so-called Holy Stone at the base of Cnoc Largie, in the shape of a symbol that Anderson calls 'a short sword with a looped handle'[2] but John Martin describes much more credibly, as a stylised depiction of a whale. The stone has a hunting scene – a deer, with just possibly a dog coming after – which seems later than the sun symbols, as well as some much later lettering, with the names of the people who incorporated it into their house, above their hearth, perhaps in the belief that the stone itself had some power to bring luck and protection. I can't help feeling that this unique and interesting artefact might have been better left in situ since there is not yet an island museum to house such relics safely.

Moving on from these earliest agriculturalists, we find that some 4,000 years ago the people of Kintyre were beginning to explore the uses of metal to construct not just practical tools, but ceremonial and artistic pieces as well. It may be more accurate to say that people were arriving whose knowledge of metalworking gave them a distinct advantage over those whose whole technology involved stone. Deposits of copper were found nearby at Crinan and Loch Fyne. Gold was present (albeit in very small quantities) in Scotland, but like the rest of Britain, these early Scottish metalworkers would eventually have to look to Cornwall or Europe for supplies of tin, without which bronze could not have been made. It was therefore essential to establish and maintain trade routes since the sourcing of materials would have gone hand in hand with the need to pass skills and knowledge to each new generation.

Early in the second millennium BC, we can detect the influence of incomers, both in the type of pottery recovered (drinking vessels known as beakers) and in burial customs, which began to involve individual burials in a single grave or cist. These incoming people were archers, and sometimes flint-tipped arrows are found in burials, presumably in case they were needed in the next life. They were also farmers, who cultivated the land and grew cereals. They buried their dead in a crouching foetal position, knees drawn up to chin, and sometimes buried their pottery beaker vessels along with the deceased, perhaps containing drink for the journey to the afterlife, as well as weapons. There is evidence of this kind of burial from all over Gigha, as well as on the whole of Kintyre but because so many graves have been destroyed over the years and their stones have been removed for agricultural purposes, it can now be difficult to decide whether certain burials were chambered cairns, later, individual cists or combinations of both, where an old grave has been used for new purposes.

Carn Ban, or the white cairn, half a mile south of *Port Righ*, in the far north of the island, is probably an example of a chambered cairn. The site is a few yards from the beach, about thirty feet above sea level. Anderson tells us that 'In 1792 the cairn was denuded of almost all its stone by dykebuilders, who were unaware of its purpose until they laid bare the internal chambers. They told how when they opened these, they were greeted with an intolerable stench which obliged them to drink spirits and keep on the windward side, and when they omitted these precautions, they had violent headaches', which suggests some build up of toxins in the air of the tomb.[3]

The central cairn contained four chambers, grouped in pairs, two lying parallel, and two more placed less regularly, and covered over with slabs. One of these was found to contain a complete skeleton but at the time when Anderson was describing it, only a few bones remained, which were reported to have belonged to a young adult. The cornerstone of one of the cists had grooves cut in the surface, which Anderson describes in some detail, obviously wondering whether they were intended as an inscription of some sort. It was customary for these people to decorate the stones of their graves (sometimes even those stones which were never intended to see the light of day) so the grooves may have been intentional.

The original account of the opening of the cairn at *Carn Ban* also states that urns were found when the grave was opened. One of them is described as being just over five inches high by five inches in diameter at the mouth, narrowing to two inches at the bottom, and made of fired clay. Anderson also points out that to the north of the group are the remains of three short cists 'evidently a secondary burial' which may, of course, be a much later use of what was perceived even then to be a sacred site.

Near Tarbert Bay, where the island narrows, and to the left of the current road to the north of the island, there is the *Uaigh Na Cailleach* or Old Wife's Grave, which is a burial cairn of some sort. As we shall see, the *Cailleach*, or old woman seems to have some deep significance for the island. Tradition has it that this particular old woman is an Egyptian, by which may be meant a gypsy, or traveller. On the other hand, some versions of the tale have it that this is the grave of a nun. All versions agree that the lady will object strongly to being disturbed (a not uncommon belief).

> *Cailleach mi as Innis Tuirc*
> *Mo chorp aig Cachaleith nan Draodh*
> *Mur tog sibh bhur n-eallaich dhiom*
> *Fagaidh mi bhur cin air raon.*
>
> I am an old woman from Innis Tuirc.[4]
> My body lies at the gateway of the Druids.
> If you do not lift your burdens off me
> I will leave your heads on the field.[5]

But which came first, the burial mound or the tradition of the Old Wife, would be hard to decide. What is perhaps most striking about this grave is the firmly held belief that a woman of some importance is buried here.

On the west side of the island, just inland from *Port a Chleirich* (Port of the Cleric, now named as *Port a Chleire* on the Ordnance Survey Pathfinder Map[6]), which lies between Kinererach and Tarbert, Anderson reports another large stone cist, covered by a cairn with other possible cist burials in the vicinity. North of Highfield Farm on the lower slopes of Cnoc Largie, is a field called *Achadh nan Caranan*, or cairn field, where a single cairn is now located on the map, but which

Anderson reports as being the site of three cairns and which from personal observation also seems to me to be a threesome.[7]

Moving further south, we find that Anderson speaks of 'a number of trench cists or their sites' in Ardminish itself, The most notable, still to be seen to this day, lies on the little rise directly opposite the school and, during excavation, a large flint knife was found there. As has been noted, this was not an indigenous material, and must have been imported, in raw form, or perhaps from elsewhere in the British Isles, as a desirable artefact, the treasured possession of some minor leader who may have called the island, or part of it, his own.

Pennant, visiting Gigha in 1772 states that there was a cairn near to a large standing stone or 'great rude column' at Kilchattan, the site of the old ruined church to the south of the village of Ardminish.[8] This, incidentally, was not the Ogham stone, which is still to be seen on the height that rises steeply above the church, and which Pennant describes separately, but was a much larger stone which has completely disappeared, although Kathleen Philip suggests that some of it may remain in the shape of a stile that leads into Achamore woods, and has 'three large cut stones as steps which are quite different in texture and working from the stones in other stiles.' She could be right. It was reasonably common for standing stones to be broken up and used for other purposes. Often a bonfire would be lit beneath the toppled stone, and then cold water poured onto the heated rock, which dramatic and rather dangerous process would cause cracks to appear. Both Pennant and Martin mention small cists on *Cnoc na Croise*, the hill of the cross, near Kilchattan.

There are other cist burials at North Drumachro, which is also the site of an ancient well called *Tobar na Tuama*, which means 'the well of the grave'. There is an oral tradition on the island that this grave was dug by one of the McNeills of Gallochoille, for his dead wife so that he could look out across the bay and see where she was buried, but even Anderson finds this dubious and wonders if the tradition might not refer to a much older burial, which was almost certainly the case. The site had been inhabited for several thousand years before the McNeills arrived. Anderson reports that one of the stone slabs in the area still bears a cup mark (often associated with Stone Age sacred sites throughout southern Scotland, if not always with burials) and goes on to mention that the old name for the site was *Tobar an Tung*, pointing out that *tunga* was an older word for grave. It certainly is older, indeed ancient, in that it is the Sanskrit word for height, or mound, but how it came to be used by Gaelic speakers, and whether it is an old Celtic usage, or dates from a previous Indo-European based language, is not known to this writer. David MacRitchie, writing in *Fians, Fairies and Picts* in 1893, mentions that the old Celtic word for a chambered cairn was a tung or tunga.[9]

Anderson mentions an old graveyard west of Ardlamey, at a place called *Cladh Goirtean nan Cisteachan* (Graveyard of the Field or Enclosure of the Cists), which seems to refer to an ancient burial place which may also have been used as a graveyard during historic times. However, when Anderson himself was writing, he said that 'few islanders remember its existence or its location'. The late Betty McNeill of Keil, who did sterling work in amateur archaeology on the island over many years, spoke of reporting a stony mound down by Ardlamey Bay to the official surveyors, which, when excavated in 1967, was found to contain the remains of a cist, and a number of white stones, although I have been unable to determine whether this cairn is in any way connected with Anderson's graveyard.[10]

White stones seem to have had some significance for the ancient peoples of western Scotland. *Carn Ban* means pale, or white cairn, and white stones were said to have been a component of that burial. John Martin told me that some friends, walking at the north end of Gigha in winter, found the remains of an ancient burial cairn, completely surrounded by white quartz pebbles, which had gone unnoticed in the summer. This white quartz is a strange and anomalous stone. It is not permitted in the ballast of a boat in the Western Isles, presumably because it is perceived to be unlucky, perhaps through its age-old association with death.[11] On the other hand, it has sometimes been (and may still be) the practice on some West Coast fishing boats to keep a white quartz pebble in the wheelhouse as a talisman against disaster.

As the second millennium BC progressed, burial practices changed again. Cremation became more usual with burnt bones being placed in a pottery vessel, sometimes called a 'cinerary urn'. It must be remembered, however, that these changes are very slow and span many hundreds of years. We tend to lump a thousand years of prehistory into one casual phrase, but we cannot know for certain how much of this change was down to local cultural evolution and how much was the result of incoming strangers, bringing new practices with them. Sometimes both factors must have worked in combination. We have no knowledge, either, of what languages any of these peoples spoke, but it has been suggested that they may have been Indo-European in origin, and it is possible that some of the less explicable place names of Scotland carry a faint echo of those long lost tongues. As we have seen with regard to *Tobar an Tung*, place names can contain intriguing linguistic fossils.

The island is so rich in such a variety of remains in stone that it has been difficult, if not impossible, to tie some of them down to any one period of prehistory. The Hill of the Bodach in the south of the island is a case in point. Anderson tells us that *Cnoc an Teamhasa*, near the march dyke between Leim and Achamore, once housed what seems to have been quite a large rectangular enclosure, '100 yards long by 20 yards wide'. He calls it a 'fort' and lumps it in with his other descriptions of Iron Age hill forts, but it sounds, and even now, on the ground, looks much more like an ancient Stone or Bronze Age enclosure of some sort, rather than our more conventional idea of a Celtic hill fort. Anderson goes on to describe the foundations of 'two huts' as being 'just discernible' one 20 feet in diameter and one about 30 feet in diameter, within the enclosure itself. These, which seem to have disappeared, may have been dwellings, but they may also have been buildings with ceremonial or shamanistic uses. Again, it is interesting to speculate, but impossible to determine.[12]

The name of the site itself was originally *Cnoc an t-Seamhasa* which means 'the Hill of Good Luck or Prosperity'. The word *seamh* translates as 'an enchantment to make one's friend prosper', which is a delightful concept for which there is no English word. All the same, *seamh* may tell us something about the ceremonial nature of the whole site. Good luck or prosperity would suggest either a genuine popular belief in the efficacy of the place to bring advantages, or the kind of naming that seeks to deflect potential trouble by ingratiating yourself with whatever powers you suppose a place – or a resident supernatural being – to possess. So in Scottish folklore, the fairies are frequently named the Good Folk, or the People of Peace, in the hopes that they will be persuaded to live up to their good name. Sometimes, of course, both explanations are possible in that the sacred sites of one culture may have been superstitiously dreaded by succeeding inhabitants.

There is, however, another association of luck and prosperity with this site. The hill which was once called c*noc an t-Seamhasa* is now known on the island as the *Cnoc a' Bhodaich* after the stone named '*am Bodach*', or old man, who together with the *Cailleach*, or old woman, stands on this hillock between Achamore Farm and Leim. There are two ways of approaching the *Cailleach* and her companion. You can follow the green lane south along the rocky spine of the island, from Achamore Farm, where a little searching will bring you to two very understated but strangely shaped stones, one slightly bigger than the other, both keeping mysterious watch over the island. Nowadays, you can also walk up the rocky road towards the wind turbines, the original trio named Faith, Hope and Charity, joined by a fourth, Harmony, tall, white towers, looming over the *Bodach* and the *Cailleach*, which lie just to the north, on their mound, very small as standing stones go, but still surprisingly visible from many parts of the island. Below them to the west, the ground falls away towards a part of the island about mid-way between Leirn and the present Achamore farm that used to be called *Chantereoch* – although it has had a multitude of spellings, over the years – and further still towards Ardlamey Bay.

It is a matter of record that in the early nineteenth century, visiting Irish fishermen would climb *Moinean Sitheil*, the 'peaceful moss haggs' up to *Cnoc an t-Seamhasa* to worship at what they considered to be a shrine. There are many such pairs of standing stones in Antrim and in Galloway and they often (albeit with a stretch of the imagination) seem to represent male and female figures, pairing a rather phallic upright with a more flowing, triangular partner, so the Gigha stones do seem to fall within a genuine tradition of some sort. Anderson tells us that these Irish visitors would tend to the stones, placing them upright if they had fallen over, or putting them together again if time and weather had seen fit to separate them. He adds that though the Gigha islanders themselves were inclined to laugh at the superstitiousness of the Irish, they themselves would treat the stones in much the same way, namely with a certain amount of reverence, as though they were somehow connected with the luck of the island. They would even have been given offerings of milk, cream or meal.[13]

The *Bodach* is taller than his *Cailleach*, with a definitely phallic shape, in spite of previous writers' attempts to bowdlerise him as 'flagon' or 'jug' shaped. The *Bodach* was a supernatural being, an old man who, in later years at least, was used to frighten recalcitrant children, like the bogeyman, with his propensity to steal the unwary away from hearth and home. However his roots may have lain with a much older and more distinguished god of fertility, like the Green Knight who so terrorised Gawain. The *Cailleach* also had a long history as the 'hag' or wise woman, the great 'mother', the fertility goddess, who was only old for part of each year, but who would be reborn in the spring, as a beautiful young maiden. Sometimes she crops up as a Celtic tripartite goddess, virgin, mother and wise old woman, depending upon which aspect of her you need to address at any one time, or season of the year. At harvest time the last sheaf was called the *Cailleach* and was believed to be very lucky, presumably because of its association with the goddess. The 'harvest home' or celebration at the end of the harvest was also known as a *Cailleach.*[14]

Anderson, in describing the site in question, adds that *Achadh an-t-Sagairt* lies to the east of the *Bodach* and *Cailleach*, which name means 'the Field of the Priest'. This seems to reinforce the belief that Anderson's 'fort' at *Cnoc an t-Seamhasa* might once have been a religious enclosure associated with the stones, rather than a later, Celtic fortification.

The terraces of Chantereoch between Leim and Achamore contain their own secrets, which may also be connected with the *Bodach* and the *Cailleach.* The remains of a place called Hilltop Town, still known by that name today, are said by Willie McSporran to be situated somewhere between Leim and Achamore, south of Ardlamey Bay. The name 'Hill Town' is often associated with Celtic hill forts. Recent archaeology seems to demonstrate that at least some of these hill towns were not so much full-time settlements, nor yet fully fortified places but more, as Piggott describes them, 'strongholds or places of refuge for use in time of emergency',[15] particularly since Celtic warfare was so often a matter of raids and skirmishes rather than any full-scale campaigns. It seems likely that people lived and worked at lower and more convenient levels, where there were springs, shelter and so on, only repairing to the windy hill tops in times of need. These may also have been places where animals were housed and finally, they may have had ceremonial uses, pre-dating even the advent of the Celts.

Anderson describes something he calls 'a Hilltop Town' (in the generic sense, rather than as a specific place) in great detail, much of which has been obliterated by the intervening years.

He also places it very firmly 'above the shore, to the south of Ardlamey Bay and one field away, in front of Achamore fort.' 'It rises in three tiers from the beach,' he tells us:

> The lowest shelf, about 40 feet broad, is at the top of a perpendicular face of rock, 15 to 20 feet high and is reached by a narrow gap cut through this rock wall. To the north of the top of this gap are some constructions, probably defensive. The second and third benches above tend to merge into each other about midway of their length and vary in breadth. On these are at least eight foundations, circular and oblong. Surmounting these is a rock citadel, 85 feet by 35 feet, showing foundations on the top. A wall of heavy blocks of stone, or slabs has surrounded the exposed parts at the sides and back. Immediately behind the fort, and at a somewhat lower level than the citadel, is a grassy stretch which has evidently been used for grazing, but has also signs of enclosures and buildings. Bounding this to the east, there is a circular pond, with marshy ground to the north and with an outlet that lets the overflow run down close by the end of the fort to the sea.[16]

This fortified place described in detail by Anderson as 'a Hilltop Town' is probably the Hilltop Town described later by Kathleen Philip, and which seems, according to her account, to have been slightly closer to Leim. Travelling south towards Leim from Achamore, but veering westwards, she and her companions come to a 'largish expanse of rocks, covered with scrubby bushes.' They find what looks like a doorstep and large flat stones. Philip notes that this occupies the same place on the map as the old, long-gone settlement of *Chantereoch*, or *Shensrioch*, but notes also that the whole thing looks much more like a hill fort than a house. It occurred to me at some point in researching this that maybe they were all describing different aspects of what amounted to quite a large site, originally dating from before the advent of the iron age inhabitants of this island, but perhaps used by them at some time and with parts of it housing a later clachan as well.

Other accounts also place Chantereoch somewhere between the *Bodach* and *Cailleach* on their Hill of Good Luck, and Ardlamey Bay.[17] Willie McSporran refers to Hilltop Town and Chantereoch in the same breath and believes that they are the same place. In old documents, the name Chantereoch has many variant spellings: Chantereach, Chanterrioch, Chantereocht, Sheanrioch, Shensrioch, Cantereach and Shansriach.

Rioghachd means 'kingdom' in the sense of 'fiefdom' – i.e. an area of interest of a particular leader, which could be quite small. Given the old pronunciation of this name, and its proximity to the Hill of Good Luck, I wonder if it might also have some connection with the word *seanns*, which – like *seamhas* – has a sense of luck. Perhaps old Chantereoch was a part of the island that took its name from its proximity to the standing stones, with all their associations of luck and fertility.

There is one final piece of speculation about the standing stones, and their relationship with the rest of the island. It has long been accepted that the name of the island, Gigha, or as it appears on some of the old maps, *Gega*, is derived from the Norse invaders of the island, who called the place Gudey, meaning either God's Island or the Island of the Good

Harbour, both of which are suitably descriptive. There is one problem with this, however. The Norse invaders came late to an island that had already been inhabited for thousands of years. Those early inhabitants must have called the island something, and it certainly wasn't Gudey. But there is another possibility, if a remote and contentious one!

All over the British Isles, but most particularly in Ireland, there is to be found a symbol of female fertility and sexuality known as a *Sheela na Gig*. Pagan in concept, she adorns buildings from churches to castles. Legs spread wide, she displays herself to the interested watcher: an immodest – to modern sensibilities at least – slightly grotesque and strangely powerful image. The *Sheela na Gig* is the female counterpoint of the similarly ubiquitous and mysterious Green Man.[18]

She often seems to possess the characteristics of an old, and a young woman within the same iconic image. There is an almost comic duality about her. There are many Sheelas and most of them share some characteristics with gargoyles, those pagan intrusions into clearly Christian mediaeval buildings, deliberately introduced anomalies. Many are carved into stones that are different (and often older and much more weathered) than the stones of the buildings they adorn, i.e. they are the remnants of something older incorporated into a Christian place of worship. The meaning and intention behind such intrusions is debatable. Many of the Sheelas seem to be clearly depicting a woman about to give birth, in the traditional squatting position. This is an interpretation which sits well with the notion of the Sheela as a symbol of fertility but which sits ill with the frequent descriptions of her as 'exhibitionist', perhaps because our culture so routinely divorces sexuality from its natural consequences.

But what is the derivation of the name? The *sheela* element seems to come from the Irish root *sil* or *siol* meaning seed, offspring, race or descendants. In Irish the word *sile* was used for an old woman, and can also refer to an effeminate person or sissy. On the other hand, the word *Geug* in Irish Gaelic means a branch, a sapling, a young female or a nymph, so there is some sense in which the *Sheela na Gig*, like the *Cailleach*, is a being who is both an old hag and a young woman at the same time. The island is actually named *Gug* in a charter of 1309, granting lands there to the Earl of Mar. If you look at the *Cailleach*, up on her Hill of Good Luck, it needs only a little stretch of the imagination to see that her strange, flowing, triangular shape has echoes of the characteristically immodest posture of the Sheela, except of course that the *Cailleach* is freestanding. In Ireland, the *Cailleach* was often associated with a healing well or spring, as well as with the ability to control wind and weather. Gigha has several notable 'holy wells', including one whose fame spread far beyond the island itself and which seems to have been associated with female 'guardians', especially older women.

Given the traditions surrounding the Gigha *Cailleach*, which have persisted even to the present day, and given the strangely evocative, not to say provocative shape of the two stones, whether natural or not, I would like, tentatively, to offer another interpretation of the name of this island, one that involves a not impossible hybrid of an original Gaelic name and a Norse suffix: *Geug-ey*, The Maiden Isle. Could it be that Gigha is not so much God's Island as the Island of the Goddess?

4

The People of the Horse

North of the Alps, from about 800 BC onwards, we find evidence of a culture of warrior horsemen who would have spoken some variation of a recognisably Celtic language. These tribes already knew how to work with bronze, but the use of iron would have been spreading steadily westwards. As Piggott tells us 'we move into a world of iron-using communities in Britain from at least the seventh century BC onwards.'[1]

There is evidence of the development of a keen interest in horsemanship in Scotland dating from around this time as well, with discoveries of various horse-related artefacts in bronze and iron, perhaps because these metals lent themselves so readily to the accoutrements of equine pursuits. It is from this period onwards that we can date the peoples whom we know collectively as the Celts, although as has recently been made clear by various archaeologists and historians, they actually consisted of many disparate groups, with linguistic similarities and some shared customs and beliefs, rather than any single group of people that can definitely be defined as Celtic. It is from this time too, that we can date the increase in hilltop fortifications, which we know as hill forts or duns. Duns are generally defined as smaller versions of hill forts, i.e. places of refuge for family groups and small communities. Gigha is very rich in these small-scale Iron Age hilltop remains.

The earliest Celtic tribes about whom we have any written information were those encountered by Caesar, and we know that they spoke a version of Gallo-Brythonic, which has affinities with Welsh rather than Gaelic. Essentially, there were two distinct families of Celtic languages, which can be loosely labelled as Brythonic on the one hand and Gaelic, in its Irish and Scottish manifestations, on the other. This is, of course, to oversimplify, but there is need of some simplification for the sake of clarity. To call Gaelic the indigenous language of Scotland is to ignore the many hundreds of years before the advent of Gaelic speakers when the language of Scotland would have been much closer to Welsh. Just as we can see the remains in stone and turf of these early Brythonic-speaking tribes all over southern Scotland, we can find remnants of their language in some place names too.

When the Romans finally invaded Britain in AD 43, with four legions and some 20,000 auxiliary troops, many of whom were Gauls themselves, they spent time, not just in attempting to subdue the natives, but in trying, with their usual efficiency, to establish just who lived where and make a record of the details. Ptolemy, a Greek geographer and astrologer, made a map of the British Isles in the second century AD, using information gained from these early military expeditions. He also tapped into the work of a Greek explorer called Pytheas, who was said to have visited Britain around 300 BC. Ptolemy calls the people of Kintyre, Islay, Jura and presumably Gigha as well (although it was too small for Ptolemy to accord it any special mention) the Epidii, which means 'the people of the horse'.

This possibly meant that they were a tribe associated with the Celtic horse goddess Epona, or some recognisable northern version of the same deity. It may also have meant that they were a tribe for whom horsemanship and horse breeding were important, something the Romans would have noticed and possibly taken advantage of. They would always have need of horses. We can assume that the Epidii too spoke a language that was not Gaelic, but Brythonic, i.e. something much closer to Welsh. It is worth noting that the Kintyre nickname for a man who comes from the peninsula even now, is '*each*', meaning horse. Within relatively recent times, until it was superseded by the more practical Clydesdale, there was a native breed of Kintyre horse, which may have carried the bloodline of the ancient Celtic beasts, although these indigenous horses have now completely died out.

We know that the Romans called the northern British tribes by the general name of Pritani, which meant 'painted people'. This probably referred to the habit of the northern tribes of tattooing or painting themselves, and is where the word 'Briton' comes from. But the name Pict also refers to this same custom of colouring the body, and the position is made even more complicated by the fact that the term Pict was often used to refer to the northern tribes in a more general sense. Even the Epidii of Kintyre are sometimes referred to as Picts, although it is very doubtful if that is what they were.

Scholars recognise the Picts as a specific and rather mysterious tribe, with a large power base in the north and east of Scotland. They were sometimes, but not always, matrilineal in their succession, i.e. the mother rather than the father could determine who should inherit what, and inheritance might well be passed down on the female side. They were builders of circular defensive structures known as brochs; carvers of detailed, stylised animals and birds in stone; and competent seamen, so that for them, at least, some of the more visible stone monuments of the islands would have been very useful in taking sightings and steering a safe course. There is some evidence that they raided the coasts of south-west Scotland, which would explain the occasional presence of broch-like structures in both Galloway and Kintyre.

We don't know what language the Picts spoke, or even if they really were the homogeneous mass of popular history. We do, however, have quite a lot of place name evidence, names that seem to differ from recognised Gaelic or British roots, although the consensus seems to be that the Picts too had Celtic origins, and were linguistically closer to Brythonic than Gaelic. The most that we can deduce from patchy evidence is that the Epidii, who inhabited Kintyre and Gigha, were probably a British-speaking, horse-breeding tribe who traded with the Romans when they could, and also tried to maintain an uneasy peace with their neighbours, the warrior Picts, to the north.

The Romans, as any schoolchild used to know (but perhaps doesn't these days) never conquered Scotland properly. They managed to get as far as Perth in AD 80. In AD 81 Agricola led an army north, and defeated the natives at Mons Graupius in AD 84. This comparative subjection didn't last long, and in AD 122, Hadrian built his wall. Nineteen years later, the Antonine Wall followed, but was never really maintained as a defensive structure, and there is some evidence that the main function of these walls was to give employment to the Roman soldiery (many of whom were, themselves, from Celtic tribes). Northern tribes such as the Epidii would have sat uneasily between the Romans to the south, the Gaels to the west and the Picts to the north: a precarious situation between warring factions and one the Gigha islanders in particular were to find themselves in with monotonous regularity. They would have maintained economic links with the Romans, supplying them with cattle, and just possibly horses, as well as maintaining contact by sea with Ireland. Gigha would have been pretty much central to this network of communications at a time when maintaining such links was problematic.

Later, in the early years of the first millennium AD, the Epidii would forge alliances with the Irish Gaelic speaking tribes (confusingly called the Scottii by Latin speakers) who, in search of new land and a more peaceful existence, were beginning to try to colonise Scotland from Antrim. Eventually these people would found the ancient Kingdom of Dalriada in Argyll, with its chief fortress at Dunadd. The Romans, with troubles of their own back in Rome, finally gave up on Britain, and went away in AD 399. Many parts of England, highly Romanised by this time, felt the loss keenly. Scotland was less concerned. Rome itself would be sacked by the Visigoths in AD 410. By the sixth century AD, the 'Iron Age' or Celtic tribes of northern Scotland had organised themselves into at least two distinct kingdoms north of the Forth.

The Dal Riata had their own long history of wars and inter-family struggles in Eire. This is not the place to go into this in any detail, or only in so far as it is the source of a thousand epic stories about the great hero Fionn MacCumhail and his followers, which provided and to some extent still does provide – popular entertainment for the peoples of Ireland and Scotland. When they came across the sea to Scotland, they brought these tales with them. Often there were similarities with the popular heroic stories of the indigenous British tribes and often the stories of these two cultures became inextricably intertwined.

There had always been contact between Scotland and Ireland, particularly of course via the Kintyre peninsula, which is only twelve miles across the North Channel, with each country plainly visible from the other for large parts of the year. Even nowadays Gigha attracts many visiting Irish yachtsmen, for whom the journey, in a small sailing boat, is seen as a short hop, even for weekend sailors.

There was probably no single moment when the tribe known as the Dal Riata in Ireland decided to colonise the country over the water, but perhaps trade turned to colonisation, as trade so often will. The grass is invariably greener, and troubles at home will always turn young men's thoughts to pastures new. However it happened, gradually in some places, more suddenly and violently in others, the Gaelic language soon began to overtake the old Brythonic language, and Gigha was no exception to this change. There is some evidence that Gaelic superseded Brythonic rather quickly in Gigha, no less than in south-west Scotland as a whole. But oral histories tell us that these Dalriadic settlers were often family men who brought wives and children with them, rather than, like the later Vikings, younger sons, unattached men seeking wives and land, who would have married into Gaelic-speaking families.

It seems to me that the profound linguistic change that occurred at this time (but not with the later advent of the Vikings) is evidence enough for the wholesale nature of the settlement. Also, there may have been some sense in which the Gaelic language and culture was stronger, much as English tends to carry all before it today. This comparative strength of Gaelic and the wholesale transplantation of families to

Scotland can be the only logical explanation as to why there are so many Gaelic place names on Gigha and so very few that hark back to the old British language. Place names, which deal with natural features, landscape descriptions, geographical juxtapositions, places of habitation and so on, are often – paradoxically – the first to be changed by influential incomers, but they can also be the last repositories of a forgotten tongue.

What this meant for the Epidii on Gigha is uncertain. Was the alliance between the two peoples uneasy or not? Elsewhere in the West of Scotland we often find Gaelic and Brythonic place names side by side with clusters of Brythonic names lingering in, for example, Ayrshire, where they seem to favour hilltop farms. Seats of power would have shifted and changed. Both peoples would have used their hill forts, not necessarily as places to live on a day-to-day basis, but as places of refuge in times of conflict. And I think that if we look more closely at Gigha, we can find a great deal of evidence in island folklore and tradition of two sets of people who were not complete enemies and yet not totally easy with each other either.

The very first 'king' of the Dal Riata – although this term meant leader, rather than our modern concept of an all-powerful ruler – was Fergus Mor mac Eirc, who came from Ireland bringing a group of family and followers around AD 497 and established his power base in Western Scotland, while still retaining a foothold in Ireland. The Dal Riata's sphere of influence spread over Islay, Jura, Arran and Gigha, and even further beyond Oban in the north. It was now becoming a kingdom in a very real sense. The centre of power was Dunadd, near modern day Lochgilphead. It was here that the Dal Riata enthroned their kings in a ceremony that involved the new leader placing his foot in a shaped indentation in the rock, a custom that is still mentioned by Edmund Spenser, writing about Irish chieftains in 1596.[2] Excavations at Dunadd have uncovered fortifications as well as the remains of a jewellery workshop. There is a stone carving of a boar, and ancient forms of writing, known as Ogham.

From Fergus, the throne passed to his son Domangart, and then to Domangart's two sons, one of whom, Comgall, was said to have encouraged Columba to try to convert the northern Picts to Christianity, not, it has to be said, from any great spiritual motive, but in order to undermine their culture. After that, there were various skirmishes and conflicts with the Picts although in 603 or thereabouts, King Bridei was converted to Christianity.

Aidan Mac Gabhrain of the Dal Riata waged war on the Picts to the north, including the Orkney Isles, and on more southerly British tribes, as far as the Isle of Man. He came to grief, however, when he tried to take on the might of the Northumbrian King Aethelfrith. By now these Northumbrian Angles had a very strong foothold in Scotland and held territories and religious foundations in Ayrshire and Dumfriesshire. Aethelfrith defeated Aidan in 603. At the same time, the kingdom of Dalriada, as it came to be known, was coming under pressure on the Irish side, and was eventually defeated by the O'Neill in 637 at the battle of Mag Rath in that country, war on two fronts never being a very good idea, even then.

After that, the Dal Riata seem to have abandoned their ambitions of retaining any power base in Ireland and instead, concentrated all their attention on their Scottish possessions, trying to maintain their kingdom in the face of encroachments by Picts in the north and Angles in the east. The still Brythonic kingdom of Strathclyde lay to the south of Dalriada, but was already part Anglian. By this stage, the people formerly known as the Epidii seem to have disappeared altogether, subsumed in the mass of Dalriadan Gaels, though perhaps not quite without trace. As we shall see, there may be traces of them in the customs, beliefs and place names of Gigha. And perhaps 'disappeared' is the wrong word in any case. As would happen to the Britons of Strathclyde, not too long after, it was as though the Irish Gaelic language and custom was stronger, almost more fashionable (if such a word could apply), and simply swept all before it.[3]

So what of our little Isle of Gigha, in the midst of all this? Well, we have already seen that there are many Stone and Bronze Age remains on Gigha, in the shape of cairn burials, standing stones and cists. But Gigha is also particularly rich in duns, hill forts, and other Iron Age remains, and as we will see, if we look at these sites with their associated legends, they seem to hold within them a remote memory of a struggle between two rather different peoples, represented – metaphorically as always – by the storytellers as 'two families' who maintained spheres of influence in different parts of the island, but who loved and intermarried, fought and fell out. Tradition has it that one of these families was called Galbraith, and as we shall see, that name is associated with the British-speaking inhabitants of Kintyre and most particularly Gigha, perhaps with the old Epidii forebears themselves.

Anderson tells us that there are the 'relics of a dozen forts that are still visible.' He goes on to describe them in some detail – some are larger, and better preserved than others, some seem to have been rudimentary strongholds at the most.[4]

'The limited size and simple appointments of most of the forts seem to indicate that they were originally the residence of the chief or head of the community.' Actually, even this may not have been the case. Forts and duns were not necessarily built to withstand a prolonged siege, and may not have been places of permanent residence either. They might have been small garrisons, and because they were high up, they would have been excellent places for watching just who was approaching. They might have been small fortifications in which young warriors were housed (thus keeping their youthful and possibly irritating boisterousness away from family life). Perhaps they were enclosures into which cattle and people could be sent in time of need. Or possibly they were a combination of all of these things.

It is worth examining one of these, *Dun Chibhich* on the Ordnance Survey Pathfinder Map, which is still very much in existence now, although there are various spellings of the name. Anderson describes it in some detail:

> At the south side of the Mill Loch, rises the peaked height of *Dun Chiofaich*, the strongest and – it may be – the oldest fort on Gigha. The whole summit from north to south stretches two hundred and seventy five feet and this must once have been a place of some consequence. The wall at the gate still shows a thickness of nine feet, but narrows to five or six feet, ranging from four to five and a half feet in height from the floor of the fort. A bare patch to the south of the gate outside shows the flat surface and close-fitting building of the stonework . . . round two sides of the Dun,

> a broad, deep gap runs in a sheltered part of which are the foundations of a house, but this is of much later date than the fort itself.[5]

The fort is positioned so that it has panoramic and defensively very useful views of Islay and Jura on one side, with Argyll and Kintyre on the other, as well as views of the whole of Gigha itself, north and south. This fort has a fascinating story attached to it. Tradition on the island tells us that *Chiofaich*, *Chibhich* or 'Keefi' as he is more phonetically spelled, was said to have been the king of Lochlin's son. Lochlin was the name often given to Norway by the Celts, or at least that part of Scandinavia from which the Vikings ventured south, while *Ciofach*, sometimes called *Ciuthach* or *Chibhich* was a hero of Scottish legend. According to Anderson, he was a 'great warrior, a leader of the Picts, contemporary with *Fionn Mac Cumhail* but opposed to Fionn'.[6] He was apparently slain by *Diarmaid*, with whose wife he had run away – or at least that's what the guidebooks tell us. When first I heard this tale, it puzzled me, since I had always associated Diarmaid with his own peculiar brand of faithlessness. Wasn't he the young warrior who had himself absconded with Finn's own betrothed, *Grainne*? And was it this same young woman with whom *Chibhich* was supposed to have run away?

In *Popular Tales of the West Highlands*,[7] we find an oral version of the tale of Diarmaid and Grainne, as related to Hector Maclean on 6 July 1859 by an old man called Alexander Macalister in Bowmore, Islay, not far from Gigha. Grainne, although betrothed to the (by this time slightly ageing) hero, Fionn, in Ireland, had fallen for Diarmaid, mainly because of the beauty spot on his face. Any woman who chanced to see it was blessed (or perhaps cursed) in that she would fall instantly in love with him.

'Grainne', according to the wonderful words of Alexander Macalister, 'was in heavy love for Diarmaid.' She persuaded him to run away with her, although for the first part of the journey at least, he resisted the temptation to lie with her and they had separate beds. She persuaded him to go first to *Carraig* without specifying exactly which Carraigh, and so they are believed to have gone to *Carraig an Daimh*, somewhere in Kintyre.

There are, of course, many *carraigs* or *carraghs* in Gigha itself, including *carraig mhor*, the big rock, on the coast near Ardlamey, which would suit our purposes very well if we were looking for an equivalent Gigha *carraig*, not too far from Chibhich's fort. However, the fort itself stands high on a crag, so perhaps it was to this ancient fortress that Grainne persuaded Diarmaid to take her.

But then, as the story goes, 'there came a great sprawling old man, who was called *Ciofach Mae a Goill* (Keefie of the Blubber Cheeks, or Keefie the Sullen) who seems to have been our Gigha Ciofach or Chibhich, and he sat and played at *dinnsirean*, which is translated as wedges. This could refer to an early game, but could also be *disnean*, or dice. To revert to Alexander Macalister's own words again:

> Grainne took a liking for the old earl and they laid a scheme together that they would kill Diarmaid. The old man laid hands on him and he turned against the old man and they went into each other's grips. The old man was pretty strong but at last Diarmaid put him under. Graine caught hold of the knife and she put it

into the thigh of Diarmaid. Diarmaid left them, and he was but just alive and he was gone under hair and under beard [presumably, in disguise].[8]

He came the way of the *Carraig* and a fish with him, and he asked leave to roast it. He got a cogie of water in which he might dip his fingers. Now there would be the taste of honey on anything which Diarmaid might touch with his fingers. Grainne took a morsel out of the fish and she perceived the taste of honey upon it. To attack Diarmaid went Ciofach and they were in each other's grips for a turn of a while but at last Diarmaid killed Ciofach and away he went. When Grainne saw that Ciofach was dead she followed Diarmaid and about the break of day she came to the strand and there was a heron screaming. Diarmaid was up in the face of the mountains. And said Grainne, 'Wouldst thou eat bread and flesh Diarmaid? Here, I will give it to thee. Where is a knife will cut it?'

'Search the sheath in which thou didst put it last,' said Diarmaid.

According to the storyteller, she found the knife, still in Diarmaid's body, and she 'drew out the knife and that was the greatest shame that ever she took, drawing the knife out of Diarmaid.'

So poor Ciofach died, betrayed by a faithless woman, leaving nothing but the name of his fort, and Grainne proved herself a knotless thread, thoughtlessly slipping away from her lovers, even, at the last, lovely Diarmaid himself. The story has a wonderful foreshadowing of the disaster to come, even in the ominous screaming of the heron. Grainne's love for Diarmaid seems shallow and superficial. She has fallen in love with him on impulse but there is also the suggestion of helpless enchantment about it. Ciofach too falls victim to her changeability. She is the death of Ciofach, just as she will be the death of Diarmaid, an event foreshadowed by the wounding in the thigh, a wound that resonates with other meanings, not least the sense of emasculation.

Anderson talks of the relics of about a dozen forts on Gigha, although I counted only five 'duns' on the present map. Ciofach's fort makes one point of what must once have been an important defensive triangle in the centre of the island, with *Dunan an t-Seasgain*, (the Little Fort of the Marsh), which lies to the south-east of Gigha's main hill, *Creag Bhan*, and *Dun Trinnse*, down at Ardailly. *Dun Trinnse* is the Fort of the Trench 'so called' says Anderson, 'because of its site on the edge of a deep trench that cuts cleanly through the massive hummock of rock, about 25 feet high, which here fronts the sea, a few feet from the water.'[9] Ardailly itself, now little more than a clachan, was, as Anderson says, 'of old a more important place in the life of Gigha than it is now.' The island's mill was down here, of which the remains can still be seen. One of the McNeills lived here too, as did the first dedicated Church of Scotland minister of the island. Looking at the geography of these three fortresses, each visible from the other, it certainly seems as though they might have been interlinked in some way as defensive positions, perhaps for the old Brythonic inhabitants against the incoming Gaels.

South-west of Drumyeon Bay were two more forts, both called *Dun Buidhe*, 'the yellow fort', possibly named for the gorse bushes that grow in profusion down here. At the head of

Ardminish Bay, behind the present manse, stands the *Cnoc an t-Sionnachain*, the Hill of the Little Fox, and although nothing remained of a fort there, even in Anderson's day, informants had told him that the hill had once been capped by what looked like man-made remains. Willie McSporran also called this the Hill of the Little Fox, but gave an alternative name as the Hill of the Witch. Ardminish Fort lay south of Gallochoille, (this is marked as a dun on the OS map) with another one, possibly, set back from the road, just opposite the gate of Achamore House, although this is much more likely to be a natural geographical feature. On the west coast at Ardlamey, there is *Dun Ni' Chrero*, The Fort of Crero's Daughter, although this name also has Norse associations in the personal name Crero.

Finally, we come to *Cnoc nan Ordac*, a hillock (not marked on the current map) that lies to the east, as you travel along the old track between Ardlamey Farm and the village of Ardachy, which once lay between Ardlamey and Ardailly. *Cnoc nan Ordac* means the Hill of the Thumbs, and this place has a story attached to it, which seems to recall a distant, but bitter feud between two island families. Once again we are told that one of them went by the name of Galbraith, a surname that has its roots in the Brythonic past of Gigha. But before we look in more detail at the traditions behind this strange place name, we must look to other sites on the island that also seem to be bound up with the history of the Galbraiths, in particular the magical and mysterious 'great well' to which generations of islanders resorted for its power to effect changes in wind, wealth and health.

5

The Well of the Winds

'There is a well in the north end of this isle' says traveller Martin Martin, writing in his *Description of the Western Isles of Scotland*, some time between 1695 and 1702, 'called *Toubirmore*, i.e. a great well, because of its effects, for which it is famous among the islanders; who, together with the inhabitants, use it as a catholicon for diseases.'

Presumably by 'islanders', he means people from other Hebridean islands because the fame of this well was widespread. He continues:

> It is covered with stone and clay, because the natives fancy that the stream that flows from it might overflow the isle; and it is always opened by a *diroch*, i.e. an inmate, else they think it would not exert its virtues. They ascribe one very extraordinary effect to it and 'tis this: that when any foreign boats are wind-bound here (which often happens) the master of the boat often gives the native that lets the water run a piece of money; and they say that immediately afterwards the wind changes in favour of those that are thus detained by contrary winds. Every stranger that goes to drink of the water of this well, is accustomed to leave on its stone-cover a piece of money, a needle,

> pin, or one of the prettiest variegated stones they can find.

Martin's word *diroch*, for 'keeper of the well', is an interesting one. There are accounts of the *derilans* – as the word is spelled in the parish registers – who were female guardians of a holy well dedicated to St Maelrubha in Loch Maree. The Gaelic word, of which these are variations, could be *deoradh*, which means a pilgrim, a stranger, an exile or destitute person, but was also applied to the custodian of a holy relic. Curiously enough, the same meaning is attached to the surname Dewar, the family who were once keepers of St Fillan's Staff and whose name is inextricably bound up with that duty. Martin doesn't specify whether his Gigha *diroch* was male or female although a later writer confirms that the keepers of the well were, in his day at least, two elderly women.

It is worth noting that St Maelrubha, as a seventh-century missionary of distinguished parentage, could be described as a *deoradh* or pilgrim in his own right. The island on Loch Maree where he built his religious cell, however, was already a sacred place, with its own holy well or spring. The waters of the well were believed to cure lunacy, among other afflictions, and such beliefs probably predated the saint by many hundreds if not thousands of years. There are many similarities between this site, and the site of the Great Well on Gigha, not least of which is that it also has an early Christian cell associated with it.

It was a common attribute of Celtic Christian monks that they tried, as far as possible, to work with local custom and belief, using it as an aid to conversion, rather than favouring the wholesale and invariably adversarial condemnation of later and perhaps more doggedly narrow-minded times. Their beliefs, when examined closely, are a mixture of asceticism, tolerance and pragmatism which twenty-first-century minds often find sympathetic or at least comprehensible. One result of this pragmatism was that the old sites frequently survived intact, retaining many of their supposed supernatural powers and attractions. They were simply given a different, nominally Christian, interpretation. There is, for example, some evidence that at Loch Maree, Maelrubha permitted animal sacrifice, in the shape of the slaughter of sacred bulls, to continue on the island. Even more astonishing is the fact that these sacrifices went on until the seventeenth century when, in 1695, the Presbytery of Dingwall woke up to the fact and took grave exception to such heathen practices being followed by nearby inhabitants. Reports of these practices, however, would suggest that pagan beliefs survived relatively unchecked alongside more conventional religious mores for many years.

Other holy wells throughout the British Isles are associated with healing powers of all kinds, both for mental and physical diseases, and also with fertility. The common denominator seems to have been some kind of association with phases of the moon, which may help to explain why our Gigha well is also associated with winds and tides as well as with cures.

The idea that fresh running water is sacred, that it contains within itself powers of both healing and divination (thus fulfilling two basic human needs – to be well and to know what the future may bring) is a concept deeply rooted in the history of human religious experience. Sometimes these sacred wells are open pools and sometimes they are contained in underground caves. Often they consist of a natural spring, protected and enhanced by ancient stone structures of various kinds. From eighteenth-century descriptions, it would seem that the Gigha well was of this sort – writers speak of the well being covered, presumably with a moveable stone slab, when not in use. It would have been natural enough to associate such places with the spiritual world, in a culture and at a time when there would have been no alternative explanation for the endless flow of water. Indeed none would have been required. There must be some source, some force that made the waters flow, and since the water was often metaphorically perceived to be the breast milk of the earth, with nourishing powers, this force was often named as a goddess: Bride, Matrona, Coventina, Rhiannon, Rigantona to name but a few.[1]

The Celts would leave coins or small objects of value around about their holy wells and springs.[2] During later years, perhaps as absolute belief in the power of the well waned, pins were often substituted for more valuable items. Well-dressing ceremonies, where the trees around the source are festooned with rags, are not unknown in Ireland and England, even to this day, although in Scotland, perhaps because of the more severe strictures of early Presbyterianism, such celebrations are almost unknown. Some English holy wells are still decorated annually with intricate collages of flower petals and leaves, seeds and other natural materials, while in Ireland, wells will be blessed by a priest, on a particular saint's day, so-called 'Pattern Days', i.e. Patron Days. Such wells are almost invariably associated with healing powers, and the Great Well of Gigha, which Martin Martin tells us was a 'catholicon for diseases', is no exception.

It is the association with weather that seems less usual, but further investigation reveals that many other holy wells were associated with this power to effect changes in the weather.

Iona, for instance, had wells of the north and south winds with similar useful properties at a time when the ability to travel relied solely on wind and wave. Pennant, touring the Western Isles in 1772, also mentions the Gigha well and its influence over the weather. 'The first wonder of the isle is a little well of a most miraculous quality, for in old times, if ever the chieftain lay here windbound, he had nothing more to do than cause the well to be cleared and instantly a favourable gale arose. But miracles are now ceased.'[3]

Quite apart from speculating as to whether the chieftain really would have wanted a full blown 'gale' to arise, we are, some time after Martin's account, still dealing with a place associated with summoning the wind, although Pennant doesn't mention the well's other magical and healing properties. By this date, of course, even people who had recourse to such a well for cures for their various ailments might not have seen fit to mention it to a casual visitor for fear that the minister might get to hear of it.

The tradition of weather magic persisted a little longer, however. Writing in 1792, the Reverend William Fraser refers to our well as '*Tabar-rath Bhuathaig*' rather than *Tobar More*, which he translates as the lucky well of *Beathag* and which he assumes is a female name, either referring to a previous abbess of Iona, or possibly a notable guardian of the well. Interestingly, this name or a variant of it, remains to this day on the Ordnance Survey map, '*Tobar a Bheathaig*'.[4]

> When a person wished for a fair wind [says Fraser], either to leave the island or bring home his absent friends, this part was opened with great solemnity, the stones carefully removed, and the well cleaned with a

> wooden dish or clam shell. This being done the water was several times thrown in the direction (or airt) from which the wished-for wind was to blow and this action, accompanied with a certain form of words which the person repeated every time he threw the water. When the ceremony was over, the well was carefully shut up to prevent fatal consequences: it being firmly believed that were the place left open, it would occasion a storm which would overwhelm the whole island. This ceremony of cleaning the well, as it is called, is now seldom or never performed though still there are two old women of the names of Galbraith and Graham who are said to have the secret but who have cause to lament the infidelity of the age as they derive little emolument from their profession.

Sadly, Fraser omits to record the 'certain form of words' that were repeated – perhaps he didn't know them himself. Although he refers to the person throwing the water as 'he', he then goes on to describe two 'old women' who still 'have the secret' of the well's power, whatever that may be, presumably a ritual involving words and actions. We can assume from Fraser's account that the well guardians were paid for their services, but at the time when he was writing, business was bad.

Anderson makes the interesting observation that Fraser was quite probably wrong in his derivation of the name, that the name was more likely *Tobar-a-Bhuadhaig* (i.e. the well of virtue) and that there is no other record of *Buathaig* as a variant for the name *Beathaig*.

There are many wells and springs on Gigha including *Tobar an Sgian-Pheanna*, the well of the pen knife; *Tobar an Tung*, the well of the grave; *Tobar Eachainn*, Hector's well; *Tobar Na Croite*, the well of the croft, situated between the Mill Loch and the east coast; *Tobar Sluichd Bhain*, the well of the white pit, at Kinererach; and *Tobar Mor*, the big well, near *Uamh Mor* on the west coast. Anderson also mentions a well dedicated to St Catan, which was once deemed to have healing properties. This well was mentioned to me by John Martin, and is still in existence near the road to Keil, opposite the lower end of the old graveyard at Kilchattan. It was said to give some of the best water on the island. 'The name . . . was recovered several years ago by Dr Kenneth MacLeod, minister of Gigha, from an old islander of over 90 years of age, then living in Kintyre, who told him that in his boyhood days the well was popularly called St Catan's Well and was a Holy Well.'[5]

It seems clear that Martin's *Tobar More* and *Tobar a Bheathaig* are one and the same well, situated in the north of the island, just south of Tarbert, where the island narrows dramatically, not far from where a great mitten-shaped standing stone called *Carraig an Tairbeart* points at the sky. *Cnoc Largie* is a smallish hill on the east side of the island, looking back towards Kintyre. It is covered with many boulders, interspersed with a tangle of inhospitable brambles, and willows, with the Sound of Gigha beyond. The site of the well itself, low down on the north-western slope of Cnoc Largie, has all but disappeared and for many years, although I hunted for it sporadically, I was never lucky enough to find it.

Anderson tells of another, possibly related relic in this area, the Holy Stone, which he describes as being situated about 200 yards to the south of the site of the well, along the base of Cnoc Largie. The beliefs about this large flat stone are associated with fertility and coincide intriguingly with traditional

Celtic beliefs about wells and holy springs discussed earlier. Anderson tells us that the stone was a place to which childless women would go, to offer prayers for fertility – a feature that is often linked to wells rather than stones, but perhaps the stone was originally part of a sacred complex that included the well.

We are not even sure if the stone is in its original place or whether it might once have been situated closer to the well and, like the well, although I had hunted for it, I had never managed to find it. Anderson gives a charming account of himself ferreting about and noticing a great slab with one of those mysterious cup marks with which Scotland seems to be littered. On this occasion, Anderson raised the turf and discovered, not only a second cup mark, but what he calls 'an incised linear cross' together with other figures. He had rediscovered the Holy Stone and great must have been his excitement.

'It had long been lost, only a faint tradition remaining of a sacred stone to which childless women were wont to travel on their knees to offer up prayers.' Since at least some of the symbols on the stone would appear to be Christian, Anderson draws the conclusion that the Holy Stone may once have been a pagan altar which was 'sanctified' by an early Christian missionary who, like Maelrubha at Loch Maree, elected to place his cell in the pagan heart of the island, close to the stone and the well. This site may also have been related to another ancient site on the southern slope of Cnoc Largie, which Anderson describes as being 'a large grassy patch, bare of heather and bracken, that looks as if it had been cultivated in olden times. In the north-east corner there are still to be found the remains of the wall of an oval enclosure, 62 feet by 43 feet in extent. Two stones standing on the south side seem to indicate the gate whilst at the upper end, a beehive hut has collapsed.'[6] This description sounds more like a monastic foundation or dwelling of some sort rather than a burial mound.

These early saints were an intriguing mixture of circumspection and bravery, interpreting their drive to convert the pagans as a battle, with Christ as the ultimate warrior king. But they would couple with this a sensitivity to the old beliefs, which guaranteed them a modicum of safety. There is some evidence that our earliest missionary to Gigha, pre-dating even the St Catan, who lent his name to the church at Kilchattan, may have been one Findlugan, a colleague of Columba, who was said to have sailed here from the larger foundation on Iona.

In the middle of a ploughed field called *Ruidh a Chaibeil*, 'field of the chapel', at Tarbert Farm, a large heap of stones is still visible, with what may be the remains of an old stone cross. The name recalls an ancient church, which must once have stood here, not far from the well and the holy stone. But this is all that is left of both chapel and graveyard. The graveyard must have been quite extensive, because over a period of some centuries scattered burials have been turned up by the plough between here and Tarbert Bay.

Anderson tells us that the cross is 'of the Celtic type, free standing, six feet high above ground level, eleven inches broad at the foot of the shaft', but goes on to say that 'there is nothing by which to fix a definite date for this cross. The type might date back to the 10th century.' As far as I am aware, it has still not been dated with any precision. What is practically certain, however, is that the chapel here in the north of the island must have pre-dated the erection of Kilchattan Church at Keil and is an indication that the focus of social and religious life on the island may have tended to shift southwards over many hundreds of years.

The well and the pagan altar would have formed an irresistible attraction for an early missionary who may have wished to demonstrate the supremacy of his own risen Christ over the forces of darkness. Anderson goes on to point out that 'It is more than probable that this chapel, (after which the field was named), stood on the site of a still earlier one.' This first chapel, if there was one, must have been little more than a simple, circular stone cell. There are no specific traditions on the island naming the missionary responsible, but the name *Fionnlagan* is attached to a little islet in West Tarbert Bay and this may be the same person as the Findlugan of the Iona community who once saved the great Columba from armed attack. Adomnan tells the tale, in his life of St Columba. Findlugan put on Columba's cowl and interposed himself between the saint and his attackers, quite ready to sacrifice himself to save his master. Fortunately, the garment had miraculous properties. It 'could not be pierced by the thrust of a very sharp spear . . . but remained untouched, and he who had it on was safe and uninjured.'[7]

We know that Findlugan is associated with nearby Islay and Jura, so it is at least possible that he may also have been responsible for setting up a cell on Gigha with the aim of converting the natives by imposing a Christian gloss on a powerfully sacred pagan site.

There is another observation to be made about *Tobar More*. The stories of the dangers inherent in leaving the place uncapped are reminiscent of a mythical Celtic well called Connla's Well, the main feature of which was that it was said, like its Gigha equivalent, to be capable of flooding the whole world. Many popular tales associated with this well have curious similarities to stories about the Gigha well. One early British version of the tale tells of Rhiannon who was the goddess of horses (presumably therefore, also a goddess of the tribes that the Romans named the Epidii, or people of the horse) and magical birds. She was also the patron of fertility and ruler of the underworld. In the Mabinogion, there is an account of a supernatural glade where a spring emerges. Cynon, an Arthurian champion, visits the glade and when he pours water from the spring onto a stone slab, there is a sudden storm. Hailstones fall from the sky to destroy all the land and the trees round about. At this point the black knight, whose land has been sadly denuded by the storm, arrives to challenge Cynon to single combat. Cynon loses the fight, but later on the heroic Owein repeats the experience and wins, the implication being that the balance of nature will be restored only when the worthy young hero defeats the older man.[8]

The one thing that all historical accounts of these sacred wells and springs seem to have in common is that they invariably had a guardian or guardians. It was the task of the guardian not just to activate the hidden powers of the well, but also to contain and control a force that could easily turn destructive if left to operate unhindered. Many old stories speak of doom-laden consequences, either when the well itself is neglected, or sometimes, when offence is offered to the women who tend it. If the water runs dry, the land will die in consequence. But the other extreme is arguably worse, and if the water is allowed to spring forth unhindered, it will flood the whole world. Either way, potential disaster looms and the well guardian's job is to maintain equilibrium.

As we have already seen, the Celtic monks were inclined to work with existing beliefs, Christianising them wherever possible. They even Christianised existing gods and goddesses in a peaceful but remarkably efficient conversion. One final point should therefore be made about the name of the Gigha well, which as we have seen, is sometimes called *Tobar a Bheathaig* or *Tabar-rath Bhuathaig* and sometimes *Tobar More* or *Toubirmore* as Martin spells it, translating it as a 'great well' although there is another, quite different, *Tobar Mor* in the north of the island. It is much more likely that the well may have been called *Tobar Moire*. This would mean that our Gigha well was yet another Lady Well or Mary's Well, *Moire* being the Gaelic name for Mary. The early Celtic saints often saw the Queen of Heaven as a fitting substitute for a pagan goddess.

Later though, the Reformed Church was zealous in trying to suppress what it termed idolatry. The regional Synod of Argyll of 1642 tells us that 'every member must give up to them idolatrous monuments within their parishes to which the vulgar superstitiously resorts to the end that the same may be abolished.'

It was this attitude that sounded the death knell for so many of these ancient places in Scotland. Ireland, by contrast, has many surviving holy wells, and still preserves the customs that go with them. Scottish holy wells, on the other hand, were ranked high among so-called 'idolatrous monuments' and even if an actual demolition did not take place, it is hardly surprising that such sites as remained fell into disuse over the centuries. Gigha is no exception and there are few people now alive on the island who even know for sure where the well is situated.

The last guardians of the well, as reported by Fraser, were two old women who went by the name of Galbraith and

Graham respectively. We have seen that the keepers of the well were perceived to be guardians of traditional wisdom, knowledge and inspiration. How interesting to discover then, that the Galbraiths were no ordinary islanders. Members of this family were once known as the poet harpers of Gigha and it seems fitting that they should be associated with a holy well, for wells were often believed to be the source of poetic inspiration in the Celtic world. For many years, these poetic Galbraiths made their home at Leim Farm in the south of the island, and it is the history of that place which we will go on to consider next.

6
Leim

If I were asked to choose one place from all of Gigha that has most inspired me, I think it might have to be Leim, at the far south of the island.

Scottish singer-songwriter Dougie MacLean is also a collector of folk song and story, and in performance, he talks about the inspiration behind one of his songs, relating how an elderly Hebridean remarked to him that the islands were 'thin' places, by which he was referring to the boundaries between the natural and the supernatural worlds. Fanciful as this may sound, it is a good metaphor for the process by which writers may suddenly find themselves in tune with certain places and a concept with which at least one distinguished past minister of Gigha, poet and folklorist Kenneth MacLeod, would have agreed. Leim Farm is one such, although there are other equally evocative parts of the island, sites where archaeology and serious folklore go hand in hand to illuminate Gigha's long history as a place where people lived, fought and worshipped.

Leim is a sturdy old stone-built farmhouse, with related outbuildings, sitting high on a hillside at the south end of Gigha. Back in the 1990s, it housed a working creamery, producing wax-covered, flavoured Gigha cheeses for the speciality food market. I remember visiting it back then and it seemed bleak and muddy in pelting rain, with a suggestion of the sea somewhere below the farm, but with the whole place so shrouded in cloud that you couldn't tell where the land ended and the sea began.

Years later, we visited Leim on a summer's day when it was standing empty. The cheesemakers were long gone and there were no other tenants. The future of the place, like that of the whole island, seemed to be hanging in the balance between renewal and decay. It was a warm day during the first year or so of the community ownership of the island and we were staying in one of the Ferry Crofts, those same crofts which once housed Captain Scarlett's enterprising and hard-working John Wotherspoon before later ferrymen moved up the hill, to the Ferryman's Cottage. The previous owner of the island had converted much of the spare housing into holiday cottages for visitors, which was hard when no new building was allowed on the island, but suddenly Gigha was on the cusp between the old regime and the new. Affordable housing was already being planned, and the Heritage Trust was welcoming all visitors who might make a contribution, however small, to the island's flagging economy. Leim Farm too seemed to be waiting for change or simply for restoration.

One warm afternoon in summer, we walked the few miles from the village of Ardminish along the road south, past the bird-haunted woods of Achamore, past neat farmhouses and cottages and then turned along the road to Leim. The road curved gently upwards, skirting green pastures. The sky was picture-book blue, the verges were full of harebells, the 'blue-bells of Scotland' of popular song, and the sound of a skylark accompanied us all the way.

Things are different in this part of the island now. For one thing, the skyline beside Leim is dominated by the four community-owned windmills, which help to power the island. The neat service road to the windmills starts from the same place as the road to Leim Farm. New people live at Leim, and new houses have also sprung up at the south end of the island, at least one of which seems to dominate the landscape at the expense of the older farmhouse. However, the skylarks are still climbing and tumbling and singing through the skies, seemingly undeterred by all this change.

Back then, a faint air of desolation hung about the place, even from some distance away, even on a summer's afternoon. The farmhouse was a foursquare, typically Scottish farmhouse, with dormers and flaking paint. The numerous farm buildings clustered about it were empty, and there was a yard where no dogs barked, no children played, no washing blew in the breeze, although the swallows still flew in to nest, and their sharp cries pierced the air. Leim was deserted, with that sense of loss and shattered dreams peculiar to empty farms or perhaps to empty places of work everywhere. Cautiously, because it felt like trespassing, we wandered about the outside of the house and yard, touching nothing, but occasionally peering in at the windows.

Somebody had left several curiously shaped stones on the windowsills. The house had once had a garden, which was overgrown, although it was possible, with a little imagination, to picture yourself sitting out here on a summer's evening, gazing down towards the sea. A rather magnificent fitted kitchen was visible through one of the windows, somewhat at odds with the emptiness and simplicity of the rest of the building. Later, we found a green lane that led down to a beach below the farm. The name of this place is *Grob Bagh*, which may mean 'Bay of the Point of Rock'. On that day, it was completely empty, the only footprints our own, except for the tracks of seabirds, particularly oystercatchers, very smart in their tuxedo plumage, foraging in pairs among the seaweed.

The name Leim itself is a very old one meaning Leap or Spout. The farm takes its name from *Slocan Leim*, which is situated at the most southerly point of the island, and is a rocky passage through which the sea rumbles inwards to spout up spectacularly on the landward side, but only when the weather is right.'

The 1793 statistical account of Gigha, describes the place as follows:

> At the south end of the island there is a subterraneous passage, one hundred and thirty three feet long, into which the sea runs. About the middle, there is an aperture eight feet long and two broad. Near the end there is another, twenty feet long and four broad. Round this aperture, there are large pieces of rock; one of which has fallen in, and being jammed between the sides, divides it in two and forms a convenient resting place for taking the depths of the chasm, which is here twenty two feet, in the middle, thirty two and at the mouth, forty . . . In a time of a westerly storm, being exposed to the great swells of the Atlantic Ocean, the sea rushes in with such violence as to discharge itself through these openings with thundering noise, rising to an immense height in the form of intermitting jetts. Hence its name *Sloc an Leim* or Squirting Cave, literally Jumping Pit.[1]

Kathleen Philip reminds us that Leim was once the site of one of the larger houses of Gigha, a fact that seems to have been largely forgotten nowadays by all but a few older islanders. Pont's map, published by Blaeu in Holland in 1654, placed a large, two-chimneyed house very precisely at the south of the island, and labelled it Leim. He drew, besides, a large house at the far north end, known as *Balmoir*, and another big one (though with only one chimney) at a site labelled *Tremyeawin* – possibly modern Drumyeon, as in Drumyeonmore and Drumyeonbeg.

At that time, however, Pont certainly perceived Leim to be one of the most important houses of the island: his inclusion of two chimney stacks denoted a significant residence. Philip, writing in 1979, says that the then tenant of Leim showed her, only a few hundred yards to the north-east of the present farm, 'the ruined walls and foundations of a large, rectangular house some sixty feet long and running over forty feet back towards a wooded cliff, forming an ideal position both from the point of view of defence and of amenity. On the rough grassy floor it was just possible to see what may well have been dividing walls of rooms.' I have not found this site and since, so far as I am aware, no architectural historian has examined it, it is impossible to confirm the age of these foundations.

Philip also mentions another discovery close to Leim of 'a hard, blackish, rough, stony substance of which he (the farmer) had found quite considerable quantities when ploughing one of his fields.' Later on, the farmer, Mr Bicket, noticed a similar material in the Campbeltown museum, as an example of vitrified stone. Vitrified forts, of which there is at least one major example on Kintyre, began life as stone forts of the Iron Age, constructed with a timber framework. If – either accidentally or in some enemy attack – the timber lacing were set alight, the temperatures achieved would be hot enough to 'vitrify' or melt and fuse the rocks themselves. To quote Stuart Piggott, 'The beam ends offered a point of weakness in that they could be set on fire by the attacking force . . . once started, such a fire would spread . . . and since many of the rocks . . . fuse at comparatively low temperatures, the whole wall would come slumping down in a semi-molten mass of vitrified blocks, slagged together.'[2]

Evidence of vitrification seems to be exactly what was discovered on Leim land, although again, as far as I am aware, no modern archaeological attempt has been made to place the site of the original fort with any accuracy. Anderson posits a fort at the far south end of the island, quite a long way south of the farm of Leim itself. 'On the south coast, near to the western corner, there is a small narrow bay with a steep outcrop of rock, 65 feet long, 35 feet wide and 35 feet in height. This rock is called *Carn Leim*, being close to the chasm of that name. According to the Ordnance Survey map, it has been a fort and close examination of the meagre remains . . . affords good evidence for the claim.'[3] Anderson mentions that – because of its position with cliffs on either side, and a good view of approaching vessels, with a reef-strewn sea passage in front – this would have made a 'good sea rover's lair' but there is no evidence of vitrification up here, so perhaps there was another fort much closer to the site of the present-day farmhouse.

Anderson himself has more to say about Leim and its environs. He mentions, for instance, that there was an old quern (i.e. grinding stones) quarry at Leim and that at the time of his writing, 'one can still see the methods of the quarriers' as they cut the old grindstones, and the smaller 'knocking stones' from the rock. This was one of several old quern quarries, the remains of which can even now be seen on the island. He also reports that, in the field immediately to the north of the farmhouse, there is a mound, 24 feet in diameter, that resembles one of the small rocky outcrops with which this landscape is littered. Closer examination seemed to show that at least part of this had been built up of stones, and that it could once have been a cairn, possibly marking a prehistoric burial of some sort.

Anderson reports also that two Bronze Age burial urns were found on the farm, at the time when the road from the beach was being constructed. Tradition states that the men who found these objects took them up to the farm and placed them on the stable window (much as we had found the curiously shaped stones). Fire broke out that very same night, a fierce storm raged outside and the animals stampeded. The farm itself was very nearly destroyed. The next day, all was calm, but the next night, as Anderson puts it 'fire and pandemonium broke out again and fears became certainty that the trouble was due to the spirits whose rights had been violated.'[4]

The farmer ordered his men to put the urns back in the exact place from which they had been removed, whereupon the farm was restored to its former peace and quiet. Anderson adds that there are no records remaining of the precise site of the urns, or any description of them and certainly there is nothing to be seen today, nor anything marked on the map. Still this account is interesting for several reasons. The discovery of what seemed to be Bronze Age burial relics on this site, at some little distance from the house itself, may be significant in terms of the long history of Leim as a site of continuous occupation.

The tale of the disgruntled ghost who, upon being disturbed, makes life difficult for the nearest living beings, although in reference to a much older burial, nevertheless bears a close resemblance to the touchy spirits of Scandinavian mythology, an interesting correspondence, on this island which the Vikings knew and used as a safe anchorage. The Icelandic sagas bear witness to a number of headstrong ghosts who – although well and truly dead – refuse to lie down, but come by night and disturb the occupants of the house with noises, knocking, drumming, riding the roof beams, disturbing the animals and every so often setting property alight. Sometimes they need to be placated. Just occasionally they have to be killed all over again.[5]

All of this goes some way towards illustrating the huge complexity of this site. We can be sure that Pont was right and Leim was a very important dwelling, with a tangle of remains that we can only begin to tease out, trying to make some sense of the patterns, if patterns there are.

Leim was also important because for many years it was home to a family with a long and distinguished history: the Galbraiths, who were the poet harpers of Gigha, a family with origins going back long before the Gaelic speakers who settled this area from Ireland, right back, in fact, to the Epidii, who were here first. Like the Starkadders of Cold Comfort Farm, it sometimes seemed to me, perusing old records, that there had always been Galbraiths at Leim Farm, so much so that I have given them a whole chapter to themselves.

However, when I first started coming to the island, the Galbraiths had finally relinquished the place. Leim was the home of the Inverloch Cheese Company. Gigha has a long tradition of cheesemaking and, in an attempt to resurrect the old Gigha creamery, a new cheesemaking enterprise was set up on the island. The Eaton family took the tenancy of the farm in the early 1990s. They had reared goats, for their milk, in the Scottish Borders and for various reasons, personal and practical, decided that the move to Gigha would be beneficial. Certainly the pastures of this island are green and lush, and if – as cheesemakers say – the flavour of the cheese owes much to the grazing of the animals, then the success of these wonderful cheeses was largely down to the island itself.

In *Life on God's Island*, Freddy Gillies remembers that cheesemaking was not a new venture for Gigha. There had been a creamery at Achamore Farm producing a hard, cheddar type 'Gigha Dunlop' from the rich milk of Ayrshire cows, but it had been closed down some years previously, following the discovery of a strain of bacteria in the water supply to the farm that proved too expensive to eradicate. The old Gigha creamery went the way of many such local creameries. The Irish seemed able to tap into European grants that for mysterious reasons were inaccessible to the Scots at this time, and Irish creameries and cheesemakers seemed to thrive, while their Scottish equivalents almost invariably failed or closed.

The Eatons raised goats (some 300 of them) and a very much smaller herd of Jersey cattle. The cheesemaking was overseen by islander Sheila McNeill but the resulting product eventually had to be processed in Campbeltown, mainly because of the real difficulty of finding people to work at the creamery, on an island whose population at that time was dwindling towards unviability. The Inverloch Cheese Company is still making the distinctive Gigha cheeses – wax fruit, pears, apples and oranges, as well as small truckles. They come in a variety of flavours: fruit liqueurs, wild herbs, mustard, garlic, whisky and so on. Drumloch is a cheddar-type cheese, and there is a smoked variety too. These brightly coloured cheeses are still on the market, in speciality food shops and some supermarkets, distinctive and delicious, especially when eaten with a sheaf of good oatcakes. But the milk no longer originates at Leim, and the whole process has now moved to Kintyre although the name Gigha remains attached to the product. The lack of workers was the main problem, but a disastrous fire at Leim finished cheese production up there once and for all. It is true that the wax was particularly flammable, although some might have wondered if the angry ghost had been up to his old tricks again.

Now, Leim is also close to the site of Faith, Hope and Charity, later joined by a fourth community-owned wind turbine named Harmony, Gigha's 'Dancing Ladies' which, from their position on the windy spine of the island, are not only supplying the community with electricity, but with income as well. The erection of these turbines, which entailed the construction of a new road, was not without controversy, though all of it seems to have come from outside, from those who wanted God's island to remain as unspoiled as possible. The decision to invest in this small wind farm was pretty much unanimous on the part of the islanders. I confess to feeling a guilty pang myself since Leim was such a favourite with me. However, the islanders, with their usual mixture of sensitivity and common sense, have been careful in their siting of the windmills. Before the buyout, the island was cantering steadily down the road to non-viability as anything but a paradise island for a chosen handful, or a useful investment for an absentee consortium. Now it is benefiting from the generation of its own renewable energy, and anything that brings a modicum of self-sufficiency is a bonus.

It was on a bright spring day in May 2006 and a few years after our first visit to Leim that we set out to find the Spouting Cave, a place, which in all our years of visiting the island, we had never yet seen. We met Willie McSporran, who had been the first chairman of the Heritage Trust, on the way there and he asked us where we might be going. When we told him, he pointed us in the right direction. 'It'll not be doing much spouting today, however!' he warned us. The weather was much too calm.

From the little car park at the south end of the island, we walked through one of John Martin's newly constructed wooden gateways, down onto the shoreline. As we crossed the first stretch of rock-strewn sand, a red-breasted merganser flew across the bay in alarm at our approach. The air was an astringent mix of land and sea, as we picked our way along a muddy shoreline. The night before, a spectacular thunderstorm had rampaged across the hills of Kintyre before going on to take Glasgow by surprise, and the going was wet and likely to get wetter. We followed the shore for some distance, with, on our right-hand side, a stone fisherman's hut, which had at that time been sold for many thousands of pounds, and which, incidentally, helped the islanders in their efforts to pay off some of their million pound loan, which had been a condition of the buyout package. But it was obvious that the little roofless hut had been bought for its position, right down on the seashore, with a panoramic view of Cara, rather than for any use it might have as a house. The new owner had a caravan in situ. Caravans are largely excluded from the island and are only allowed with special permission, as temporary dwellings for those who are involved in building or rebuilding their own houses under the new dispensation. This seemed like a very worthwhile project.

Soon though, we had left the hut and the road and the pier far behind, and were striking off towards the very southernmost tip of the island, picking our way among bent grasses and muddy pools, and stretches where the seaweed lay deep and slippery, interspersed with flat white sheets of firm sand. Once or twice we stepped into what looked like a solid swathe of sand only to find ourselves practically up to the ankles in mud, but other than that there were no mishaps. Spring had come late, and the clumps of thrift along the shoreline were only just coming into bloom. At the back of the shore, the low hillocks were threaded with primroses and violets, while everywhere the starry celandine was in evidence. The rocks were yellow too with crotal, the lichen the Celts once used to dye their clothes the golden colour so much favoured by the Irish and the Scots.

There is an edict of Henry VIII forbidding them to wear articles 'coloured or dyed with saffron'[6] by which was meant not so much the plant, as the characteristic colour that seems to have been deemed by Henry to be as inflammatory as the Scottish tartan would become to later English monarchs. The Latin word for saffron, *crocotus*, is similar to the Irish word crotal, used for the yellow lichen, which makes a clear yellow dye. The forerunner of the kilt, as worn by the early inhabitants of Gigha, was the saffron shirt, an outer garment made of linen, dyed yellow gold, often with crotal. Looking at the Gigha landscape in spring, one can see how saffron garments would provide excellent camouflage so maybe Henry had a point.[7]

On this occasion, the subtle yellows of crotal and celandine were picked up and intensified by the ubiquitous yellow of the gorse, another substance that was also used in making dyestuffs by the Celts. The shoreline was still busy with oystercatchers. Lapwings and curlews were calling, while, almost on the very edges of sound or at least our ability to hear them, the skylarks were singing. There are otters at this end of the island too, and seals, but we didn't see either, although we did see the heron sailing past, with his pterodactyl legs trailing out behind him.

On a remote beach, we found a piece of treasure from the sea: an ancient oaken block, from a sailing ship. It looked as though it might have been in the water for a hundred years or more – the holes in it peering up like two dark eyes. 'It'll make a fine sculpture' said my husband, and fashioned a little piece of rope into a carrying handle so that he could take it with him. Many a sailing ship foundered in these waters between southern Gigha and the Isle of Cara, so who knows what wreck this little piece of maritime history may have come from, dislodged from its resting place by the previous winter's storms?

It was a long scramble, but at last we found the rocky bay we were seeking. We were warned away by voluble gulls, alarmed at our proximity to their nests, but we left them in peace, and they soon calmed down. A forty-five degree cliff barred our way. Unsure as to whether we could get around it on the landward side, we clambered up what looked like the easiest face, cushioned by tussocks of grass, and as we hauled ourselves up, we became aware of a most extraordinary sound, a groaning, whooshing, echoing roar, as though some great giant were lying asleep beneath our feet, and – with his head back – was snoring for all he was worth. We had found the spouting cave and Willie had been right. It wasn't spouting today. But for now, the sound was enough. We perched on top of it and listened for a while. As the waves came roaring in, time and again, you could hear the noise of stones, tumbling about inside the tunnel. It sounded like a giant stone-polishing machine, and several people subsequently told us that certain islanders had been known to clamber down into the cave beneath, and come back with finely polished stones for their gardens.

On the way back we took a detour uphill to the cairn, which was said to be the site of a beacon once used to direct vessels into the sound and into the harbour at Gigalum, speculating that perhaps our old wooden block belonged to a vessel that hadn't quite made it. Here, we sat down and gazed across to *Grob Bagh*, and to Leim again, the farm named for the spouting cave we had just heard roaring and grumbling away beneath our feet.

Back down at shore level again, and as we made our way in the direction of the pier, we found a circular rock pool, cauldron shaped, very high on the shore, and only occasionally tidal. It was surrounded by turf and rocks, and the contents were completely still. Deep within the pool, brown as caramel, sat a perfect clockwise spiral, like a galaxy in miniature. Pools at either side contained similar phenomena, but not so well formed – eerie swirls, which looked as though they might eventually evolve into what the central cauldron had become. I have no idea what natural phenomenon might have caused this strange effect, some form of spiral algae, possibly, but it seemed very odd indeed.

In his *Antiquities*, Anderson observes that 'a little to the north of this, (i.e. the spouting cave) there is a smaller cave of the same type, thirty-six feet long, called *Sloc an Tranan* (*Sloc an t-srannain* on the present pathfinder map) the Snoring Pit, so called from the kind of noise it emits in storms'.

These spouts and holes in the landscape from which peculiar noises or strange jets of water emerged were often associated in the popular imagination with the 'otherworld', the kingdom below the turf, which belonged to the fairies, a kind of parallel universe existing alongside our own. Logical explanations for these landscape anomalies must have existed side by side with more fanciful conjectures, since fishermen and farmers, even hundreds of years ago, would have had some idea of their causes and there is little evidence that the spouts of Leim were ever deemed to be of supernatural origin. But such places were also perceived to be entrances, doorways, 'thin places', where it was possible to make the perilous passage between our world and another less predictable kingdom.

On this island, as in so many other places, this otherworld was perceived to be dangerous, if not treated with proper caution and reverence. There were definite rules, and woe betide you if you broke them. There is no fairy gold to be found in *Slocan Leim*, but the highly polished stones lurking deep inside might be sufficient enticement to a Gigha man who is brave enough to dare the cavern and the snoring giant within. Perhaps the poetic Galbraiths, who called Leim their home, listened to these same strange noises emanating from deep within the earth, and were inspired by them.

7

The Magical Galbraiths

There are traditional stories on Gigha of two families who once dominated the island. Surprisingly, these tales do not refer to the McNeills, who came later, but to the Grahams and the Galbraiths. Quite apart from the fact that the guardians of the Great Well were once named as Galbraiths and Grahams, there is also a story that Gigha was once divided between these families, the north end of the island, beyond Carraig an Tairbeart, being more or less (although by no means exclusively) populated by Galbraiths, who were, for the most part, farmers. The south end was said to have been the domain of the Grahams, who were mostly fisherfolk and to some extent this was true. But we now know that there were Galbraiths at Leim in the south of the island as far back as the Middle Ages, as well as people of both surnames tenanting various other farms and inhabiting clachans and larger settlements throughout the whole island. However, the division of the island between two sets of people with quite different traditions is an interesting one.

This legend of an ancient divide between two different clans or tribes is also to be found in a much older popular tale about the island. On the west side of the island, between Ardlamey and Ardailly, runs the old track which used to serve those western settlements which looked out towards Islay and

Jura, until people deserted them for economic reasons, either emigrating to the mainland or America, or simply decamping to the more sheltered eastern side of the island. It is still possible to follow the remains of this old track even now, as it negotiates the rocky and occasionally precipitous western side of Gigha. I have walked the west of the island, and been amazed by its beauty and intrigued by the fact that this side was once so populous, but is now almost completely deserted. Of the old clachans that were once sited here, only Ardailly with its mill wheel and a scant handful of cottages remains at the western end of the valley that cleaves the island, along the foot of Creag Bhan. Of the deserted village of Ardachy, which Kathleen Philip calls 'an eerie, lost world' and the clachan known as The Glen, and the dozen or so other houses which once thronged Ardailly itself, there is now almost no sign, and such masonry as survives is usually so overgrown as to be invisible, though the green spears of water-loving irises will often mark the site of an old spring which served some lost community.

The island is deceptive. Casual visitors assume that Gigha is so small, that the landscape must be correspondingly simple, but closer acquaintance reveals its true complexity. At the back of Ardlamey, a hill called Cnoc nan Ordag rises to the east of the old track. There, Kathleen Philip describes a 'roofless ruin of a cottage which had, in the mid 19th century, housed three families' but the name means 'the hill of the thumbs' and the place is so called after an old and somewhat savage story of which Anderson gives two versions.[1]

One concerns a chieftain of mixed Norse Celtic blood who went by the similarly mixed name of *Gothfuigh*. This intermarrying between Norse settler and native Celt gave rise to a people who came to be called the *Gallgael*, foreign Gaels, recognised as populating the islands and outlying peninsulas of western Scotland in the early mediaeval period, of which we will hear more later. This tale, which Anderson attributes to the Reverend J.F. Mackenzie of Gigha, is said to have been collected from an unnamed islander. He tells of an old warrior by the name of Gillony, said to be a branch of Clan Cameron, who landed at Ardlamey (from where is not reported) with his six sons and stole some sheep. The sheep belonged to Gothfuigh who was an island chieftain, but after an initial quarrel, which threatened to turn violent, an uneasy peace was restored. A little later, one of the six Gillony sons was married to Gothfuigh's daughter, in order to seal an agreement between the two parties to the dispute. Later still, old Gillony died in suspicious circumstances, and the funeral was held at Ardachy. But the two families soon began to quarrel again and after the resulting battle the Gothfuigh victors savagely cut off the Gillony losers' thumbs and heaped them on *Cnoc nan Ordag*.

The other version of the same story is, I think, the one that has survived longest and is most pertinent to this chapter. There were, according to this version, two perennially warring clans living on Gigha, *Clan Fhamhair*, the Sons of the Giant and the incoming *Clan Bhreatan*, who are believed to be the forebears of the present-day Galbraiths. The idea that the Western Isles were once inhabited by a race of giants is found throughout Irish Celtic mythology, in the many legends about the Fomorians. Sometimes they are said to be 'huge, misshapen, violent and cruel people',[2] while at other times they are merely described in human terms as being tall and occasionally exceedingly handsome, as with *Elathan*, who was the father of the (mixed race) Irish hero *Bres*. As is so often the case with folk tales, there seems to be some small germ of truth lurking behind the legendary exaggeration and elaboration. They were invariably excellent seamen: 'the Fomors of the bright sea' with a knowledge of dairying (and presumably farming) and the stories may hark back to one of those early Bronze Age tribes referred to by Piggott, whose knowledge of sailing and farming had allowed them effectively to colonise an island such as Gigha. The name *Bhreatan*, however, seems to hark back to the Brythonic-speaking inhabitants of the Kintyre peninsula and these southern isles, the Iron Age tribes, who came somewhat later.

Eventually, so the story goes, one of the Gigha Galbraiths took a wife from *Clan Fhamhair*, and all was well for a time. The couple strove to bring the two warring factions together, but they still loathed each other. At length, the girl's Fomorian father took ill, and the Galbraith son-in-law went to see him before he died. Even on his deathbed, the old warrior of *Clan Fhamhair* had concealed a sword among the bedclothes, hoping to be able to kill his daughter's husband. Galbraith, however, saw what was going on, and left without recriminations, 'saying that they would have another day of it.'

After the death of the old man, the two clans did indeed have another day of it. They met in battle to settle things once and for all. The Galbraiths won a decisive victory, cut off the thumbs of the defeated men of *Clan Fhamhair* and drove them away from Gigha altogether. The hill where the battle was fought is *Cnoc nan Ordag*. Chopping off the thumbs of men who might be fisherman or farmers or both is a good way of making sure that they can no longer fend for themselves. However, since many popular accounts of the Fomorians describe them as being 'one eyed, one armed and one legged' the loss of the thumbs may be just another instance of legendary mutilation. There is an ancient Irish ritual, which refers to *Clan Fhamhair*, usually associated with cursing, known as '*corrguíneacht*' or 'crane-prayer' in which the ill-wisher stands on one leg, with one eye closed, one hand behind his back and chants a curse on his enemy.

The important point here is the tradition that *Clan Bhreatan*, the forebears of the Galbraiths, ousted some previous inhabitants (as well as intermarrying with them) to become pretty deeply entrenched on the island and although later histories talk of disputed ownership between the powerful McNeills and the even more powerful Macdonalds, I think we must look to the *Bhreatans* to find our links with some of the earliest inhabitants of Gigha. We have already noted that well guardians, including those who looked after the Great Well on Gigha were called by a Gaelic name which meant 'Pilgrims', 'Wanderers' or 'Strangers'. We have also seen that at least one of those well guardians (and we should bear in mind that often the guardianship of a sacred site was a hereditary position within a family) went by the name of Galbraith. But the Galbraiths were not just *dirochs* and farmers. They were also, so it seems, poets. And as poets, they may also have been wanderers, strangers or pilgrims, since, for many hundreds of years, Celtic poets were expected to travel.

To understand the nature of these early Galbraith poets who lived on Gigha, it is necessary to know that in the Celtic world, poets were uniquely powerful. In his history of Columba, Ian Finlay gives a detailed analysis of the ancient status of poets within the community. Poets constituted one of three social classes, which also included the warrior aristocracy and the serfs. Poets were of extremely high status and they would travel freely between Ireland and Scotland. 'The main task of the bard was to extol his patron and to recite his genealogy when necessary' says Finlay.[3]

Sometimes a bard would win the patronage of a particular nobleman with poems of praise as an enticement. 'A eulogy was sometimes rewarded by a silver cup' says Skene, analysing the same institution. 'Even poetry had need to be purchased'.[4]

Prophecy, miracles and incantations were also attributed to poets. The poet was a historian and storyteller with – in early Celtic society at least – a mantle of crimson bird feathers and a golden wand as badges of his office. The bard had something of the laureate and something of the satirist in his make-up, and because poetry was so often associated with magical powers, this satire could be deadly. Moreover, the poet was uniquely protected from retribution by his status as a bard, and as Finlay observes, was therefore in a position to exert what might amount to 'a sort of blackmail.' Poets were trained for many years. Those from Scotland would travel to schools of poetry in Ireland. The poet would possess a great store of knowledge, all of it memorised, while there were strict rules of composition, which must also be learned and obeyed. Comparisons have been made with Celtic arts and crafts, which so often involve enormous complexity within very strictly regulated forms.

Within these formal poetic structures, the poet could use his own talents to construct and compose anthems in praise of his patron, or satires with which to harangue him. If the medium could be said to be the message, at a time when all news was hearsay, and the written word as a way of transmitting knowledge and opinion was restricted to the educated few, the memorable compositions of a recalcitrant or disgruntled poet might make or break a leader. Words (and words made memorable by music) could disproportionately harm or bolster a reputation. There are irresistible parallels with the power of the tabloid press today.

As late as 1596 Edmund Spenser was to be found declaring that Irish poets were 'held in so high regard and estimation . . . that none may displease them, for feare to runne into reproach through their offense, and be made infamous in the mouths of all men.'[5] while in late eighteenth century lowland Scotland, Robert Burns styled himself a 'bard' and was accorded a certain licence while also being feared for his satire. The mediaeval Scots and Irish poets certainly had the unique freedom to move across political borders without let or hindrance, and would be given the best available accommodation at all times. Moreover, their job was not to fight, nor to get involved in any way, if they could possibly help it, but to observe and report on the battle. Skene quotes a heroic poet called Fergus the Bard, who, when asked if he would be joining in the battle, told his chief, 'That is not my business. You fight and I'll relate.'

The relevance of all this to Gigha is that the substantial house at Leim once housed a family of poets by the name of Galbraith. In the Advocates' Library in Edinburgh is a little handwritten book, a collection of poems compiled between 1512 and 1526 by one James MacGregor, who was Dean of Lismore. Graeme J. Baird, writing in the *Kintyremag*[6] in 1999 seems to have been the first to point to the fact that several of these poems had an apparent Gigha connection.' The poems were written in classical metres, and were written down in a kind of phonetic Gaelic, which tells us a great deal about the pronunciation of the time. At least two of them were written by one *Giolla Criost Bruilingeach*, who was a member of the *MacBhreatnaigh* family of Leym, on Gigha. A third poem, by Sir Duncan Campbell of Glenorchy, refers to another bard, *Lachlann Mheic an Bhreatnaigh*, possibly of the same family.[7]

Skene, a nineteenth-century Gaelic-speaking scholar, analysed some of the poems from The Book of the Dean of Lismore. He makes the point that many of the verses that MacGregor collected may have been much older than the specific date at which they were gathered. The poets and musicians of Highland and Island tradition were part of an oral continuum with a long and distinguished pedigree. Trained musicians often accompanied them, but sometimes the poets themselves performed both functions, i.e. they were poet-harpers.

Although poets could perform prodigious feats of memory (a skill that is largely lost to us), they also had recourse to various formulaic lines which would give the poet breathing space and carry him forward to the next part of the story.[8] These would also act as points of reference for the audience (for this by its very nature, was performance poetry, largely aimed at those who could not read), their very familiarity reassuring the listeners that this was a poet who knew his craft. Such formulaic lines might also have acted as an aid to memory, in the same way that a cue is used by an actor. As part of his training, the poet would have learned a lexicon of stock descriptive phrases, which could be slotted into different poems. These poems would fulfil various functions including entertainment, newsgiving, the keeping of the history of a tribe or race, the memorising of laws, the declaring of love, and the celebration of the natural world in which the Celts invested a great deal of power.

Poets would attach themselves to a particular chieftain, but only as long as that leader was generous. These poets thought nothing of moving from island to island. They frequently journeyed between Scotland and Ireland and travelled the length and breadth of each country, all this at a time when – although there were acknowledged connections between the two countries – such journeys were hazardous and many people would have been born, lived and died in the same small village, or in the case of Gigha on the same small island, without ever seeing what lay beyond the next horizon.

There is a traditional belief that the roots of the Celtic Travelling People lie with the ancient '*seannachie*', wandering bards such as *Giolla Criost Bruilingeach* of Leim, whose function was to entertain, to teach and sometimes to reinforce the social status quo. In turn the *seannachie* claimed descent, however unlikely, from the mythical Danaan people, who, like the legendary chieftain of *Clan Bhreatan* at *Cnoc nan Ordag*, defeated the more practical Fomorians (whoever they might have been) and whose chief skills lay in music and magic. The surname Galbraith or its earlier incarnation of *MacBhreatnaigh*, as we have already seen with regard to the battle of the Hill of the Thumbs, is a very old one, already associated with Gigha. *MacBhreatnaigh* means 'son of the Britons' with the *bhreatnaigh* or *bhreatan* element, referring to those earlier inhabitants of Scotland, who spoke Brythonic rather than Gaelic.

One of the *Bhreatnaigh* poems in the Dean's collection is actually a satire by Sir Duncan Campbell of Glenorchy, in which he describes one *Lachlan Mheic an Bhreatnaigh Bhinn*

– sweet-voiced Galbraith. Although Lachlan may have had a sweet voice, he was also something of a miser, demanding a variety of gifts from all and sundry, as of right. Poets expected to be constantly rewarded and Celtic leaders habitually wore bracelets that could be handed out like a kind of currency, but Lachlan is depicted as demanding an increasingly bizarre list of items including soles for his shoes, a peacock's feather, an old felt hat, maidens' shifts and a headless pin, all from contributors as diverse as young women, little dogs and weasels. Nobody is spared his outrageous avarice.

There seems to be no mention of the provenance of this greedy poet and we know that the *Bhreatnaigh* family had connections in Kintyre and Wigtown as well as Gigha but since the Dean collected two more poems, by a bard calling himself *Giolla Criost Bruilingeach* (the latter word referring to a form of metre or style of poetry – an 'inferior' form, according to a thirteenth-century Irish poet who said the work of the 'bruiling' was but a 'crooked lay') who was also of the *Bhreatnaigh* family, and who was said to be a Bard in Leym, it seems a reasonable assumption that Sweet-Voiced Galbraith, the Miser may also have been a Gigha Galbraith, or at least may have been connected to them in some way.

The first of the *Giolla Criost* poems was written for *Tomaltach MacDiarmida*, Lord of Moylurg in Connacht and we know that he died in 1458. It contains a request for a harp, as a reward for poems praising Tomaltach. By harp, the Gigha poet no doubt meant the portable and very beautiful *clarsach*, an instrument which was itself often deemed to have magical properties.[9] That the request was fulfilled, we know by a later poem, in which *Giolla Criost* praises his chief again, but also satirises one Tomas Maguire, King of Fermanagh, who was presumably, not so generous because *Giolla Criost* resorts to satire and calls him an 'outlandish starveling cripple'.

Whatever the quality of his poems, this man is described as the 'Bard in Leym' which is believed to be a variant of Leim, that same farm at the south end of the Isle of Gigha whose prehistory we have already discussed. It is interesting to note that the family connection persists. Some 200 years later, there is a list of Gigha men concerned in Argyll's Rebellion of 1685 and one of them is 'John Roy McVretiny in Leim', which is also a variant of the same surname, *Bhreatnaigh* and one which eventually translated itself to Galbraith although when this change occurred is uncertain. Graeme Baird posits some time during the eighteenth century, and certainly by 1793, the surname Galbraith is common throughout Gigha as it was throughout much of Kintyre and south-west Scotland.

The *Bhreatnaigh* family were known to have populated the old kingdom of Strathclyde, with its fortress at Dumbarton, whose name itself means the Fortress of the Britons and variants of the name are found throughout Ayrshire and Galloway. By the end of the twelfth century the Galbraith's first designated chief was *Gilchrist Bretnach* (meaning servant of Christ, the Briton) who is to be found witnessing a charter in 1180. The family home was Inchgalbraith, an island in Loch Lomond. The Galbraith name itself means Foreign Briton.

Historically, the Galbraith family had ties with the House of Lennox, which meant that they fell foul of James I of Scotland in the early 1400s. James was sent to France in 1406, at the age of twenty-two, after his elder brother the Duke of Rothesay was murdered. On the way there, James was captured by pirates and handed over to King Henry IV of England who kept him prisoner for eighteen years while the Duke of Albany became regent of Scotland, making little effort to free his sovereign. James was well treated during his imprisonment, as befitted his royal status, but when he was eventually released and returned to Scotland to be crowned at Scone, he immediately sought retribution on those families that had betrayed him: the houses of Lennox and Albany and their adherents, the Galbraiths.

The chieftain of the Galbraiths at the time was said to have fled to Kintyre and Gigha with some 600 families – a very large number of people. However, logically, one would assume that they fled there because it was already a Galbraith stronghold. Baird suggests that the McNeills of Gigha or the Macdonalds may have been patrons of the Galbraith poets, especially since before 1476 Leim was not included in that portion of the island over which the McNeills held authority.

As a member of the Gigha *MacBhreatnaigh* family, as Keith Sanger points out in another interesting paper for the *Kintyremag*,[10] the poet musician *Giolla Criost* may also have been related to a *MacBhreatnaigh* family of harpers who are mentioned in the Exchequer Rentals for 1471 as holding lands near Wigtown in Galloway at that time. The names Martin, John and Lachlan *MacBhreatnaigh* are to be found on record between the years 1471 and 1513 and this family of musicians may have originally held their lands under the patronage of the church at Whithorn, which also held lands in Kintyre. Bearing in mind that these poet-harpers were still accustomed to travel widely, it doesn't seem to be stretching the imagination too far to propose Leim on Gigha, a large and important house at that time, according to Blaeu's map, as being the home of members of a distinguished family of poet-musicians who were well known throughout the whole of south-west Scotland.

In *Highland Folk Ways*, Grant observes that – even when she was writing in 1961 – the country people still had a wealth of stories and traditions handed down by storytellers. These might be the *Ursgeulan* or wonder tales, which had much in common with tales from other cultures. Besides these were the familiar Gaelic epics, which survived throughout the Lordship of the Isles, and were well remembered right until the early years of the nineteenth century. Even then, visitors to a small community would be asked if they knew anything of the *Fheinn*. If the answer were in the affirmative, the whole clachan would gather together to listen to the storyteller.

These were tales of Finn MacCoul, and of his band of warriors, of Deirdre and Grainne, of Diarmaid, and Cuchullin. So familiar and well loved were the stories that references to these heroes and heroines of myth were often quite deliberately placed in a local landscape. This may even have been a poetic convention. As we have seen, something very similar must have happened on Gigha, in that Diarmaid and Grainne feature so prominently in the Gigha landscape in connection with Keefie's fort.

The records of successive Gigha Galbraiths are very sparse, but in 1794 we learn that Galbraiths were elders of the kirk, and presumably still well thought of on the island. Neil Galbraith is recorded as being responsible for the suitable Sunday behaviour (and compulsory kirk attendance) of various farmsteads and clachans, including Keil, South and North Drumachro, and Cara. Notably Lachlan Galbraith, who was himself an elder of the kirk was involved in a dispute which resulted when a considerable quantity of wreckage was cast up on the Leim shore, on a wild Sunday in February. The records of the kirk session tell the tale.

'On this day was convened on Leim shore a great number of the people of this Parish during the time of divine service, waiting what wreckage might be cast ashore by the waves and behaving themselves in a riotous and indecent fashion.' Not only was it a crime to miss divine service, no matter how urgent the enticement, but simply working on a Sunday was a punishable offence. Nevertheless, there were obviously times when practical matters overrode the fear of the kirk and this was one.

Lachlan Galbraith excused himself thus. 'I was sitting at home in my house, not having any shoes to go out in. On a girl coming to my door she told me about the throng securing timbers, so I went to their assistance.'

The gathering of scarce and much-needed timber, of which the island had scant supplies for building, repairing or for fuel, was deemed to be worth the penalty even on the Sabbath. Martin, writing in the late 1600s, observes that 'the isle affords no wood of any kind but a few bushes of juniper on the little hills' and the fact that the situation is somewhat different now is a fairly recent occurrence. Gathering of wood on a Sunday involved a reprimand and a fine, which was quite substantial at two shillings and sixpence. However, the reprimand was seen as being rather worse than the fine, and there is evidence that islanders, when they could afford it, would offer to pay higher fines, so as to be excused the public humiliation of the reprimand which was usually given in the kirk, in front of friends and neighbours, on a Sunday. Money from these fines was given to the poor, so at least somebody benefited and it seems as though the kirk elders (ever realists in these matters) were not averse to commuting the reprimand if a higher fine was forthcoming.

That there were still Galbraiths (or Galbreath as it is often spelled) at Leim in the late 1700s is also evidenced by a memorial in the graveyard at Kilchattan erected by 'Donald Galbreath, Leam, in the memory of his father Donald Galbreath who died November 1794 aged 89' along with a nearly obliterated inscription to a Galbraith who was married to a McQuilkan, both living at Leim, and one of whom had died in the 1720s.

Kathleen Philip points to the dramatic drop in the island population, around the 1850s and 1860s, which seems to have been largely due to the sudden exodus of members of the Galbraith family, who had, in the early 1800s, been tenants on many an island farm.[11] 'Popular legend on Gigha centres around the strange and sudden decline of the numbers of the once flourishing Galbraith family.' Early that century there had been Galbraiths at Tarbert, North Ardminish, Highfield, Ardailly, Drumyeonbeg and North Drumachro, but by 1871 they seem to have left all but Drumyeonbeg. The exodus seems to have been mostly young people, leaving to find work elsewhere, either in flourishing Scottish cities, where the industrial revolution was providing and had provided employment for some years, or emigrating to America or Canada to seek greater prosperity and a potentially easier way of life. At least some of the apparent population decline, however, can be accounted for by the prolonged absence of young men who would have been working at the herring fishing.[12]

There are accounts of island families suffering in the factories of Glasgow, but this does not seem to have been a clearance in the regular understanding of the term, with families being evicted from their crofts to make way for more lucrative sheep.[13]

There is little evidence of enclosure and subsequent sheep rearing on Gigha, and indeed the landscape of this small island would hardly be such as to lend itself to this. It seems that people were leaving very much of their own volition, although economic and social pressures must have been a major factor: a clearance by default. Those who cannot make a reasonable living where they are will, if the opportunity arises, go elsewhere. This motivation is, after all, what had brought incomers to Gigha itself over many thousands of years.

They were seeking, as young people will, a better and less difficult life elsewhere. In fact the exodus of so many people, albeit for temporary work at the fishing or in service on the mainland, left the island farms so depleted of healthy young labour that the lairds must have found it a considerable inconvenience. This seems to have been the start of a process that only looks likely to be halted and possibly reversed in the next few years, by the recent community buyout of the island. The Galbraiths were part of a much wider movement, and as usual we find that Gigha provides a microcosm of many of the challenges and problems besetting the Scottish isles and rural south-west Scotland from prehistory to the present day.

As a postscript to this, it is interesting to note that when I originally researched this book in 2006, there were no Galbraiths left on Gigha although there are plenty of their descendants. According to Rona Allan who was then working for the Gigha Heritage Trust, in 1827 there were 113, in 1841 there were 85, in 1881 the numbers had sunk to 24 and by 1891 there were only 16 left. Rona points out that 'the name died out here as many left in the mid 1700s and early 1800s.

Those that stayed seemed to be women who married and obviously took another surname.'

Rona points out that her own great-great-grandmother was a Galbraith who died in 1894. This observation would seem to bear out Kathleen Philip's contention that these Gigha families were not so much cleared as tempted out by the promise of greater economic prosperity elsewhere. Perhaps it was mostly the younger and stronger Galbraith men who left the island, taking their wives and families with them. The older members of the family died out, while the young women who stayed on, married and of course changed their surnames.

8

Kilchattan

At some point in the history of Gigha, the main focus of Christianity seems to have shifted from the north of the island at Tarbert, where we find the Holy Stone, the Field of the Chapel and the ancient cemetery, and moved further south to Keil (a name that generally denotes a monastic cell) where we find the remains of a church dedicated to an early Celtic saint called Cattan or Cathan. Kilchattan is *Cille Chatain*, i.e. Cattan's Cell. The map of the island, published by Blaeu in Holland in 1654, but based on maps and plans drawn by Pont some fifty years earlier, also confirms the association with the saint.

It is worth quoting Martin Martin's 1695 description of the church in full here:

> There is a church on the island called Kilchattan, it has an altar in the east end and upon it a font of stone which is very large and hath a small hole in the middle which goes quite through it. There are several tombstones in and about this church; the family of the Macneils, the principal possessors of this isle, are buried under the tombstones on the east side the church where there is a plot of ground set apart for them. Most of all the tombs have a two handed sword

> engraven on them and there is one that has the representation of a man upon it.
>
> Near the west side of the Church, there is a stone of about 16 feet high and 4 broad, erected upon the eminence. About 60 yards distance from the chapel there is a square stone erected about ten feet high; at this the ancient inhabitants bowed, because it was there that they had the first view of the church. There is a cross 4 feet high at a little distance and a cavern of stone on each side of it.[1]

Another church named for Cathan is to be found on the isle of Bute and there are references to him in Kintyre and elsewhere. Colonsay and various other islands can lay claim to him too. Cathan was said to be of Dalriadan royal lineage, and some traditions say that he was King Aidan's son and was educated by Saint Patrick himself. However, most other accounts equate him with a sixth-century bishop of Bute in 563 when King Conall was ruling the Scottish kingdom of Dalriada.

In common with many religious men of that rather ascetic branch of Christianity, the Celtic monastic tradition, Cathan preferred to espouse the solitary life and eventually relinquished his office and lived out his days in great simplicity on the Isle of Bute. The other patron saint of Bute, St Blane, was said to be Cathan's nephew, the son of his sister Ertha. The monastic foundation on Bute remained well into the twelfth century, after which the church there was rebuilt. At some point, however, tradition tells us that Cathan visited Gigha and spent time on the island, leaving little else but his name and a handful of remains in stone, with only Martin's 'square stone' and 'cross' indicating the Celtic monastic origin of the site. Since his name is known and commemorated on other western isles, there is a possibility that he may have spent at least some of his life on pilgrimage, a traditional way of life for monks of the Celtic faith, bringing news of Christ to the people of the Inner Hebrides.

The only thing we know with any certainty, however, is that the present ruined church of Kilchattan post-dates the saint by many hundreds of years, and dates from the twelfth- or thirteenth-century Europeanisation of Irish religious tradition, but there is a chance that beneath these stones lie the traces of an earlier cell dedicated to Cathan or one of his community. Between the cottages at Keil and the church itself, not far from the Ogham stone (which Martin describes as the 'square stone'), is a circular enclosure where Betty McNeill of Keil told me that her father used to grow his potatoes. It has the appearance of an old enclosure for animals of some sort, perhaps an old garden or an allotment, which is obviously what it has been used for, but, given its position, close to the Ogham stone, and the similar siting of such ancient circular enclosures elsewhere on the island, I have occasionally wondered if it might have a much longer history as the site of an original 'cell' after which the place was named.

Cathan's reported impulse to withdraw from the world and lead the contemplative life is absolutely in accord with the nature of this early Christianity. As Finlay tells us in his history of Columba, even in biblical times, holy men would go off into the wilderness, to fast and pray. These early Christian monks were following in that tradition. They wished to be simply and completely self-sufficient, to live a life of pure spirituality, which could only be achieved by fasting and meditation. They would set up cells or bothies, often built of little more than wood and wattles, in a style that had been in use for the construction of domestic dwellings for thousands of years. These cells would be grouped around a central oratory, which would also have been of basic wooden construction, wherever timber was available.

On western isles such as Gigha, however, where timber was very scarce, these small settlements would have been constructed of stone. If this desire to live in remote places, for the love of God, seems strange to us, we need only look to the remote religious huts at Great Skellig, off the coast of Kerry in Ireland, to grasp some idea of the mindset of these men. These fifth- and sixth-century monks would have led lives of chilly austerity.

The rewards of this bodily hardship, of course, were all in the next life, and yet standing up at Keil on the spine of Gigha, with the Kintyre peninsula to the east and the broad sea and the further islands to the west, there is something in most of us that responds to the desire for solitude and enlightenment which drove these early Christian monks, although they certainly seem to have had an eye for beauty in the sites they selected. The Celts with their love of nature, of intricacy in poetry, in music and in art, as well as their inherent appreciation of heroism, seem to have responded in a unique way to this early version of Christianity. The tribe, or *tuath*, in this society was a group of families who owed allegiance to one another, through ties of kinship. They were ruled over by a *ri* or king, though the term is closer to our 'leader' in meaning. There were also overlords to whom groups of *tuatha* owed a kind of communal allegiance.[2]

The early monastic communities, familial, and with ties to a local leader, from whom they might be granted small parcels of land, fitted very smoothly into the Celtic pattern of closely interlinked families, as did their belief in Christ as the ultimate heroic king, to whom all might owe allegiance. These monks would have spoken Gaelic and Latin and, as the possessors of literary skills unknown to the masses, some of them would have written down the poems and stories and beliefs of their own Celtic heritage. They also – like the wandering poets of Gaelic tradition – thought of themselves as wanderers upon the face of the earth, seeking to be anywhere, for the love of God, spreading the word of Christianity to the unenlightened, but also understanding the complexity and entrenched nature of the existing belief systems of the people whom they were seeking to convert. Wherever possible, they sought to replace, rather than displace.

Sometimes these men fell foul of unrepentant pagans and were martyred for their beliefs like many who were to succeed them. Mostly they sought to convert with a light touch, slotting their belief in the heroic risen Christ smoothly into the wisdom and intricate spirituality of the past, partly because of their own lingering fondness for their Celtic heritage. It is a pity that successive and much more heavy-handed proselytisers, on Gigha, no less than elsewhere, seemed set on destroying what had endured for so many hundreds of years.

While we are on the subject of these earliest Christians on Gigha, it is worth mentioning another ancient relic at Keil. We have already referred to the lost standing stone mentioned by Martin and later by Pennant, in the vicinity of the church, but the Ogham-marked pillar may still be seen, a short walk to the north-west from the church, and beyond the modern cemetery. This sits on a hill called *Cnoc an Charraigh* (the Hill of the Pillar), looking across to Kintyre and, as Martin described it, is square in section. Like the tombstones in the church this pillar is now very badly weathered, but it is just possible to make out the original indentations along the edge, which constitute the ancient stone script known as 'Ogham'. Various interpretations of the script have been made, among which are *Vicula Maq Comgini* (Fiacal, son of Coemgen) or *Viddosamo Qoicogini* (Viddosamo son of Qoicogino).[3] The former would be a Pictish-influenced Scottish inscription, while the latter would seem to be a native Pictish inscription. Either way, the pillar seems to have been a very early Celtic Christian memorial, cut and erected in memory of a deceased island leader.

Our next direct mention of St Cathan in connection with this site comes much later in 1510, when we learn of the 'Ecclesia Sancti Catani in Giga' in the Register of the Privy Seal. In that year King James IV presented Angus Makkane to the rectory of St Catan, Gigha, vacant through the death of Sir John Judge. In 1549, Dean Munro mentions 'ane paroche kirke' on the island and a hundred years later, as we have already heard, Martin Martin similarly refers to it in his own description of the Western Isles. As Kathleen Philip points out, 'that is the sum total of references to the Church of St Cathan during the course of some four centuries.'

Although the written references are few, the ruin that remains can tell us a good deal more. This building itself dates from as long ago as the twelfth or thirteenth century, which would already have made it quite a venerable church when Angus Makkane was appointed rector in 1510. In the same way that it is only tradition which tells us that Cathan once had a cell up here at Kilchattan, we do not know who built this early mediaeval church and named it for the Columban saint, and opinion is divided. Primary sources are silent, although Anderson speculates that it might have been the Macdonalds, while Philip wonders (with more justification in my view) if the Cistercian monks from Saddell Abbey on Kintyre might have been responsible for constructing the church as a monastic outpost of Saddell. There, the relatively simple early church has disappeared, so we cannot make comparisons.

Kilchattan was quite small, with a steep roof and according to Anderson would have had lancet windows in all its walls. If Gigha was still maintaining its reputation as a holy place, it may have attracted the monks of Saddell to build a church for the use of the islanders, and perhaps for their own use, as a place of retreat. The church is very well built and Irish masons may have been employed on its construction. There are few surviving documents about the Cistercian foundation at Saddell, so we will probably never know the truth although as we shall see in due course, there are parallels between Saddell and Kilchattan in more than the church itself.

In the early eighteenth century the Gigha parish church was re-sited closer to the village of Ardminish, and subsequently this chapel fell into the ruin that remains to this day although the graveyard stayed in use, with the later addition of a new cemetery, sited on the gentle slope to the west of the church, below the Ogham stone. The church at Kilchattan is oriented east-west. The eastern gable is 13 feet high, and in it is an elegant lancet window, 6 feet in height and 6 inches wide. When Anderson was describing the ruins in the twentieth century, he was able to tell us that the altar that Martin saw in 1700 had gone, although he wondered with some justification if it might not have been relaid among the grave slabs at the rear of the church. The octagonal stone font remained in position, although that has now been removed for safekeeping to the current new kirk, built in 1923, down in the village of Ardminish and where it can still be seen. These old stone fonts are a rarity throughout Scotland, most having been vandalised or put to secular uses.

Anderson tells us that 'almost the whole floor of the church is covered with graveslabs, the total number including fragments being thirty-three'. He laments the fact that many are indecipherable, and this is a situation that has certainly not improved with the passing years, since it is now practically impossible to see any of the once beautiful and intriguing designs that characterised these stones.

We can do little more here than offer old accounts from *Archaeological Sketches in Scotland* by Captain T.P. White, published in 1875 and from Anderson's later account, and leave the interested investigator to decide whether he or she can match any of these tantalising descriptions with their well-worn counterparts in situ. According to White, whose analyses of his own drawings are somewhat sketchy, there had once been a mermaid, or merman, with a substantial head of hair. There was also an otter, 'grabbing at a fish'. There was a beautifully sculpted design with a sword and 'a kind of griffinish animal common in Knapdale, but in this case headless'.[4]

These ornate stone slabs are part of a long tradition in Argyll and the isles, which seems to have seen its greatest flowering at the time of the Lordship of the Isles but the stonemasons who carved these were working in a tradition of intricate intertwined lines at once free-flowing and formal, coupled with depictions of birds and beasts (with a sideways, and very Celtic, glance towards animism) that stretched back over many hundreds of years. There are more such stones in

Knapdale, over on Kintyre, but the Gigha stones must once have rivalled them in complexity and beauty. Anderson writing somewhat later than White describes what he calls a row of 'monuments of Heads of the local House' in some detail.[5]

On one of them, 'the surface is filled with a decorated cross and ornamentation. The upper part of the design consists of an equal-armed cross with the arms intersected by two flat concentric rings.' There is a slab with 'three vertical lines of ornament: a four-cord plait, a chain of conventional leaves and a vertical scroll of formal foliage. The three series of ornaments join in the angled floor of the slab in an ornamental swastika.'

Of those which Anderson calls 'Great Slabs', one has a broadsword, with 'depressed quillions and lobed pommel' and is 'probably of early 15th century date'. The second 'suddenly flowers out into the fully developed, highly decorative foliaceous and animal ornament, characteristic of so many of the gravestones in the West Country and Islands. A procession of animals is seen. There is an otter, following a salmon, next a dog or otter and finally two dogs side by side; the whole reaching to the tip of the blade. On the right are two intertwining stems ending in the figures of two wolves.' This stone also depicted a cat and a beaver and White's aforementioned mermaid. Above the mermaid in the right-hand corner is a pair of shears with another sharp tool of some sort and what Kathleen Philip describes as a comb – perhaps that which was traditionally said to belong to the mermaid. The mermaid was an emblem of certain Scottish families, but in the Middle Ages and after it was also used to represent the dangers of vanity and promiscuity. Its most famous depiction is perhaps as a deliberate insult to Mary Queen of Scots. As such it might have been carved on a gravestone as a 'memento mori' to those who might come after, much like the skulls and crossbones on later graves – remember that you will die, and that the vanities of the world are fleeting. We should remember that women would have been buried beneath these ornate stones as well as men, married couples perhaps, beneath the same emblematic stone. Primary sources offer us little in the way of detail, and most histories, even modern analyses, make little mention of them.

This mermaid grave slab is thought to be of the fifteenth-century type, but as usual we have lost the key to what these carvings may have signified to the stonemason who made them and those who commissioned them for their deceased relatives. Certainly they belong to a time when symbols took the place of inscriptions, and when written inscriptions would have been superfluous, because few could have read them and in any case everybody on the island would have known what these things symbolised, and who would have been buried beneath. Such details would have been passed on to those who came after.

Hunting obviously loomed very large for these people, who would have been important in their community. Deer would have been hunted, not just for sport, but as a valuable food source. Weapons of course would have been important, and the sword would have been a personal and precious item for the man who wielded it – made for him alone, or passed on from father to son. But we know that other creatures had a deeper significance within this society, such as the salmon's association with wisdom, the dog with loyalty, the wolf with bravery. Once again we are faced with the lost language of these stones, like hieroglyphs that we could read if only we had the key.

The third stone had an intricate four-cord plait, with 'elaborate detail'. And the fourth had, according to Anderson 'considerable grace and variety' with various animal ornaments including a bull, a hind and a crouched dog 'ready to spring'. Even by the time when Anderson was describing these, he tells us that the fifth slab was 'almost wholly defaced and the design beyond recovery'. The sixth slab depicted a stag in flight before a dog, 'a vital presentation of animal life' and the seventh, which is broken in two, seems to have been later than the others, of sixteenth-century date, again showing a sword and foliage but no animals.

Slabs survive, but in sadly worn form so that it is almost impossible to match them with Anderson's descriptions. It is a moot point as to whether it would have been better to remove these examples of early Scottish grave art to a museum where they might have been preserved, but understandably enough, there are always strong community objections to such removals. As it is, they have been left in situ, where the elements have done their worst. Wind, rain and time have worn the designs away, but at least the stones themselves remain in evocative and atmospheric remembrance of those leaders of Gigha who were buried here.

Perhaps the most striking grave at Kilchattan is one mentioned by Martin. It is set apart from the other McNeills, on the east side of the church. Anderson describes this as: 'The figure of a warrior in camail and jupon, carved on the graveslab in high relief; and the rest of the surface, very much worn, still shows that there has been foliaceous ornament.' He goes on to suggest that this slab marks the grave of Malcolm McNeill, a fifteenth-century chieftain, whose predecessors were constables of Castle Sweyn or Sween in Knapdale, also a centre of the stonecarver's art, and who are buried on the mainland. Kathleen Philip tells us that the islanders called it 'Malcolm's Grave'. This Malcolm seems to have had a particular attachment to the island.

When the Lords of the Isles resigned Kintyre and Knapdale, Malcolm is found in possession of Gigha or a large part of it. He habitually signed himself 'Malcolm McNeill of Geya', the island was his little kingdom, and when he died in 1493, this was where he was buried, in an enclosure, just outside the church dedicated to St Cathan. We can speculate that he might have lived in the big house shown on Blaeu's map at the north end of the island, and named Balmoir, since this seems to have been the seat of the lairds of Gigha for many hundreds of years. But we can't know for sure. Still, there is something profoundly moving about this surviving tomb, with its shadowy, still powerful warrior in stone, one of the ancient lairds of the island; and whenever I walk up to Kilchattan I find myself leaving a flower or two on his grave. Once or twice, I have found that other people have done the same thing.

The simple truth is that we do not know who carved these stones. Kathleen Philip talks of 'Gigha masons', and this is possible, but unlikely. The carving on these stones is of such a high standard that it suggests a more specialist school of carving than might have been found on such a small island. If there was a group of Gigha masons, then they may have learned their craft in Knapdale or elsewhere. But it is not hard to find a potential source for that very specialised knowledge. There is a striking similarity between the Gigha warrior and a group of gravestones carved with equally striking warriors at Saddell Abbey on the east coast of mainland Kintyre, looking towards Arran, and since there are other connections between this place and Gigha, it is worth exploring the nature of this Cistercian Foundation in a little more detail.

Saddell Abbey has been researched (not without difficulty, since documentary evidence seems to be very slight) by Professor A.L. Brown of Glasgow University.[6] Tradition has it that the abbey was founded by Somerled, the most powerful leader in Argyll and the West, and a leader who succeeded in freeing Argyll from Norse rule. Some accounts say that he is buried at Saddell, but it seems more likely that his son, Reginald, was responsible for building the abbey. Somerled was killed in 1164 and Reginald died around 1207. The earliest documents refer to Reginald as founder, rather than his father, but perhaps the son was left to carry out his father's plans in this respect. The motherhouse from which this abbey sprang was Mellifont Abbey in County Louth, near Drogheda in Ireland. Mellifont itself was founded in 1142. A papal bull, dated 12 July 1393, confirms the election of Macratious, one of the monks, as new abbot of Saddell and implies a long-term link between Mellifont and Saddell, which was well established and flourishing at that time.

Professor Brown tells us that the earliest buildings on the site were possibly constructed by Irish craftsmen, which would have been at a time when the Irish religious tradition was gradually being Europeanised. Gigha was mentioned in connection with Saddell Abbey in the saga of Haakon in 1236. In this account, the abbot of a monastery of 'grey monks', which surely refers to the Cistercians of Saddell, comes to King Haakon at Gigha, where his fleet lay at anchor before the Battle of Largs, and asks for his protection and for the protection of the abbey from marauding Norsemen who would have made short work of whatever treasures were kept there. The Viking king grants the abbot his request and gives him a charter to mark the deed.

There is also a mention in this saga of a priest named Simon, who was a Dominican monk and who was of some importance to Haakon. He died at Gigha, and was taken ashore in Kintyre, and buried in the monastery of the 'grey monks' with a silken cloth to cover him. Given the possible twelfth-century date of Kilchattan, it is also possible that the Gigha church was an offshoot of Saddell Abbey, built at a time when it was felt that a larger and more distinguished church was necessary on the island, which would have had a large Christian population.

Certainly Saddell Abbey was in possession of 'two mark-lands at Craigvan in Gigha' in the fifteenth century, but where this was situated in relation to the present-day Creag Bhan is impossible to say. The monastery was important enough to attract gifts of land in the 1400s. It was still in existence in 1498, but by 1508 it was seemingly deserted and then suppressed. Brown calls this a 'mystery' and wonders why it happened. He points out that Saddell, which had always been provincial, had probably come under increasing lay influence.

The Cistercians as an order were usually involved in agriculture, and worked as horse and cattle breeders, all of which were settled occupations. But writing in the *Kintyremag* in 1998, D. Rixon and A.I.B. Stewart both discuss the possibility of a distinct Kintyre-based 'Saddell Abbey School' of stone carving, which was thought to have started about 1425 and continued until approximately 1500, when, as we have seen, the abbey fell into rather sudden decay. By 1508, we learn that many of the ordinary abbey stones were removed for the construction of Saddell Castle for the bishop of Argyll, but the carved tombstones were kept within the old abbey walls for many years. From the nature of the stones themselves, it was apparent that many had been carved locally, although some were of Iona stone. Recently, the Saddell tombstones were taken to Edinburgh for cleaning, and are now preserved back on site beneath a purpose-built shelter.

There are many secular tomb slabs among them, warriors with swords, like our Malcolm of Gigha, and it seems likely that in the century before its demise, Saddell would have become increasingly associated with this carving school and its relationship with various local lairds, who would have taken advantage of the skilled stonemasons and rewarded them accordingly. In consequence of this, there may have been only a few monks left there, and the Cistercian rule may have been poorly observed. Stonemasons were often itinerant craftsmen. This was a profession inextricably linked with travellers who (like poets and musicians) often moved from place to place, exercising their skills in situ. Given the pretty exact correspondence of dates, it may well be that the carved tombstones of Kilchattan on Gigha, like so many other carved stones on Kintyre, belong to a school of carving that was linked with Saddell Abbey on the mainland. If there were stonemasons on Gigha, they may have learned their craft at Saddell itself.[7]

During the summer of 2010, an extensive conservation project was undertaken at the church with funding from the Heritage Lottery Fund, Historic Scotland, private donors and the islanders themselves. This beautiful building has now been stabilised and preserved although donations for ongoing maintenance will always be gratefully received by the Gigha Heritage Trust. Rona Allan has also done sterling and detailed research on the inscriptions in the adjoining graveyard, with the information being of particular interest to genealogists or those with island connections. All of this means that the lovely old stones of Kilchattan have resumed their role at the heart of island tradition once more.

9

The Norseman's Scales

It is impossible to visit Gigha without wishing to view the landscape of the island from the sea. Many of the islanders have their own small boats, and it is possible to go fishing, or simply rowing along the coastline, to see it as early incomers must first have viewed it. Seen from a boat on a fine day, the island is a fertile place, surrounded by turquoise seas over pure white sand, seas which must once have teemed with life. Gigha is some seven miles long by less than two miles wide, but has twenty-five miles of coastline. There are places where a shallow boat can navigate long corridors between rocky islets, where seals bask in the sun, too lazy to do more than lift an indignant head and bark at you, with the bark sometimes turning to a yawn, as you pass by.

Below the boat, a looking-glass garden is spread out in the clear water. Iridescent fronds trail upwards, while clinging to the rocks below are great heaps of spongy growths where tiny fish dart in and out. Peer more closely and you will see crabs, lurching along the bottom, with their curious gait, or common (and harmless) jellyfish like so many floating lampshades, slowly pulsating along. At certain times of the year, they come ashore in great numbers, to lie stranded on the beaches, alien life forms among the rocks. More dangerous, and feared by fishermen, are the long trails of pinkish tentacles called 'scalder', with a painful sting, disproportionate to their size, which wrap themselves around fishing lines. The shallower pools, where seawater is trapped upon the rocks by the receding tides, are home to strawberry sea anemones, hermit crabs, blennies and gobies, and transparent shrimps.

All of these things would have been apparent to the Norse incomers as they circumnavigated the island, viewing its excellent harbours and fertile landscape with an astute and acquisitive eye. Gigha was to become a useful base for these Vikings, a strategically valuable place, where they could lurk, take stock, seek shelter and food, and make decisions about the next move in their ongoing attempts to colonise Scotland and the Hebrides in particular.

In the late eighth century, Scotland saw these incomers as a new and terrifying threat. As so often in the past, this threat came from the sea. It would have started in a small way, with a handful of dragon-prowed longships making exploratory forays along the Scottish coast, but by AD 800 the Vikings would have been raiding in good earnest. By AD 1000 Islay was part of a Norse kingdom that was growing in size and confidence, and the inhabitants of Gaelic-speaking Gigha too would have seen the feared longships navigating the shallow straits between Gigha and Cara. The custom of these Northmen, from whose fury the churchmen of the time prayed for heavenly deliverance, was to farm in spring, go on raiding expeditions in the summer, returning in time for the harvest, and then setting off again from harvest time until December, before sailing north again to spend the dead months of winter in the comfort and enjoyment of home. However, if the evidence of the sagas is anything to go by – and they were factually pretty accurate – these hot-headed young men (egged on by equally hot-headed and passionate young women) were as likely to pass the dreary months of winter in the pursuit of a few home-grown blood feuds, which would in turn make the following spring expedition not just desirable, but necessary as a way of escaping revenge.

Although these Scandinavian warriors and seamen shared a language and culture in common, their own society was politically unstable and rather fragmented. The climate and landscape of home could be inhospitable and yet there was a constant demand for fertile land, for these people were traditionally farmers as well as sailors and raiders. Large families were the norm, but new land was hard to come by, and wealth, or even the means of acquiring it, in very short supply. Inheritance generally went to the eldest son and small farms could not be divided. This in turn meant that vast numbers of younger sons, legitimate or otherwise, were turned loose to fend for themselves. They were good seamen, they were land hungry, and they came south and west to seek their fortunes, in the search, quite literally, for pastures new.

They were greatly assisted by the sheer skill of their ship-builders. By the middle of the eighth century, the Norsemen had become expert shipwrights. The longship, efficient and manoeuvrable, reached its apogee just as the seamanship of the Picts had fallen into decline. Early raids on the coasts of Scotland were small – a handful of longships in company – and swift, taking whatever they could seize and retreating, but word spread rapidly that there were rich pickings and fertile land to be had over the water, and so more ships came. Although accounts of the Vikings, often from churchmen who had suffered most from their depredations, and had the skills to write about it afterwards, told a tale of savage, merciless, godless robbers, it would also be true to say that from very early on, many of these young men would have come with less violent intentions, seeking only a place to live and farm. They would have married local women, often converting to Christianity in the process, and would have adapted to life in Scotland with relative ease, since many customs and habits were shared between the two peoples.

Within a few generations, many of them would have settled down to a reasonably peaceful existence, although old habits die hard, and by the end of the ninth century, at least some of these settlers were actually returning to plunder the Scandinavian mainland while bands of young warriors, the descendants of Gaelic Norse intermarriage, resorted to piracy along the coastlines of Galloway, Kintyre and the Isle of Man. Early church annals – true or not – maintain that under Norse influence they had also reverted to paganism. They became known as the *Gall-Gaedhill*, Gallgaels, or in Norse, the *Gaddgeddlar*, an almost legendary people, warlike and mysterious.[1]

A related word *Gallowglas* was used for many hundreds of years to describe groups of Hebridean mercenaries. Much later, Shakespeare himself refers to them in Macbeth: 'The merciless Macdonwald, from the Western Isles, of Kerns and gallowglasses is supplied.' The gallowglasses of Shakespeare's time were heavily armed foot soldiers, often Scots fighting in Ireland, and were deemed to be of extraordinary bravery and determination.

The term *Gallgael*, which seems to have been used to describe a race of people of which *Gallowglasses* were merely a warrior faction, means, literally, 'foreign Gael', in the same way that the Galbraiths were the foreign Britons, and it is often used with reference in particular to the people of Galloway (it is, in fact, the derivation of that place name) but also to the inhabitants of Kintyre, and the southerly Hebridean islands including Gigha. Since the Vikings were as much colonists as plunderers, and there is some evidence that they may have regularly intermarried with the Gaels of Dalriada, it seems likely that the *Gallgaels* were their descendants, a people with some of the characteristics of both races – like the great Somerled himself who, although he would later restore the old Dalriadic claim to Argyll, was evidently the product of mixed Gaelic-Norse ancestry.

Long before the time of Somerled, however, the Isle of Lewis had become an important Viking station, and from there, the Norsemen began to colonise further south. In *The Lords of the Isles*, Ronald Williams comments that Islay, Colonsay, Oronsay and Gigha were Viking stations. He points out that Viking settlements were by no means so extensive as in the north, although we know that Norsemen did settle in Mull and Kintyre, and as far inland as Loch Fyne.

From the sagas we know that many of these young men would have been adventurers and farmers looking for new prospects. It would be safe to assume that at least some of them would have settled on Gigha, which they knew as *Gudey*, a name that can be translated either as God's island or possibly the Good Isle, perhaps as a description of its useful harbours. But there would also have been travelling tradesmen from the Norse world, people who may have been involved with commerce, without settling in any one place, and it was, perhaps, to one of these traders that a most interesting Viking find belonged.

In Glasgow's Hunterian Museum, there is a little set of folding scales with a Norse provenance, which were found at Tarbert Bay. They were accidentally dug up some time in the 1900s by two men who were making a potato pit a few hundred yards from the beach at the south end of the east bay. Fortunately the scales were so curious and attractive that they were preserved. As Anderson relates the story, one Sarah Galbraith of Carnvickoye said that they used to dig their potato pit beside a huge boulder at this spot, but eventually, when the stone became a nuisance, they rolled it out of the way, and found a square stone box buried beneath it and in the box was the balance. Anderson remarks that the hilt of a sword was also said to have been found in the vicinity, but it has now disappeared.[2]

This area was once a large burial ground, with remains being found over the whole area between the site of the Great Well, the Holy Stone and the Field of the Chapel, as far as Tarbert Bay. The scales have been dated to the tenth century. The set, which is very beautiful, consists of a bronze balance beam, with hinged arms, although one arm is missing. There are two pans of tinned bronze with a geometrical decoration, which was drawn with the aid of compasses, and then made by scraping away the surface tinning. The two pans would have been suspended by fine chains from two little birds made of metal, which hung from the end of the beam. Lead weights were also found with the balance, the largest weighing 100.3 grams, another lead block weighing 47.7 grams, and a small cube with an iron handle, weighing 10.2 grams. There is also a broken perforated disc or whorl, which weighs 27.1 grams, although it is obviously now lighter than originally intended. The Hunterian suggests that the Vikings used a system based on multiples of a unit of 12.5 grams, so that the Gigha weights may have been intended as 12.5, 25, 50 and 100 grams.[3]

The scales may have been used to weigh small amounts of silver but does East Tarbert Bay contain a full-scale Viking burial? Well, perhaps not. It is much more likely that the owner of the scales was a travelling merchant, carrying his scales with him, possibly even a Christian, who finally came to grief on Gigha and was buried in the island's main burial ground at the time. It is equally possible, of course, that he may not have been buried here at all, since no bones were reported and there is no account of a skeleton being discovered in the box with the scales. Perhaps the scales, as a precious object, had been buried for safekeeping during a time of trouble on the island. Perhaps they had even been handed down from father to son over a period of many years and buried after the time of the Vikings was past. On the other hand, the owner may have been an islander, perhaps even one of mixed parentage, who acquired his scales from a Norse trader, because they were useful and beautiful.

Anderson tells us that 'before the 9th century, Gigha had already seen the scouts of the fighting Norse sweeping past, prophetic of 400 years of foreign rule, of tragedies innumerable and of transmutations radical and abiding.' Iona itself was first attacked in AD 795. We know that eventually, the Hebrides became linked with the Isle of Man, and that many high-born Icelandic families held lands there. Ketil Flatnose, one of the heroes of Icelandic saga, became the first Norse ruler of the Hebrides in the ninth century. Still, these incomers seem, on the face of it, to have made very little real impact on Gigha.

Place names are often a very good indication of Norse influence, but a quick scan of Gigha place names gives us very few that are indisputably Norse, and even the name of the island is arguable. The Norsemen certainly named the island for themselves, but whether they influenced the later name is debatable. Similarly, it is traditionally supposed that the little island of Cara is named for an eponymous 'Kari' (perhaps 'Kari-ey' or Kari's Island), but since there is an old Gaelic word *Cara* meaning friend or companion (and since the small island is undoubtedly a companion to the larger Gigha), it seems just as likely that this could be the derivation of the name.

Craro Island is possibly a Norse name as is *Dun Ni' Chrero*, which Anderson translates as 'The Fort of Crero's Daughter' although we have no knowledge of who Crero might have been, except that he sounds Norse. Craro Island has a bull-shaped rock formation, which was familiar to Gigha fishermen, and there is a story on the island of a ship being attacked by pirates, Gallgaels perhaps, or accomplices of a later pirate, known as *Allan nan Sop*, who proceeded to put her crew to the sword. The cabin boy prayed to God to bless his mother in Gigha, since he wouldn't be returning to her. The pirate captain asked him to say which direction the Craro Bull faced. 'North-east' said the cabin boy, whereupon the pirate, who had Gigha connections, spared him. This same pirate is reputed to have buried his ill-gotten gold at Ardlamey Farm although it has never yet been discovered.

Gigalum may be a conflation of Norse *Gja* and *Holm.* The *nish* suffix, meaning inlet as in *Achamhinish* (the field of the narrow ness) is partly Norse.[4] This combination of Gaelic and Norse elements within one name does at least indicate the mixed nature of the society of these islands.

The only other partially Norse name of any significance is *Cnoc Haco* and even this is arguable. The mound, sometimes called Round Hill, on the farm of Drumachro, opposite the main entrance to Achamore House is supposed to be associated with the Norse King Haakon, and was reputed to be the burial place of the Norsemen who died at the battle of Largs, but Anderson disputes this with what seems like good reason. We know that Pennant first described it as a 'large artificial mound' and proposed that it might be 'the work of the Danes' but this was only because of a supposed resemblance to an ancient hill in Sweden, and since one hill looks very much like another, we can probably discount this explanation. Besides, he had not attempted to excavate it. If he had, he would have discovered that the hill is not, in fact, artificial at all, and is an outcrop of rock with earth and sand on top, like many another on the island.

Writing about Gigha in 1824 MacCulloch describes the hill as a 'Law Ting' or 'Tynewald Hill' but there seems to have been no real tradition on the island that this was the nature of the mound in question. Fraser, in his statistical account some years after Pennant, says, 'Of the beautiful earthen mount at a farm called Drum-a-Chro, the name and intention of it are equally unknown.' But surely, if there had been a Norse tradition associated with it, he would have known about it and mentioned it. There is an outside chance that this may have been a much earlier Judgement Mound as used by the ancient Celtic *brehons* to administer justice. There is, however, above the shore of the east bay of Tarbert a hill called *Cnoc an Eireachdais*, the hill of assembly, which was sometimes called a Court Hill on the island, and which is much more likely to have fulfilled this function at a time when the main settlement on the island seems to have been situated at the north end.

In spite of persistent Norse associations with the island, there is precious little evidence that Norsemen settled here in any great numbers. By AD 900 the Vikings considered the Hebrides to be their own territory, calling them *Sudreyar* in their sagas. Some 250 years of – by no means peaceful – Norse rule followed, until the great chieftain Somerled, as Ronald Williams says, 'embarked on the reconquest of his ancestral patrimony in old Dalriada.'[5] Williams points out that 'Gaelic was again becoming the prevalent language in the Hebrides' if it had ever gone away, which is very doubtful although it had certainly borrowed extensively from Norse. Somerled, for his part, claimed that he was descended from the ancient Celtic kings of Dalriada although there is some evidence that he too was of mixed race. Whatever the truth of the matter, he was the ancestor of Clan Donald, the Lords of the Isles. Somerled was a brave warrior, and an astute politician but above all he seems to have been a clever seaman with a knowledge of boat design and building which allowed him to beat the Norsemen at their own game. Ultimately, Somerled would win back the Isle of Man, all the Southern Hebridean Isles, including Gigha, as well as Kintyre, Knapdale and Lorne; in other words a large slice of the old Dalriadic territories.

Another hundred years would pass before the true Norsemen would again turn their attentions to Gigha but when they did so, it was in spectacular fashion. In the summer of 1263, King Haakon Haakonson came from Norway to settle his dispute with Alexander III of Scotland as to the ownership of the Hebrides, once and for all. Magnus, Earl of Orkney travelled in company with him from Bergen and as the sagas report, 'the king gave him a good longship.' The fleet stayed at Bressay Sound in Shetland for two weeks. Then they sailed to Orkney, where they lay at anchor in Elwick Bay, near Kirkwall. They sailed round South Ronaldsay, and stayed for some time in Ronaldsvoe, while men were sent to Caithness to 'levy a contribution' – in other words extort money and supplies from the natives, as was their custom.

In the words of Haakon's poet – for like the Gaelic chieftains, the Norse leaders had their own travelling bards whose job it was to extol their deeds for posterity – he 'imposed tribute on the dwellers on the Ness who were terrified by the steel-clad extractor of rings', which is a poetic way of saying that they got what they wanted by brute force and threats. From there, he sailed south to Lewis and Skye where he was joined by another Magnus, king of Man. His fleet had now grown to more than a hundred vessels. This was divided into two squadrons, one of which, fifty strong, was sent to plunder the coasts of Kintyre and Mull, before rejoining Haakon at Gigha where they lay at anchor for some time.

They positioned themselves in the quiet sound between Gigalum and the south-east shore of Gigha, close to the pier where, nowadays, the little car ferry, bright in its CalMac colours, is tied up every night. Among the ships was one that was grander than all the rest. This was the warship of King Haakon himself, specially constructed of oak, at Bergen in Norway, with thirty-seven benches for the oarsmen, and with the highly carved dragon's head, which Hollywood producers would later find so irresistible, all plated with gold in honour of the king. It must have been an extraordinary sight for those on Gigha, the like of which they had never encountered before, nor would they see the like of it again. And yet there is not a breath, not a ghost, not a murmur and barely even a commemorative name of all this in island tradition. Which is curious, considering how firmly the memories of these fighting Norsemen are entrenched in – for example – the history of Largs.

Haakon must have spent many weeks at Gigha, preparing for battle. We know that, after some prevarication on their part, he received the renewed allegiance of Murdoch and Angus of Clan Donald, of Kintyre. They probably had little choice in the matter, and must have agreed to provide both supplies and manpower to Haakon on the understanding that their lands would not be raided, or more likely, would not be raided more than they already had been. Ewen of Lorne, (named John, in the saga), great-grandson of Somerled himself also came to visit the Norse king on Gigha. This man held the Southern Isles from Haakon and therefore owed him allegiance. Haakon's allies, however, had reported that Ewen had changed his mind and was about to side with Alexander instead. Haakon, who must have been fond of the young man, steadfastly refused to believe them.

The position was complicated and Ewen of Lorne was in an invidious position, since he held more land on the mainland, which was within Alexander's sphere of influence, than he had on the islands. Moreover, he had rashly sworn an oath of allegiance to Alexander as well. On the horns of an unpleasant dilemma, he begged Haakon to take back the isles, and thus release him from his promise, which Haakon agreed to do, but all the same decided to hold him prisoner on Gigha in the meantime, in case he, Haakon, should need to communicate with Alexander. If this eventuality arose, Haakon must have known that he would be able to send Ewen, who had Alexander's ear, but who could also be relied upon to favour the Norse king, in return for the mercy that had been shown him.

Meanwhile Haakon also agreed not to plunder Kintyre if Angus Mor and his brother Murdoch would formally surrender to him, which they duly did, whereupon Haakon laid a tax of a thousand cows, a huge number, upon Kintyre, a place that Haakon's poet called, with some justification, the land of 'drizzling rain, of western storms'. It was also, as we have already seen, while Haakon was at Gigha that he had some dealings with the Abbott of Saddell, agreeing to spare the foundation from the depredations of his men, and also utilising the abbey for the burial of one of his priests. He was, after all, a professed Christian.

Haakon was detained in Gigha for some time by unfavourable winds. One wonders why he didn't try to harness the powers of the Great Well, which must even then have been famous, but perhaps he did and perhaps it led to his downfall since one can imagine that the *dirochs* of the day would not have had much sympathy with a Norse king. Eventually he and his fleet set out for Arran. He sailed his whole fleet around the Mull of Kintyre, no mean feat when even modern yachts find the journey daunting, and they anchored in Lamlash Bay on 8 September. From there, Haakon sent Dominican monks as his envoys to entreat for a peaceful settlement with Alexander. The negotiations were long drawn out, perhaps deliberately so on Alexander's part, for the Scottish leader would be well aware of how prone this coast is to stormy weather in autumn. Receiving no very favourable reply, Haakon then advanced to the Cumbraes, off the Ayrshire coast, where on 1 October, a violent storm arose.

A merchant ship and nine longships were driven ashore, some were dismasted and others dragged their anchors. Haakon's own longship broke its moorings and very nearly

TOP. Waiting for the ferry at the Gigha pier. Note the old perambulator.

ABOVE. Cargo vessel MV *Lochshiel*, approaching the pier, at 8 a.m. on a wet and windy day.

TOP. The pier with small steamer leaving – possibly the *Pioneer*?

ABOVE. The steamer *Lochiel*, the fourth MacBrayne vessel of that name, leaving West Loch Tarbert, Argyll. Gigha was a regular port of call. The *Lochiel* replaced an old paddle steamer called the Pioneer in 1939.

Young Willie McSporran (see Chapter 14).

TOP. The *Arran* took over from the *Lochiel* after the *Lochiel* struck a rock in Loch Tarbert in 1960.

ABOVE. The *Bodach* and the *Cailleach* at the south of the island (see Chapter 3).

Islay Allan on the pier, which was under renovation when this peculiarly evocative photograph was taken in the 1950s. Islay Allan was a gardener like his father Malcolm. He left the island to work in Kent, in Windsor Great Park and then at Drummond Castle in Crieff, where he was head gardener for 25 years.

Carraig an Tairbeart, the so-called Druid's Stone, at Tarbert, where the island narrows spectacularly between two beaches.

Kilchattan – the remains of the old church dedicated to St Cathan. This is the surviving eastern gable with its lancet window.

RIGHT. Malcolm McNeill's grave at Kilchattan. Malcolm was a 15th-century chieftain of Gigha, and the only one whose probable grave is remembered by name.

BELOW. South Ardminish Farm and the Gigha Hotel, still recognisable today.

TOP. Corn stacks, very neatly built, at South Ardminish when it and the small hotel were being run by the MacPhersons. This farm was 'immaculately run, a showpiece of a farm' and 'the stacks were beautiful', says Willie McSporran.

ABOVE. Another view of the orderly South Ardminish land.

TOP. Malcolm, Betty and Kenny McNeill's brother Duncan. This photograph was taken looking down towards the old village of Ardminish.

ABOVE. Sandy Orr's Shop in Ardminish Village – licensed to sell tobacco.

LEFT. The Rev. Kenneth MacLeod, minister of Gigha from 1923–1948. He is best remembered as the author of 'The Road to the Isles'.

BELOW. Malcolm Allan, head gardener at Achamore, with Kitty Lloyd Jones. Malcolm worked in the gardens at Achamore for 52 years. Kitty Lloyd Jones came to the island as a close friend and horticultural advisor to Sir James Horlick.

Malcolm Allan (left) in the gardens at Achamore with Peter McCallum (centre) and Donnie McNeill (right).

TOP. From the left, Katie Wilkieson, district nurse; Helen Allan, Katie's husband Angus Wilkieson, who farmed at Drumyeonbeg for many years; and Mary McSporran, far right. This photograph was taken at Gallochoille, to which the Wilkiesons retired.

ABOVE. A three-horse yoke. 'It was a real art to get the beasts to pull together,' says Willie McSporran.

Carting in the old way at Ardlamey Farm

TOP. Building a stack at Ardlamey Farm.

ABOVE. Old Mill Wheel at Ardailly. The wheel was brought in by sea.

TOP. Waiting for the steamer. Angus Allan notes of this photograph that the people seem to be dressed up for some special occasion.

ABOVE. Waiting for the ferry with a small flock of sheep and sheepdog in attendance.

TOP. Mr Sinclair of Ardlamey, transporting his sheep.

ABOVE. Harvest time at Ardlamey. Note the size of the pair of Clydesdales compared to Mr Sinclair, who was not a small man.

ABOVE. Donald and George Allan, sowing in the field around the house at North Drumachro, late 1950s.

RIGHT. Malcolm Allan and companions at North Drumachro. Laird Sir James Horlick built a new house here for Malcolm and his family.

LEFT. Angus (with the pipe) and Hugh McVean, Helen Allan (wife of Angus Allan, who left the island and is a retired minister of the congregational church) and Mary McSporran.

BELOW. A shipment of sheep awaiting the ferry in the 1960s. Note *Lochiel* skipper in his 'captain's hat' in the background.

RIGHT. Sheep on the pier. A very young Seumas McSporran is facing the camera, in the centre.

BELOW. Tarbert Farm, to the north of the island.

TOP. John Martin rediscovering The Great Well on the lower slopes of *Cnoc Largie* (see Chapter 16).

ABOVE. The Holy Stone, thought to be a fertility stone, one of a number of interesting prehistoric remains on, or close to, *Cnoc Largie*, near Tarbert Farm.

TOP. Typical Gigha landscape, looking east towards Kintyre.

ABOVE. Summer pastimes with the Gigha hotel and Donald Allan's bungalow in the background. Parts of North Drumachro, and North Ardminish Farms were amalgamated with the hotel farm at South Ardminish, and Donald Allan and his wife Carole (part-time district nurse) took over the tenancy of the combined farms.

TOP. The *Lochiel*, coming into the pier on a fine calm day.

ABOVE. From Ardlamey.

LEFT. Willie McSporran, aged 30 (see Chapter 14).

Tigh Mor, Gigha, May 2010

Willie McSporran, the author and her son, 1993.

came to grief, golden dragon and all. These vessels had been designed to transport men, not as warships. In what came to be known as the Battle of Largs, although it was more of a skirmish than a full-scale battle, the mainland Scots attacked the stranded Norsemen and plundered the vessels that had run aground. Alexander arrived and attacked the Norwegians on shore. Haakon's men fought bravely, and managed to wade out to their ships, which limped back from whence they had come, by way of Gigha, to Orkney where the aged King Haakon died at Kirkwall, at midnight on Saturday 15 December 1263.

The battle, though far from momentous, and influenced as much by the Scottish weather as by strategic planning, marked a turning point for the whole area in that the Norwegians effectively abandoned their Hebridean campaign from this point onwards; while afterwards Alexander wisely granted an amnesty to the chieftains of the Isles who had previously supported Haakon, recognising that most of them had had no alternative.[6]

The Norsemen have left little behind on Gigha to remind us of their presence – a mention of the island in a nobleman's saga, a handful of place names and a set of scales isn't much to go on. However, as we have seen, there may be a more enduring connection than the remaining evidence would suggest. The Norsemen and the Celts had much in common, including a love of the sea, of song, and of story. Although our clichéd view of the Vikings is of boatloads of ruffians, engaged in rape and plunder, the truth contained in the sagas is much more equivocal. They were in search of land and new places to settle. There were, among them, fine craftsmen, musicians and poets, and one can imagine that after the first raids, and once contacts began to be established, the two peoples might very quickly establish some kind of rapport.

Certainly some of the larger Hebridean islands such as Lewis have many surviving Norse place names but it was the Gaelic language that persisted and survived after all, and maybe Gigha – as so often – simply reflects an overall picture, i.e. that the Gaelic culture largely absorbed the incomers, while the Norse culture gradually adapted itself to that of the Gaels. Perhaps, too, we forget the unique power and influence of the mother tongue. In the islands of the far north, which were perceived to be Norse by right anyway, whole families would have settled, bringing Scandinavian culture with them. In the west, there may have been more of a propensity for young men to arrive alone and seek brides from the indigenous population. If, in the Hebrides, the majority of Norse incomers were young men, intermarrying with Gaelic-speaking women, it would certainly be Gaelic, rather than Norse, which would become the first language of the resulting offspring. The Gallgael – foreign Gaels – may well have been the result. But in the end it was the Gaelic language and Celtic customs that triumphed on Gigha, as in the whole area. Although the blood of the Norsemen may still run through the island families, and their descendants, more tangible remains are – like the Norsemen's scales – deeply buried in the landscape of the island.

10

The Lords of the Isle

The story of the people of Gigha, during the Middle Ages and after, is inextricably linked with the political struggles of the Lords of the Isles, the legendary Macdonalds, who traced their ancestry back to Somerled, and before that to the ancient Kingdom of Dalriada and before that again to an Irish king known as Conn of the Hundred Battles. It is, of course, a tale of grandeur, poetry and nobility. It is also a mind-numbing tale of mostly young men, (although some of them were certainly old enough to know better), who seem to have been almost constantly engaged in rivalry and infighting, and an endless jostling for superiority, land, power and political influence. It is besides a tale of overweening pride without conscience, of the indulgence in rash acts without responsibility, and of betrayal and savagery beyond belief.

It is only necessary to read a brief account of the infighting that occurred over many hundreds of years, to see the sheer waste of it all. When we speak nostalgically about the grandeur of the Lords of the Isles, we all too often forget the ordinary majority who must have suffered for the aspirations of the few. In fact no one side seems able to lay claim to more nobility than the other. As I ploughed my way through the swithering fortunes of these clans, and their victims, the ordinary men, women and children of these islands, struggling to live, work and feed themselves as best they could, in the face of war, robbery, waves of infectious disease and the occasional famine, I could only pity the poor souls who surely did not deserve such rulers to add to their tribulations. It takes only a little reflection to understand why so many Gaelic songs involve beautiful but tragic accounts of the death of the beloved and the waste of a bright future.

However, as the title of this chapter suggests, we are only concerned with Gigha here, and only with the Lords of the Isles in so far as their politicking impinged on our own little isle. After our account of the Norsemen, we left Alexander III in possession of the throne of Scotland, having sent King Haakon homewards, not only to think again, but to die a sad old man in Orkney. John, or Ewen of Lorne, the man whose original desertion of Haakon at Gigha precipitated that ruler's eventual defeat, might have seemed the obvious choice for Alexander to appoint as his lieutenant in the isles, but there is no evidence of this, although he was certainly restored to all his lands, with some additions, while Angus Mor, who had been forced to surrender his lands to Haakon under threat of having them plundered, was pardoned and confirmed in his own existing possessions. If Haakon's invasion had taught the mainland Scots anything it had been the strategic value of these southern isles, and it was at this time that the islands of Arran and Bute were given to the Stewarts, while the Scots rulers sought ways of both controlling and currying favour with the remaining island chiefs.

Ewen's successors were, on the whole, favoured by King Alexander's successors, throughout the dreadful struggles against the hostile English which followed. The descendants of Somerled in the Western Isles were pretty evenly divided between Bruce and Balliol interests. It is doubtful if Bruce would have been victorious at Bannockburn without the help of the men of Argyll and the Isles, under the command of Angus Og, Angus Mor's son. But, as Ronald Williams so succinctly describes it, 'Bruce never forgot that Angus had been his ally rather than his servant.' Robert the Bruce was no doubt very grateful to those Highlanders who had fought so bravely at Bannockburn, but that battle had also opened his eyes to other factors.

Like others before him, Bruce could not help but notice that these western chiefs represented a formidable and fiercely independent power in their own right, and one, moreover, which could form a serious threat to the Scottish mainland, if times and allegiances changed, as they were so prone to do. He knew that these men came from ancient stock with long memories, and that those memories included a strong sense of their own kingship. Bruce advised his successors to ensure that the Hebrides should never be governed by one man alone, i.e. there should be no single 'Lord of the Isles', but he tempered this caution with the advice that the Isles should always be treated with justice. But what great king has ever been able to dictate the course of events after his death?

Angus Og had a son, John, by Agnes O'Cahan, and he was the first to be called 'Lord of the Isles', which isles included Gigha. The McNeill family – who were to be prominent throughout the history of Gigha – had been associated with settlements in Kintyre since the time of Haakon's defeat. There is a grant of lands in Kintyre, which includes the Island of *Gug* (as has already been suggested, perhaps an instance of the old, pre-Norse name), dated 1309. It is from Robert I to the Earl of Mar, but in 1335 there is another mention of Gigha in connection with the treaty of alliance between John of the Isles and Edward Balliol, at Perth, ratified by Edward III. This confirms John in his ownership of a long list of Hebridean islands, which also includes Gigha.

However, by 1341 we find Balliol fleeing to France, David II crowned King of Scotland, and the islands of Islay, Gigha and Colonsay being given to Angus MacIain, a man who was descended from a younger son of Angus Mor. John of the Isles simply ignored this decree and since nobody seemed at all inclined to wrest the islands in question from him, he just carried on as before. Besides, David had other matters on his mind, namely the invasion of England, and he made his peace with John, confirming him in possession of the isles.

It is doubtful if any of these machinations among the high-born had much effect on the people who were living and working on Gigha at the time. John, in his turn, shared out his territories among those most loyal to him. His son Donald, who was born about 1362, had inherited a huge territory. The Lordship of the Isles then consisted of Lochaber, Moidart, Arisaig, Morar, Knoydart, Morvern, Knapdale, Kintyre, Glencoe, Islay, Mull, Colonsay, Jura, Scarba, Tiree, Eigg, Rhum, Lewis, Harris, the Uists, Benbecula, Barra and Gigha, all of which would eventually pass to Donald's son, John's grandson, Alexander. It was in 1449 that this Alexander, Lord of the Isles, close to the end of his life, granted title to lands in Gigha upon one Torquill McNeill, who was constable in Castle Sweyn. Alexander had been imprisoned after a rebellion against King James, but on his release, became a force to be reckoned with in Scotland. Torquill had been his loyal servant for many years and Alexander obviously wished to reward him before he died.

This Torquill McNeill was given one eighth of Ardailly, one eighth of Ardachy, two-eighths of Drumyeonmore, an eighth of Ardminish, an eighth of Ardlamey and an eighth of somewhere known as Fairyfown, which may possibly have been at *Carn na Faire* in the north of the island. This name is common enough in the Gaelic-speaking world and was often used of an outlying watch or guard hill associated with a larger dun or fort. In the lowlands, it was frequently translated into English as Fairyknowe. Included with all these lands were various forts and sheltered harbours, of which Gigha was well supplied so the lands were strategically very useful.

Torquill McNeill was the grandson of Neill McNeill, the founder of the southern clan McNeill. The McNeills were astute fence-sitters, managing to remain loyal adherents of the Lords of the Isles, while at the same time retaining the favour of the Stewarts. In 1455, Alexander's son John, Fourth Lord of the Isles confirmed the grant of the Gigha lands to another Neill, this time the son of Torquill, who had succeeded his father. Then Hector succeeded Neill, and still managed to keep a toehold in Gigha.

In the power struggles between the Macdonalds, the McLeans and the Campbells for the mastery of Argyll and the isles, the McNeills cleverly trimmed their sails to the prevailing winds. In 1476 the lands of Kintyre and Knapdale were attached to the crown, with Colin Campbell, Earl of Argyll, whose star was very much in the ascendant, now becoming Constable of Castle Sweyn. Hector McNeill, however, seems to have been a trusted friend of this Campbell of Argyll and remained in favour, in spite of his Macdonald connections. In a charter of 1478, Malcolm, possibly a son of this same Hector McNeill is found in possession of the island, signing himself 'of Geya'. This Malcolm or *Gillecallum* as he was called, was in possession of 'the £20 lands of Geya and other lands' and seems to have been well thought of on the island since he is believed to be the chief whose grave at Kilchattan is still remembered as 'Malcolm's Grave' to this day, the only one of these ancient lairds who is accorded the honour of being remembered by name in the oral traditions of Gigha. Malcolm died in 1493 but in 1514 we find Neill McNeill of *Gaeya*, possibly Malcolm's son, associated with Colin Campbell of Argyll as 'friend and servitor'.

During the 1520s the terrible *Allan nan Sop*, Allan McLean, the younger son of Lauchlin Cattanach Maclean of Dowart, had taken to roaming the western seas, killing islanders, plundering their homes, and thieving cattle, like his Viking ancestors before him. He was a pirate and a brigand, sailing as far afield as Ireland in his reckless raiding. His name, which means Allan of the Straw, was said to describe his habit of burning out his victims with their own stacks. In 1530, Allan emerged from his piratical lair in West Loch Tarbert, and sailed to Gigha where, it was related, on very little provocation, he killed Neill McNeill of Gigha, murdered many of his fellow islanders, stole or destroyed their property and imprisoned some of them.

Anderson describes the ruins of a long building, some 100 feet long by 16 feet wide, in the 'hollow' between the Fort of the Marsh and Craig Bhan, on the cross road to Ardailly. A local place name *Cuil nan Ciomach*, the Prisoners' Corner, is connected with this site, 'a sunken marsh surrounded by steep heights and under the grim shadow of the fort' and Anderson speculates as to whether this building, which had four divisions, might once have been the place where the dreaded Allan imprisoned the 'poor inhabitants of Geya', an event about which the islanders were forced to petition Mary of Guise, who subsequently commissioned Argyll to proceed against 'certain Macleans' the chief amongst whom was presumably Allan nan Sop.

Neill had an unmarried daughter, Annabella, and an illegitimate son called Neill, neither of whom could inherit the lands of Gigha without a royal charter, and so Torquill, the murdered Neill's brother, received the grant of the Gigha lands in 1531 from King James V, as the surviving 'chief and principal of the clan and surname of Maknelis.' Torquill seems to have diligently sought the required royal charter to secure Gigha for his nephew, of whom he must have been fond, but had to contend with Allan nan Sop who was reluctant to give up such a strategically useful island to anybody, never mind its rightful owner. Tradition has it that Allan treated the inhabitants very badly, and in view of his obvious ruthlessness there is no reason to doubt this account. This must have been a particularly miserable time for the islanders and may account for the fact that Malcolm of the previous century is remembered with such affection.

In 1539, in what seems to have been a move to secure more influential assistance – and since Argyll seems to have been less than helpful – Neill McNeill sold his financial interest in his Gigha lands to James Macdonald of Dunnyveg, which was a stronghold on Islay, fourteen miles west of Cara. In that same year, however, Macdonald – who obviously wished to curry favour with the formidable Allan – in turn gave the revenues of 'Geya, Comeravoch [modern-day Kinererach], Tarbert and other lands' to the pirate, 'until the entry of the rightful heir.'

This move, while not entirely discounting McNeill's claim to the island, seemed calculated to cause trouble and trouble was what ensued. Various skirmishes between disgruntled McNeills and Macdonalds resulted but at last, in 1542, the crown stepped in to settle the dispute and we find the younger Neill McNeill being granted the entire island of Gigha at the behest of the king 'on narrative that the deceased Neill Makneille of Geya and the greater part of his Clan had been slain by the rebellious Islesmen and that Anabela Makneille had resigned her lands to her natural brother Neill, the son of the deceased.'

However, this was by no means the end of the affair and to complicate matters still further, in 1544, after the king's death, we find James Macdonald again being granted a charter of the lands of Gigha, although in 1549, we also note that the Lord of the Isles has his own Council among which were 'four thanes of lesser estate' one of whom was the McNeill of Gigha. But there was a difference between being a thane and being a laird, in receipt of income, as Dean Monro pointed out at the time: 'The auld thane of Gigay [presumably he was referring to the elder Neill's brother, Torquill] should be laird of the same, callit McNeill of Gigay and now it is possessit by the Clandonald.'

After this, however, and somewhat surprisingly, we find Neill McNeill, Allan McLean and James Macdonald all involved on the same side – the wrong one as it turned out – when King Henry VIII tried to force a marriage between his son Edward and Mary, the infant queen of Scots in what came to be called the 'Rough Wooings'. All three of them are noted as being involved in the resulting intrigues with England against the distracted lowland Scots, but the consequences for them were not too grave, perhaps because Allan and James, at least, were too powerful for the authorities to tackle in any meaningful way.

Allan continued to draw the rents of Gigha while James was officially recognised as the owner of the island until in 1551 Allan nan Sop died in his bed at Tarbert, having – as so many before and after – belatedly repented of his evil ways and sought forgiveness for a lifetime of murder, rape, pillage and ruthless self-indulgence. He was buried with the saints on Iona but his son Hector, a chip off the old piratical block if ever there was one, decided that he wanted to keep Gigha for himself and paid the crown handsomely for the privilege.

In 1554, the disappointed McNeills, Torquill and his nephew Neill, again relinquished their theoretical rights in Gigha to James Macdonald, his wife, and his brothers, perhaps in a move to oust the unpleasant Hector Maclean from the island. James died on an expedition to Ireland in 1565 and Neill McNeill died the year after. Angus Macdonald then became chieftain in his father's stead, whereupon the Macleans dug up the imperfectly buried hatchet and renewed their old quarrel with the Macdonalds. In 1567 Gigha was 'ravaged by the old enemy' according to Anderson, and Mary, Queen of Scots (who had troubles of her own with Bothwell, and a murdered husband in this same year, troubles moreover which were about to end in disaster for her) accused Hector Maclean, both the elder and the younger, of 'burning the houses, barns and cattle of the poor inhabitants of Geya, killing some and imprisoning others'.

Things seem to have settled down somewhat after this, until in 1576 Angus Macdonald gave his natural son Archibald a charter of the lands of Gigha, for life. In 1582 a new charter was given and this was to be confirmed by the crown in 1598. The McNeills of Gigha (at least some of them must have still been living on the island, even if they didn't own it) are reported at this time as joining in the still simmering Macdonald quarrel with the truculent Macleans and in 1587 history repeated itself all over again and Gigha was again put to 'fire and the sword' along with Islay, by marauding Macleans.

In 1590 a now-impoverished Angus sold his holdings on Gigha to John Campbell of Calder. In an ironic (and probably pre-plotted) twist, this same John Campbell immediately resold the island back to Neil McNeill of Taynish who instantly granted it to his brother Malcolm. We should remember at this point that the McNeills were, and had remained, very thick with the Campbells, and this transference not only returned the island to its erstwhile McNeill owners, but also kept it very firmly within the Campbell sphere of influence.

In 1605, Mary's son James, who had fallen heir to both thrones after the death of Elizabeth in 1603, summoned the island chiefs to meet his Commissioner at Campbeltown, then called Lochkilkerran, where they were commanded to pay all their arrears of rent, and show title deeds to their lands. Angus paid his arrears and gave Archibald Macdonald of Gigha as his surety. Archibald (presumably because his title to the island was by now false, though one could be forgiven for becoming a little confused at this point) was imprisoned in Dumbarton castle but escaped. Angus died at Rothesay in 1614. His eldest legitimate son James was also in prison but he too escaped and fomented open rebellion.

In 1615, he went to Kintyre, hoping to make one more attempt to retake the old Macdonald family estates there and thus regain his power base. He made his camp on Cara, which was, and had been for many long years, the property of Macdonald of Largie, of which more in due course. He also made various attempts to capture Hector McNeill of Taynish and Gigha, hoping to add the men of Gigha and Knapdale to his fighting force, but McNeill remained resolutely loyal to the Campbells of Argyll. The Macdonald fleet was at anchor around the head of the island, while their army was encamped on the coast of Kintyre, opposite Gigha. Meanwhile Campbell of Calder (he who had bought the island from the Macdonalds and immediately resold it back to the McNeills) had gone ashore on Gigha with a detachment of fighting men. James Macdonald was warned about this, but inexplicably didn't believe the spies who told him so. James beached at Gigha, only to be promptly and devastatingly attacked by Calder. He and his men only escaped at the cost of several boats and a number of casualties. On the other hand, Calder tried to make a surprise attack on the Macdonalds on Cara but the servants at Largie in Kintyre lit warning beacons and so pre-empted the attack. Finally, the Macdonalds were forced into an ignominious retreat. Anderson tells us that there is a tradition on Gigha of 'so many lords dining in Gallochoille', which was one of the McNeill's old mansion houses by the jetty at North Drumachro, and also in the mansion house of Cara, which was the seat of the Macdonalds of Largie, all of which perhaps constitutes a folk memory of this skirmish and the musters that preceded it.

That might well have been the end of the matter, but for the fact that in 1618 Argyll himself was sent into exile 'because he had made open defection from the true religion and that he had entered into very suspicious dealings with Sir James Macdonald'. The former is believable but the latter accusation seems incredible, in view of all that had gone before. Argyll was proclaimed a traitor while Sir James Macdonald was recalled from exile, but made to live in London since it was considered too dangerous to allow him to come home.

Archibald of Gigha was murdered at *Eilean Mhic Carmaid* in 1618 and in 1619 John Macdonald was made heir to the 'barony of Geya.' In 1631 however, he sold his holdings on Gigha to Archibald McNeill, Lord of Lorne because in 1673 (one heaves a sigh of relief to write it) the McNeills of Taynish were the acknowledged lairds of Gigha, holding the island from the Campbells of Argyll. This branch of the McNeill family retained the island until in 1780 it was eventually sold to the McNeills of Colonsay from whom it passed away from Clan McNeill altogether in the nineteenth century. We shall go on to look at some of those later owners and their tenants in succeeding chapters.

As Kathleen Philip points out, however, a major factor in the various acrimonious disputes was that, throughout the whole of this confusing time, the island was far from being united under one laird. The McNeills themselves granted parts of the island to various younger branches of the family and when documents refer to 'McNeill of Gigha' we can never be sure who exactly – or which parts of the island – they are referring to. Perhaps the most important division came in 1673 when we find that Roger McNeill of Taynish granted a portion of the island to his kinsman Donald McNeill of Galdchailzie on Loch Sweyn. This portion included Leim, Drumyeonbeg, Drumachro and Gigalum.[1]

It might be useful, finally, to make a small digression into the history of the island of Cara, which throughout all this time remained as a possession of the Macdonalds of Largie. The island is small at a mile long and something less than half a mile broad. It is noted nowadays for a herd of feral goats, which can be seen grazing its slopes. There is a small chapel on the island, which is associated with Findlugan, and which Anderson suggests dates from the fifteenth century, but since there are also sites associated with this saint on Gigha, namely the religious remains and burial ground near the Great Well at Tarbert, already described, there may possibly have been an older cell on Cara too. Anderson suggests that since *Fionnlugh* was the patron saint of the House of Islay, the Macdonalds may simply have named their chapel in his honour but it is interesting to note that there is a document dated 1456 that refers to the 'monkshaven' on Cara and there are traditions of an Iona connection. There is also a large seawater pool on the south-eastern shore of the island that is known as the *Pol an Aba* or Pool of the Abbot and there is some suggestion that monks may have used the island as a place of retreat, although in view of the possible connections between Kilchattan and Saddell the monks in question may have been Cistercians from the mainland abbey, rather than Iona.[2]

On Cara stood Cara House, with the ruins of a much older house nearby, perhaps that old mansion house at which the rebel Macdonalds met to plot their insurrection. The later history of this little island includes a rather tragic connection with Flora Macdonald who, after her historic encounter with Prince Charlie, stayed with her cousins at Largie on the Kintyre mainland for a year. Her brother sustained a fatal injury while on a shooting expedition to the island and it was after this that Flora herself departed for the Carolinas.

In the late 1700s, Cara was sustaining a population of around twenty people, among whom were crofters and fishermen, and the occasional smuggler, according to island tradition. But there was, and always had been, one other inhabitant whom it was perilous to ignore or annoy. Near to the farmhouse on Cara you will find the Brownie's Well, a spring never known to run dry, and high up on the eastern slope of the Mull of Cara is the Brownie's Chair, a huge stone seat commanding fine views.

The Brownie or the 'wee brown man' as Willie McSporran calls him, was a familiar spirit of the Macdonalds of Cara, although such legendary and frequently diminuitive beings are to be found attached to many ancient Scots families. He had the qualities of most of these strange supernatural creatures, and a few more besides, which seem to have been peculiar to himself alone.

A brownie was a domestic sprite, and a great help about the house. He was bound by magical ties to serve a particular family as their help and protector in time of need and the Cara Brownie was attached to the Macdonalds. On a day-to-day basis, the Brownie would work hard at various household tasks, although there is a suggestion that he preferred to do most of these jobs unseen, by night. Housewives and maidservants who were kind to him would come down in the morning to find the kitchen tidy, the dishes clean, the butter churned. He was particularly fond of children, and nursery maids who fell asleep at inopportune times would find themselves roughly shaken awake. But he was of a mercurial and unpredictable temperament, like most of his race, and sometimes he would choose to let the slackers sleep and mind the children himself.

Freddy Gillies relates how Angus McGougan, the last man to work a croft on Cara, had crossed to Gigha for supplies from the island shop, taking his family along for the trip. Unable to make the return crossing because of a sudden storm, the family were forced to spend the night on Gigha, leaving the cows on the island unmilked. When the storm abated the next day, they went back to Cara to find – much to their amazement – that the cows had all been milked and were peacefully grazing again. As Freddy relates 'there was not another living soul on Cara at that time.'[3]

Besides these useful domestic and agricultural skills the Brownie was possessed of various supernatural abilities. He was popularly supposed to have power over the weather and could induce storms to wreck enemy vessels. Legend has it that he was sitting up on his chair one day, when he saw one of the hated race of Campbell landing on the island. Rushing to intercept the old enemy of his family, he found a stone in his brogue and stopped to take it out. He tossed it over his shoulder, and the stone (some twenty feet high) still stands on the Kintyre mainland.

Macdonald tradition also relates that the Brownie was the ghost of a murdered Macdonald and that (naturally) a Campbell was responsible, but in fact, a creature of this sort is not usually associated with ghosts, but is believed to be all too real, a useful but unpredictable servant who stays because he is bound by spells, but is not above grumbling about his situation or taking revenge on those who upset him. Woe betide those who do not accord him due respect. In the old days, people who spoke of him 'with levity' might find themselves physically assaulted. Anderson relates the story of a visiting tailor who, all unaware of the real presence of the sprite, scoffed at the very idea, only to find himself the recipient of a hearty, albeit invisible, punch on the jaw.

The Brownie would work for free, or for food and drink, but if he were offered money or possessions or even, in one instance, a second-hand suit of clothes, he would go and never be seen again. Whether he saw this as an affront to his dignity is never explained, but this taboo is one that seems to apply to his entire race. This fate does not seem to have ever befallen the Cara Brownie though, and he is still said to be a permanent resident on the island.

Some years ago, architect and town planner Harry Teggin leased the island from Cara's proprietor Macdonald of Largie and renovated Cara house. The Brownie, whose name seems these days to be Angus, lives there still and is reported to be on very friendly terms with whoever visits the island as long as they accord him due respect. Freddy Gillies writes of Harry and his sons walking the island in chilly weather, having set the fire all ready to be lit when they came back. Two hours later, they came home to find the fire blazing as though somebody had set light to it, just a few moments earlier.

In the old days, the Brownie was given his own attic room in Cara house, and visitors to the island were expected to doff their hats to him as they came ashore. A few years ago, my husband took a party of friends to visit Cara in a small boat with an outboard motor. The engine worked perfectly all the way there and the visit went well, but not one of them remembered to doff his or her sunhat, or even call out a greeting to the Brownie, which might have been enough to avert disaster. As it was, they spent a pleasant few hours on the island, but when the time came for them to return to Gigha, the engine steadfastly refused to start. Help had to be summoned and the little boat with its occupants had to be towed ignominiously home. No doubt the Brownie watched them from his chair, all the way across.

11

The Kirk and the People

As we have already noted, Christianity on Gigha has a long history of interaction with the earlier pagan beliefs, which it supplanted or simply absorbed. Between 1626 and 1638, Gigha (which we find written as Gia at that time) along with Jura and Colonsay were all part of the same bishopric but the island became Presbyterian from 1638 onwards. The difficulties of ministering to such scattered and disparate parishes quickly became obvious. By the year 1640, one John Darroch is to be found serving the three above-mentioned isles as minister; but in 1641, surely for the sake of practicality, Gigha was joined to Saddell on Kintyre, and minister Murdoch McCurrie was 'ordained to repair to Gigha every six weeks.' In view of our speculations about Kilchattan, it is interesting to note the continuing connection of the church with the parish of Saddell on the mainland, long after the Cistercian monastery there had ceased to exist.[1]

Gigha always seems to have been something of a problem for the Kirk because in 1642 the Synod of Argyll recommended that Gigha and Killean become one parish, while during the subsequent ten years from 1644 to 1654 the Presbytery of Kintyre was under the power of the supporters of a rebellious Montrose so that, as Anderson tells us, 'church life and work was greatly disorganised.' Much else must have been disorganised at the same time, for the poor islanders who never seemed to know any peace from the effects of the political disputes of others, and the disposition of the Kirk was probably the least of their worries. Gigha was in a sad state amid the upheavals of the whole century, too small to be completely self-sufficient, and yet much too close to its warring neighbours to remain immune from their problems.

Sometimes that lack of immunity was literal as well as metaphorical. The mid 1600s saw plague rampaging through the island, a wave of sickness that resulted in the deaths of many islanders, although those at *Ardachadh* (later Ardachy, on the west coast) were said to have been spared, because of the miraculous properties of their well. This was possibly pneumonic plague, which was rife in the cities in 1646 and 1647, although on the whole the Highlands escaped the worst of the epidemic. But perhaps Gigha's relative proximity to the mainland meant that it was vulnerable to infection.

On the mainland too, whole districts were being depopulated, not just by disease, but by warring factions in what were essentially religious wars. The so-called Covenanters were anxious to keep the church independent from the English-based state machine, and in the ensuing battles and religious persecutions, some 18,000 people died. Ayrshire and Galloway were particularly affected and it is at this time that we find many people fleeing from southern Scotland to the protection of the all-powerful Earl of Argyll, at least some of whom must have settled on Gigha.

In 1642 Synod, in one of its frequent attempts to simplify places of worship, acted not only to prevent 'Burials in Churches' but also to do vandalism to those that remained, decreeing that 'sepulchres and church staines should be removed out of the body of the Church to the churchyard'. But this rather drastic requirement was never properly enacted upon many of the islands including Gigha and the gravestones rest inside the church at Kilchattan to this day.

By 1654 Gigha was to be found petitioning Synod about the 'desolate condition of that Isle' in religious terms at least, and in 1656 David Simpson became minister of the Parish of Killean, with Gigha included. By 1658 all was not well again, but this time the troubles seemed to originate on the island itself, in the shape of rebellious rumblings from the parishioners and we find Synod instructing the Presbytery to censure 'Gyga' for 'refusing to transport the victual due to them here [i.e. tithes which were due to be paid to Killean], refusing to ferry over the minister when he is to preach to them, in not preparing a house to preach into in said Island and delaying to build the kirk.'

The islanders were certainly protesting vehemently, but whether this was because they objected to the part-time nature of their minister, or whether they disliked the man himself, is hard to decide from this rather thunderous rebuke. It sounds very much as though they were holding out for a minister of their own, but whatever the reason, the independence and defiance of the islanders in the face of outside interference or indifference (both equally unwelcome) seems to have been a characteristic of many interactions past and present, between Gigha and the mainland.

It would seem that a new kirk was certainly planned instead of the old building at Kilchattan and this change, as well as the forbidding of burials in churches, would accord with the fifteenth- and sixteenth-century dates of the grave slabs inside the Kilchattan church, although obviously the graveyard outside continued in use for many hundreds of years afterwards.

From 1660 Gigha became Episcopal again for a brief spell. David Simpson went to Southend on Kintyre and Angus Macdonald, grandfather of the more famous Flora, succeeded him at Killean, while Gigha was once more unceremoniously lumped together with Jura and Colonsay, under the charge of one John McSwine. This man appears to have lived up to the letter, if not the real derivation of his name, by being charged in 1691 with 'drunkenness, profanity and flagrant neglect of his duties', although he evaded retribution until 1703 when he was finally deposed from his ministry. From 1687, in any case, John Cunnison, a Presbyterian minister, had succeeded Angus Macdonald, who left in some haste, presumably because of political and religious differences between the Episcopalians and the incoming Presbyterians.

The political upheavals, which were running as a counterpoint to all these religious switherings, were the defection of James II, the arrival of William of Orange and the war against France over the Spanish succession. The religious uncertainties of a small Scottish island seem small beer by comparison, but must have caused considerable inconvenience and worry to devout islanders. On the other hand, perhaps they were glad to be on the fringes, largely overlooked by the protagonists in the various disputes.

As far as Gigha was concerned, this same John Cunnison who succeeded the defecting Angus Macdonald seems to have substituted adequately enough for the neglectful Episcopalian McSwine, by taking an 'informal oversight of Gigha's interests' until his resignation in 1697. The year 1698 saw Patrick

Campbell as minister of Killean and Gigha together, but he seems to have found it a difficult charge, since he is on record as complaining that he has 'five places of worship' to oversee at a time when travelling between his various churches must have presented some problems. He also complains of 'the want of a roofed church or preaching house in all the bounds of his charge upon which he is necessitated either to preach and dispense the ordinances of Jesus Christ under both rain and snow and tempests, or surcease from his dewties at such tymes.' He points out with some justification, 'the vastness and discontiguousness and numerousness of his charge', which he is obliged to look after for a stipend of 700 merks, with no proper manse or glebe on Gigha or, it seems, anywhere else for that matter. He therefore asked for an assistant. James Lea took on this role, and between them they must have made a reasonable job of church matters on the island (or perhaps some local McNeill landowner took a hand in things), because, between 1707 and 1712, the successor to the old church at Kilchattan was finally built to the north of Ardminish village, some fifty years after we first found Synod complaining about unfulfilled promises in this respect!

With the new church planned, (just opposite the present-day hotel) in 1708, Gigha applied to have its own minister, which seems to have been what was wanted all along. The islanders followed this up with a formal appeal to be disjoined from Jura and made an independent parish, along with the island of Cara to the south.

Finally, in 1717 the Reverend Neil Simpson, the first Church of Scotland minister of the parish of Gigha and Cara and none other, was admitted to the parish. It had been many years in coming, and the minister seems to have been much appreciated. This same Neil Simpson died in 1759 and is buried in the churchyard at Kilchattan so his ministry lasted for some time. The inscription on the slab ends with the rather pathetic line 'and his children', who may well have predeceased him.

In 1761 we find the Presbytery at Ardminish proposing to designate a glebe (i.e. a portion of land that goes with a clergyman's benefice and provides him with revenue). In seeking to arrange this they find that the 'town of Keil was church lands and that there was still remaining there the ruins of a church and manse'. However, Anderson tells us that the 'first minister of the present parish', by which we must assume that he means Simpson, 'had his house and glebe' at the clachan of Ardailly, at the western end of the glen that bisects the island, and where the remains of the island's mill can still be seen.

Why he elected to live there is unknown, but we must deduce that the fifty-odd years between the building of the new church and the establishment of this glebe must have seen the old church and manse at Kilchattan fall into disuse and decay until, in the late 1700s, we find the minister, William Fraser, referring to the 'old manse at Kilchattan' in connection with Mr John McNeill of Gigha, the laird, who, he says, is using it as a 'temporary mansion house' for himself. This has led to speculation as to whether the presentday Achamore House might be sited where that old manse once stood, since the present Achamore is certainly not very far removed from Kilchattan.

The new church, built in the early years of the eighteenth century, can't have been a particularly sturdy construction, since 1772 finds William Mowat, then minister, complaining bitterly that the 'church of the Parish was fallen to the ground and that he had no sufficient grass for two soums' (or beasts).[2] These complaints about the poor quality of the various designated glebe lands, which were essential if the minister was to sustain himself and his family on an island where there were few other resources and little wealth, were to be repeated in future years and one can only make the assumption that the islanders were reluctant to endow their successive ministers with land that might be of more use elsewhere. In 1780 a new church, seating 260 people, was built on the same site as the 'fallen' one and in 1787, when one Dugald MacDougall was minister, the Presbytery designed a new glebe, more convenient for the church, and presumably more convenient for the parish minister since even now, travelling to and from Ardailly can present some problems in the wet winter months.

In this same year of 1787, it was also decided that the church needed repairs and renovations in the shape of two side galleries or lofts for the accommodation of the parishioners. We know that the island population was thriving at this time, and that by 1791 Gigha was home to over 614 people.[3] Numbers had been increasing for some time although they would decline in the following century. Couple this with the absolute necessity of church attendance, under pain of stringent financial penalties, and the need for a larger building becomes obvious.

The present-day manse was only erected in 1816, close by the ferry, just to the north-east of the village of Ardminish but it seems as though by the time the Reverend William Fraser was appointed to the parish of Gigha and Cara, some twenty-five years previously, the manse was no longer at Ardailly. Fraser's manse may have been where South Drumachro farmhouse now stands, since there are references to kirk session meetings being held at Drumachro from this period.

The story of William Fraser's appointment to the ministry of Gigha and Cara is, in itself, an interesting piece of social history and there is some discrepancy in dates between the various accounts. We know that Dugald MacDougall left the ministry some time in 1789, taking the previous kirk records with him, and then unfortunately mislaying them so that we know very little about church business before Fraser's accession. In 1790, the Duke of Argyll himself and Gigha Laird John McNeill presented a clergyman called Samuel Peat to the living of Gigha and Cara in Dugald's stead. However, he was not found to be a competent Gaelic speaker, and consequently his parishioners – for whom Gaelic was their first and in most cases their only language – objected strongly to his appointment due to his 'lack of proficiency in the Gaelic tongue.'

The unfortunate Mr Peat was interrogated first by the Presbytery of Kintyre, and then by the Synod of Argyll, and, somewhat surprisingly, in view of the fact that he had been supported by the powerful Duke of Argyll, found to be wanting in the necessary linguistic skills. The islanders were well within their rights to object, but it seems that Peat dug in his heels and appealed to the General Assembly. At this point the indefatigable Mr McNeill himself wrote to the Synod, pointing out that the island had been without a minister for long enough, and the Reverend William Fraser was duly presented and appointed, some time between 1791 and 1794. Perhaps in the absence of Peat, who seems never to have been officially retired from the post, William Fraser had gradually begun to undertake duties on the island. Certainly his work of writing a

Statistical Account of the island seems to pre-date his formal accession as minister in 1794.

In the last decade of the eighteenth century, then, we find the Reverend William Fraser writing a Statistical Account of his parish, which paints a vivid picture of the social and economic life of the island and the islanders at this time. It was also from the period of Fraser's ministry that we have the earliest kirk session book still in existence, although this is largely due to MacDougall's carelessness with the previous records. From both these written accounts, we learn a great deal about the day-to-day life of the islanders. This sudden burgeoning of detail is fascinating – like a clearly differentiated voice emerging from a mishmash of interesting but obscure sound.

In so far as the Statistical Accounts tell us so much about the everyday life and work of the islanders, we will leave a closer examination of these for another chapter. It is worth noting here, however, that if one were to examine only the Statistical Account, one would make the obvious assumption that Fraser was a popular and much loved figure in the community, working within a calm and well-disciplined parish. The kirk session records, however, tell a different story or at least contain a rather abrupt change of tone. In 1801 the rumbling discontent, which, until this point, has been pretty much a constant of kirk history on the island, seems to have erupted into a dispute marked by bitterness and exasperation on the part of the minister and a certain malice on the part of his parishioners.

The Presbytery of Kintyre is summoned to Gigha, to deal with the minister's complaints. Essentially, he feels that his parishioners are not providing for him as they should.

In fact they are subjecting him to what is described, in the extraordinary words of the Presbytery as 'a studied system of oppression'. He is, not to put too fine a point on it, completely fed up. His manse is so uncomfortable as to 'endanger his health and that of his family'. His glebe is too remote for comfort. He has nowhere decent to stable a cow or a horse, and when the well runs dry he is 'denied the use of a neighbouring well to get a supply of clean water'. In short, he is not at all a happy man, and after investigating his complaints and finding them fully justified, the Presbytery advises him to leave, which he does in 1802. From 1803 until 1806 we find Duncan Rankin as minister, followed by Malcolm Macdonald from 1807 until 1826 and the long ministry of James Curdie from 1827 until 1877.

The cases that are recorded as having come up before the Session at this time mostly involved 'disorder', 'calumny' and 'immorality'. They are illuminating as to the way of life of the island at this time and although the disputes seem somewhat petty and nitpicking, when followed through the original documents, they also paint a picture of the problems that can beset small communities everywhere, where tiny disagreements can become magnified out of all proportion and where some form of community-sanctioned arbitration is necessary to maintain authority and perspective, and in short, to keep the peace.

The plain fact is that the church was a huge arbiter of public morality and behaviour at the time, an institution of enormous power and influence within a community. But the constant tensions between the power of the church to control the islanders and the intrinsic free-spiritedness of the people are also apparent from the records. It is a tension that is observable from many accounts of the relationship between the Kirk and the people throughout the whole of Scotland at this time, not least in the life and work of Robert Burns.

The strict observance of the Sabbath was paramount, as it is today in many Hebridean communities. As we have already seen, with regard to the crime of gathering wood from the Leim shore, on the Sabbath day, no excuses were permitted. Even heads of households must 'attend Divine Service, keep due order in their families at home, and oblige them to render an account of their behaviour while out of the parents' or their master's sight'. Elders were allotted particular *clachans* or parts of the island which they must oversee, sometimes in the role of 'whippers in' to reluctant parishioners who thought that they had better things to do with their Sundays.

Church attendance was an onerous business by modern standards. Morning service would last for two full hours, while afternoon service meant sitting on a hard wooden bench in a cold building, listening to the minister preach for up to an hour and a half without stopping. Psalms could go on for a long time as well, but at least they were participatory and there was robust chanting or singing (line and line about), to warm you up a little. Sinners, particularly those accused of fornication (what Robert Burns, writing only a little earlier, knew as *houghmagandie)* had to stand up, own to their sins and suffer a stern public reprimand. The only saving grace was that men were as open to censure as women. Prayers were made up by the minister who could, and frequently did, go on as long as he liked.

The kirk session books deal with the minutiae of absence from the kirk (often drink, in the shape of whisky, possibly illicit, is a factor in taking people's minds off the legitimate business of the Sabbath day), while the usual disagreements and allegations that always occur within a small community seem to take up a disproportionate amount of time. The elders were, however, appointed to maintain peace between neighbours and bring the benefit of age and wisdom to bear on their disputes, fulfilling an important function in such a society. One is reminded of a community policeman, reporting to a neighbourhood watch meeting in a present-day village. 'If discord arises' they were told, 'they must first try appeal and only if that fails are they to bring the matter to the Session.'

Crimes of 'calumny' involved name-calling or slander. This may seem unimportant to modern-day urban dwellers, but as anyone living in a small community knows, such tales can spread like wildfire and can do a disproportionate amount of damage. As Kathleen Philip drily observes, after her own perusal of the records, 'nobody would ever own up to anything.'[4] Elders had to devote vast amounts of time to witnesses who often blatantly contradicted one another, or resolutely backed up members of their own families at the expense of others.

There are two excellent examples of situations in which 'calumny' could have had very grave effects for those concerned, although both occurred many years after the Reverend Fraser's time. One was dealt with by the sheriff court in Campbeltown, while the other merely came before the kirk session. The first must have happened during the well-documented ministry of James Curdie, in the mid 1800s, although we find records of it in the Scottish Law Review for 1939, where the tale is told as something of a Gigha curiosity and an example of 'old beliefs which still linger in this little isolated community'. It is also a curiously modern example of a woman not being prepared to put up with slanderous talk.[5]

The story was related in the Steamboat Tavern, in Port Ellen, Islay, so we can assume that drink had been taken and may well have been a contributory factor. A Gigha farmer told a story to the assembled company, about a female neighbour who came to his smallholding, asking to borrow a 'graip' or fork, (usually used for digging potatoes). He went off to find it, but when he came back, he declared that she vanished, while in her place was a brown hare, which looked at him in a sinister fashion and then made off across his field. He must have been a good storyteller, because one Archibald McDonald, elder of the kirk, testified that his hair stood on end while the tale was being told. Perhaps the storyteller himself thought the tale harmless enough, but – as is the manner of such things – the story gained currency in the district, with the farmer being asked to repeat it many times.

Not long afterwards, the tale must have got back to Gigha, where the female neighbour in question, outraged at being so slandered, took the farmer to court, declaring that she was being accused of witchcraft and that she 'felt very sore about it'. We must remember that a couple of hundred years earlier an accusation of witchcraft would have had very serious consequences for the woman concerned and some fear of being so labelled may have lingered long after wiser counsels had prevailed. In his defence the farmer denied everything, but added that since there was no such thing as witchcraft, the accusation had no substance anyway. The sheriff, wisely and somewhat surprisingly, found for the woman. Perhaps he was angered by the farmer's too-clever defence. He said that although the belief in witchcraft was no longer prevalent, there were still places where such an accusation might cause not just ridicule but active persecution. He fined the defendant ten pounds, which money was given to the woman. He also fined the Gigha ferryman twenty shillings. *He* had been called to court to testify as a character witness on behalf of the woman, but had failed to turn up. The farmer paid promptly, and the sheriff summed up the whole affair by declaring that whatever 'idle superstitions' people might entertain in private they should keep them to themselves, and not slander their neighbours – which seems a very enlightened judgement on his part.

The second tale of calumny with potentially damaging effects occurred during the ministry of John Francis Mackenzie. It never got as far as the sheriff court, but seems to have been settled by the kirk session. In 1882, two Gigha men appeared before the session to complain that they had been accused of being 'corprisers' (i.e. body snatchers after the manner of Burke and Hare in Edinburgh and drunken ones at that), a very serious allegation. They stoutly denied this, claiming that they were burying the bodies of shipwrecked sailors from a ship called the *Challenge*, which went down near Gigalum and since the bodies were in such an appalling state, they needed strong drink to assist them in their task. The session duly made enquiries, found that they had been speaking the truth, commended them for their actions and made their accuser apologise in the kirk for his calumny. Records show that a vessel called the *Challenge* was indeed wrecked in a storm off Gigha, and since it was carrying heavy wooden pit props, the bodies of the sailors who were forced into the water would have been mangled beyond belief, so the story rings completely true.[6]

Cases of immorality were taken equally seriously to those of calumny, but the kirk records show a strong, and somewhat unexpected concern with the welfare of the young people involved, rather than any too unrealistic condemnation of sexual relations. At a time when it was possible for a young man to scatter his seed without fear of retribution (or proof of patrimony), the kirk session would often redress the balance in favour of the young woman involved. Kathleen Philip reports one dispute about patrimony about which the decision of the elders was to 'wait till the child is born when it will be clear'. Why this would be the case is not explained, but I have heard of similar tales from other areas, and since many families have strong genetic traits it doesn't seem beyond the bounds of possibility to be able to judge a child's father by its appearance. In one instance an uncle is castigated for his irresponsibility and is made to contribute towards the upkeep of the child, for allowing a very young couple to sleep together in his house, with the result clearly demonstrable in nine months time. But the decision shows a good deal of wisdom and compassion operating among the elders of the kirk within a small community.

The poor were very much the concern of the Kirk, but once more the surroundings of a small island exert their influence, and the elders are more concerned with assuring themselves that those who are too old or sick to work, those without families to provide for them and those who need food, warmth and shelter are given access to it, rather than wholly being concerned with financial handouts. Nevertheless the session did pay small regular sums to the poor, as well as the occasional one-off payment as a contribution towards funeral expenses.

As we have seen, the ministers who followed the disgruntled William Fraser were Duncan Rankin, from 1803 to 1806, Malcolm Macdonald from 1807 to 1826 and James Curdie from 1827 to 1877. James Curdie wrote a new Statistical Account of the state of the Parish in the 1840s, and noted that the church was in a satisfactory state, though a little troubled with damp and also commented that his manse, which had been built in 1818, had been repaired in 1828. It was from his account that we glean much about the state of the ferries to and from the island. He has much to say about the fluctuating population of the island and the economic tribulations which resulted from 'the failure of the potato crop' and other problems. He also mentioned that 'there are two mansion houses on the island, used only occasionally by the late proprietors but now occupied by tenants'. One of these must have been Achamore by this time, but the other is unspecified. Elsewhere, this was said to be down at Gallochoille, although as we have seen, Blaeu's much earlier map, based on Pont's sketches, has placed mansion houses at Balmoir in the north and Leim in the south. Although the landscape of the farms remained largely unchanged, it seems that the siting of the mansion houses on the island underwent significant changes in the 250 years between Pont and Curdie.

Duncan Black succeeded Curdie in 1869, and in 1877 John Mackenzie became minister, being succeeded by the much-loved Donald MacFarlane in 1907. Sydney Smith wrote a biographical sketch of this man, who was minister of Gigha and Cara until 1923. I have a copy of this in my possession, with a photograph of MacFarlane as a frontispiece, a benign, individual with deep-set eyes, wispy fair hair and a fine handlebar moustache – the man's humour and gentleness shines out of the picture. In his account, Smith describes MacFarlane in Celtic terms as a true *caraid-anama* or 'soul friend'. This is, of course, a concept, the idea of a mentor for the soul, which has its roots in that early Celtic Christianity which we have already discussed and which would have been recognised up at the old foundation of Kilchattan as surely as Smith recognised it in MacFarlane in his new manse.

> The order of *Caraid-anama* receives no official recognition in the Presbyterianism of the Church of Scotland, but the order survives. Of this lineage was Donald MacFarlane. The sound of his name is music to my heart and the music is often there.[7]

It is worth quoting Smith's description of Gigha itself here:

> Gigha slumbered in the haze of a summer morning under a patchwork cover of yellows and greens and the three hills which repeat themselves in as many hummocks were as the rumples of it. Little Cara lies like a lion couched, the face of it the high broad cliff at the Southern end in whose brow Nature has set an eye, quiet, piercing, keeping watch over the waters.[8]

MacFarlane was minister in Killean and Morvern before moving to Gigha in February 1907. Smith calls the Gigha manse a 'bare, gaunt, narrow-gabled high building, its harl always dull in colour but turning to darkest mud drab when soused with rain by the winds and its face always with something of a frown on it.'[9] The old manse seems to have been repainted, and looks much less grim nowadays.

Nevertheless MacFarlane clearly loved it. He and his sister took the garden in hand and planted it up. He set his heart, however, on building a new church for Gigha, finding the old kirk somewhat makeshift for his taste. Smith details the progression of the plan:

> the scheme is advanced a considerable stage by the generosity of one of the parishioners and the proprietor of the island at that time; in twelve years he has £800 in hand: not long afterwards a grant from one of the Church Trust Funds, subscriptions from the congregation and outside friends, and contributions from Campbeltown, amounting to £100 collected by himself in the course of a single afternoon, would have made it possible to start, were it not that the Great War has put up the cost of labour.[10]

MacFarlane was a staunch teetotaller, though one with a sense of humour. He himself told a tale of threatening one of his parishioners with a daily visit if the man did not moderate his drinking, to which the man replied 'God bless me minister, is it as bad as that?'[11] Smith credits the minister with 'large hearted kindness' and quotes from his letters of sympathy, for example one sent to the relatives of a young man who had been drowned saying that God had taken him 'home by way of the waters'.[12] He was fond of collecting and using Gaelic proverbs, among which were: 'It's the heaviest ear of corn that bends the lowest', 'A friend's eye is a good looking-glass'[13] and, one of his favourites, 'Your mother's kindness will meet you when she cannot meet you',[14] meaning your mother's influence will be felt even when she is not there.

Smith notes that MacFarlane was a born sailor with a great love of the sea. He had his own small boat, and sailed whenever he could. But during the whole of his ministry on the island, his mind was set on the new church. He even chose the site for it himself, of which he remarked, 'Instead of saying as you do in English, at the end of a story that "they lived happily ever after" we say that "they lived in a little spot at the back of the wind and in the face of the sun". Our site for the church reminds me of that. May many receive blessing here.'[15]

In 1917 he had an accidental blow to the chest when working on his boat, which eventually caused him to seek treatment. In 1918, he spent three months in a nursing home in Glasgow before returning to Gigha. After a few years he began to suffer vague symptoms again. In February 1923, he was working in his garden when he slipped and fell, stumbling against one of the fuchsia bushes, and suffering with acute pain in his side. A member of the congregation was visiting the manse, and he told her that she must have some early flowers from the garden and some apples from their winter stores to take home for her little boy. Then he went to bed, where his brother sat and read to him in an effort to take his mind off the pain, but he died in the early hours of the morning of 10 February 1923, a day before his sixty-second birthday. He died just when the new church was about to be built and is buried up at the old graveyard, at Kilchattan where his inscription commemorates 'a faithful and beloved minister'.

The new church which he had planned was finished and opened a year later and it stands, very fittingly, on the old 'Hill of Music' one of the ancient 'Fairy Hills' of the island, from which it was thought that music might issue on certain nights, and the sound of singing and merriment, from the good folk who were thought to live in the hollow hills. Within the church is a stained glass window, set up by the people of Gigha and MacFarlane's friends, showing the boat in which St Columba has come from Ireland, and the saint kneeling on the shore of Iona.

There is something very fitting about Columba as a memorial to the spiritual power of this man. And unlike Mr Peat, so many years previously, MacFarlane had the Gaelic. Smith quotes an account of the minister from Norman MacLean, who spent some time with him in 1892 when he was only thirty-one years old. 'He had a beautiful voice and he loved to use it. An old psalm tune or a Highland ditty, whatever it was, he would pour out his heart. It was the Gaelic that he loved best and it was in Gaelic that he preached, breaking into a chant at the end, sending forth his appeal with a rhythmic beat. He was in truth the friendliest of men.'[16]

This simple account of the simple life of a Presbyterian minister on a small Hebridean island is unexpectedly enthralling. MacFarlane, it seems to me, was part of an old tradition on the island. He would have sat well with those brave travellers from the early years of Christianity: Cathan, Findlugan, Columba himself, and perhaps that was why he was so well loved.

He was followed in 1923 by Kenneth MacLeod, from the Isle of Eigg, not just a minister of Gigha, but a distinguished collector and translator of Gaelic song and story, as well as a superb songwriter himself. The 'Road to the Isles' was written before MacLeod came to Gigha, but published while he was minister of that island:

It's a far croonin' that is pullin' me away,
As take I wi' my cromak to the road,
It's the far Coolins that are puttin' love on me
As step I wi' the sunlight for my load.

> Sure by Tummel an' Loch Rannoch an' Lochaber I will go
> By heather tracks wi' heaven in their wiles,
> If you're thinkin' in your inner heart, braggart's in my step
> You've never smelt the tangle o' the Isles.'[17]

Few people now remember, if they ever knew, that the song was written as a remembrance of home. It was, in fact, a marching song 'for the lads in France, during the Great War' to whom it is dedicated. But even now, the scent of 'the tangle o' the Isles' is as familiar and evocative to visitors to Gigha as to more northerly isles.

12

Farmers and Fishermen

George Mackay Brown, writing about his beloved Orkney, described Orcadians as 'Fishermen with Ploughs' but this would be an apt description of most Scottish islanders, including the inhabitants of Gigha, since farming on the island was often supplemented with fishing, or vice versa.

We have many details about the way of life of the Gigha islanders from the Reverend Mr Fraser's statistical account of the late eighteenth century, when agricultural changes were overtaking the island. Each Gigha family, so Fraser tells us, had three children, on average, (which seems quite a small number, but many children simply did not survive infancy) while approximately twenty-two families lived in each clachan, or 'farm village'. Before the eighteenth century, most of them would have lived, not so very differently from the way their ancestors had lived for thousands of years, in fairly rudimentary cottages with damp earthen floors and a roof that was liable to let in the rain. Isabel Grant, writing in *Highland Folk Ways*, describes very graphically from elsewhere in the Highlands how 'drips of inky black water were liable to fall on the inhabitants' whenever rainwater percolated through the sooty roofs. There was even a Gaelic word, *snighe* for this rain that filtered through the roof. Chimney flues were a late addition and only began to be incorporated into the gable ends of cottages in the eighteenth century.

In the preceding centuries, farms had been held 'in common'. Land was held by groups of people who cultivated it together. The strips were mixed, and periodically reallocated between people so that there was some fairness in the system. There was also common grazing of whatever pasture was available. This method of farming had been carried on in the Highlands and Islands for many hundreds if not thousands of years, but at the time when Fraser was writing his account, the practical deficiencies in the system had been recognised by landowners and things were changing. 'They are now beginning to divide one farm from another by dykes' says Fraser. 'They are beginning to subdivide each farm so that each tenant may have his marked off and enclosed.'

From Fraser's account, we learn that it had once been the custom to kill all but a few animals in winter, since the dearth of winter feedstuffs for the beasts had been a constant problem in the past, but meat could be preserved in various ways, such as salting and smoking. Enclosure was now allowing people to grow hay for winter feed, so that beasts could be over-wintered with much more success. Other crops consisted of oats, barley and potatoes. Oats, which are largely impervious to the Scottish weather, were always a staple in these northern climes but we are told that this grain often went by the name of 'corn' in Kintyre and on Gigha.

Bear, or bigg, an early type of barley, was also grown here. It was ground and used to make 'bear bread' but in 1772 we find Pennant reporting of Kintyre as a whole that a great deal of bear was grown, but that there was 'often a sort of dearth, the inhabitants being mad enough to convert their bread into poison, distilling annually 6000 bolls of grain into whisky.'[1] But perhaps Pennant knew little of the hardships of a Scottish winter when whisky might have seemed even more important than bread! Apart from its obvious use as bread flour, barley could also be useful in thickening soups and stews and making them both more appetising and more substantial, but its main value was certainly perceived to be for malting, and distilling into whisky.

Mr Fraser the minister tells us that 'there is one distiller on the island' but this is surely a devout wish, rather than the truth of the matter. Angus Martin, in his *Kintyre Country Life*, devotes a whole chapter to illicit whisky distillation on the Kintyre peninsula, with at least one mention of Gigha in connection with a still, purchased from Robert Armour, a well-known maker of distilling equipment.[2] The more taxes rose, the more likely illicit distillation was to thrive, alongside smuggling of the products of the stills to mainland Scotland, and tales of illicit stills are many. *Tar an Tarbh*, the Loch of the Bull, the mysterious haunt of the Gigha water kelpie, below *Dun Ciofaich*, was traditionally the resting place of illicit whisky-making equipment when the excisemen paid unexpected visits to the island.

Barley was also milled and used to make malt for brewing beer, which was, of course, legal. Ale was the everyday drink of choice in Scotland for many hundreds of years. Writing in *The Scots Cellar*, F. Marian McNeill tells us that 'in rural communities, copious libations of the national beverages – ale and whisky – attended each and all from the cradle to the grave.'[3] Even in prehistoric times, there is some evidence that ale was made and flavoured with meadowsweet.

Later, home-brewed ale would have been flavoured with various herbs and spices and could range from a mildly alcoholic everyday beverage to the much stronger brew which might be drunk at – for examples – weddings. Writing in 1772, Thomas Pennant tells us that 'ale is frequently made of the young tops of heath, mixing two thirds of that plant with one of malt, sometimes adding hops.'[4]

It was drunk by the whole family, women and older children included. (In fact in towns and cities, ale may have been a much cleaner and therefore healthier drink than water, although obviously this would not have applied on islands such as Gigha, which were well supplied with freshwater springs.) There were professional brewers on Kintyre, but there would have been no need to import ale to Gigha. It was customary for farms to brew their own ale and was one of the skills for which – along with her baking – the woman of the house might be noted, and had been praised since the time of the Vikings.

Flax was grown on the island at this time, although Isabel Grant reminds us that it was 'a troublesome crop' which had to be hand weeded, usually by women.[5] Once it was picked, it was soaked, until it rotted, a very smelly concoction, after which the fibres would have been beaten by hand, and then combed with iron combs so that it could be made ready for spinning and weaving into linen. We know from nineteenth-century census records that there were linen weavers living and working on the island. Kelp was harvested at low tide, burnt in kilns and the resulting material was exported to the mainland, where it was used in the glass-making industry. According to Fraser in his Statistical Account, Gigha already had a connection with a glass-making factory at Dumbarton, where sand from its shores was sent, so perhaps the product of kelp burning was sent there too.

This so-called 'silver sand', the fine white sand found on Gigha as well as many another Hebridean beach, had a variety of household uses. It was frequently to be found as an ingredient in home-made cleaning materials, mixed with lemon juice and much appreciated for its mildly abrasive properties. It was even used in the Victorian kitchen as a layer of insulation on a baking tray, when range ovens meant that heat was not well controlled, and the essential teatime cake would burn at the bottom before it was properly cooked on the top.

Potatoes were also widely grown on the island. They did very well on the west coast, being cultivated in 'lazy beds' covered with decaying turf and earth, after the Irish fashion. Potatoes and seed potatoes were exported to Ireland, which seems a little like carrying coals to Newcastle, but as Angus Martin points out, the Irish had great need of seed potatoes, particularly after the failure of the Irish potato crop due to blight in 1845–8, which resulted in famine in that country. Sometimes, however, the potato crop would fail on the Kintyre coast as well. Angus Martin quotes the Campbeltown Town Council initiating a public fund for the relief of the poor because of the dearth of potatoes and there was a similar failure in 1831. We must assume that where there was scarcity in Campbeltown this would also have applied on Gigha and since potatoes were such a staple of the island diet their absence would have been disastrous.

Angus Martin tells a story about a shipment of potatoes from Gigha in 1838. It concerned Donald and Hugh, whose surname is not given. They owned a smack called the *John Bull*, which they loaded with 32 tons of potatoes. Half of this cargo belonged to their brothers Archibald and Neil while the other belonged to David Smith, of Kinererach Farm. Since the price in the Glasgow market was deemed to be too low, they took their potatoes to Dublin instead, leaving David at home in Kinererach. But on the return journey, the boat ran aground in a fog, and broke up. Or at least that was the tale that Donald and Hugh told when they got back to Gigha. They said that they had been forced to take to the water in a small boat, leaving the money behind. David was – not surprisingly – enraged, refused to believe their story and took the brothers to court, although there is no record of the outcome or whether he ever received his share of the proceeds.[6]

A most interesting postscript to this story comes from the old graveyard at Kilchattan, where as many of the inscriptions as possible have been very carefully and lovingly documented by Rona Allan, within the last few years. There, we find a stone erected by 'Donald, Archibald, Hugh, John and Neil Henderson, in memory of their father Duncan Henderson, Seaman, Gigha, who died 12th February 1825.' These must surely have been the same brothers, and perhaps their father Duncan was the original owner of the ill-fated *John Bull*!

'There are twenty four ploughs on the island, each drawn by four horses,' Fraser tells us in his statistical account. The ploughs would have been wooden, fastened together with wooden pins or leather straps, the only iron being the coulter, while the eighteenth-century horses would have been a native Kintyre breed, which is quoted by Angus Martin as being 'long bodied, long legged, hard and high in the bone and ill to support.' One wonders if these were descendants of the original ancient horses bred in this place by the Epidii but in any case, they were soon to be superseded by the more powerful and perhaps more practical Clydesdale. Harrows with wooden teeth were used and in Gigha were then tied to the tails of the horses, which can't have been very pleasant for the poor beasts involved, hard and high in the bone as they were.

Fraser tells us that 'black cattle' were exported from Gigha to England. These would have been descended from the old Highland breed, which were small and hardy, but there is some evidence that Kintyre cattle were a less desirable cross between Highland and Irish breeds. They were rather thin and deemed to be poor specimens, because dealers would have to transport them from islands such as Gigha and fatten them on the lush grasslands of lowland farms before exporting them south. They were, however, said to be good milkers, and the tradition of butter and cheesemaking on the island can be traced back a long way.

During the Napoleonic Wars, the price of cattle rose quite steeply, because meat was needed to feed the navy. Mr Fraser's account speaks of a price of £4.00 an animal for an export figure of some 120 black cattle in a year – a valuable source of income for each farmer involved. One huge drawback to the system, at least from the point of view of the islanders, was that the dealers would buy the beasts, but payment would be delayed until the cattle had been sold. The dealers would not expect to pay anything until they returned to the island for the next consignment of cattle. Added to this the presence of a certain amount of counterfeit money in circulation at any one time (what the Kirk Session Minutes refer to as 'bad money'), and the problems of the Gigha farmers become obvious.

As well as meat and meal, the islanders reared poultry for their own consumption, and for sale as well. Fraser tells us that 'the only prolific wild animals are rabbits', which is still the case today, and one must assume that these also formed a useful part of the diet of the people. Fruit and vegetables (other than potatoes and some carrots) were not thought to be an essential part of the diet at the time when Mr Fraser was writing his account, meat or fish and meal of some sort being the main constituents of the day's fare. The Scottish aversion to fresh fruit and green vegetables has a long history and there is some evidence that from as long ago as the sixteenth century, the consumption of fruit in any quantity used to be thought injurious to the health. Turnips were grown mainly as fodder for cattle.

Back in the late 1700s, we find the good Reverend Fraser describing fishing as well as farming on Gigha. It seems that fishing is an industry that causes him some concern, or at least those who earn their living as professional fishermen certainly do.

'Sixty or more of the Islanders who engage in this lucrative business' (i.e. the herring fishery, these fish being both prolific and much in demand) 'being away from home from June till January each year are rarely married and so, when they are at home, live with relatives where they exert a bad influence as they have no specific work to do.' When they return to Gigha these fishermen are much the richer and consequently 'from the habits they acquire aboard, they are not inclined to work hard ashore' and constitute a poor example to the rest.

Fraser can't have known very much about the life of a fisherman at this time if he attributed laziness ashore to the way of life at sea. The herring fishermen would have worked long hours, at a difficult and dangerous job, in open sailing boats. There are stories of oilskins that rotted and fell off, from repeated immersions in salt water. Still, Fraser must have disapproved of their relative independence. These would have been young men for the most part, with sufficient money to buy them a breathing space from the rigours of life at sea during the winter months. These men would not have been without occupation in the off season. Boats had to be maintained for one thing. They would also have been expected to help with the necessary island tasks, including farm work, but still, as far as the kirk was concerned, these young men who had travelled away from the island, and for whom money would have spelled a certain amount of freedom, might have been seen as disruptive elements upon their return.

Fraser's censure of these fishermen, who were often people of consequence and influence in their community, as well as independent thinkers, may well have had something to do with the poor esteem in which he was eventually held by the islanders, when they subjected him to the 'studied system of oppression' of which he later complained. Tact and sensitivity were not among his more obvious virtues.

In later years, salt cod from Gigha was exported to the mainland and was a popular feature of the diet, both on the island and in neighbouring Kintyre. As well as commercial fishing, however, families would take fish and shellfish for their own use, particularly 'cuddies' after which Cuddyport, below Ardlammy is named. These fish are young saithe and were taken with a hook or bent pin, using ground bait to attract the fish, in the traditional manner.

Fraser tells us that 'Everyone fishes for himself, except when the whole party joins in pounding the bait, the flesh of a black whelk, and then throwing it into the sea when these beautiful small fish make their appearance in large numbers, darting at once from all directions like the radii of a circle.'

These fish were very palatable, when cooked in the right way. Kathleen Philip tells of a fish soup called *savas*, made on the island, with cuddy flesh, milk, butter, onions and salt, after the manner of the better-known East Coast Cullen Skink.[7] The late Angus McAlister used to dry fish for his own use.

Fraser details the other occupations of the islanders in the late 1700s. There was a miller (at Ardailly), a blacksmith, five weavers, four tailors, and a shoemaker. Three apprentices worked variously with these men, while there were two boat carpenters (an absolute necessity on an island), a mason, an (official) distiller, two innkeepers, one fiddler and two pipers, although presumably all of these people must have been engaged on other occupations, much as islanders today work at several jobs at once. In more recent times, ex-postmaster Seamus McSporran, who was regularly photographed by the press wearing his many working 'hats', was only following an old established tradition. In Fraser's day, for example, and for many years after, the smith would be responsible not just for shoeing horses, but for making and mending various iron artefacts such as pails, chains and anchors for boats, implements for the farmers, girdles for scone-making and the swee, which was used for suspending the pot over the fire. Iron cooking pots would have been a precious possession for most families, imbued with ideas of hospitality and plenty, which are descended directly from the sacred 'cauldron' of Celtic mythology.

From the eighteenth century onwards, education would have played a part in the life of the islanders. From 1791 until 1912, we know that the island school was situated in the building that is now the post office and shop. There is no record of the existence of a school anywhere in Kintyre before the seventeenth century. In the Middle Ages, most people could neither read nor write and learning was the province of the clerics and the lawyers. It is no coincidence that for many years the lowland Scots word for lawyer was 'writer.' As Andrew McKerral tells us, 'even the greatest chiefs in the Highlands were ignorant of letters.'[8]

During the sixteenth and seventeenth centuries learning became more prized and the sixth statute of Iona, enacted in 1609, decrees that every gentleman in possession of sixty cattle (a marker of his wealth and status) should send his eldest son, or, failing male children, his eldest daughter to school in the Lowlands and maintain his child there till it had learned to speak, read and write English. This inclusion of the daughter in the statute is surprising, in view of the prejudice against educating women to be found elsewhere Britain. Throughout the sixteenth century young men went from the Kintyre peninsula to Scottish universities, but again these were the sons of gentlemen. The first parish schools began to appear in Kintyre in the 1600s.

It had been John Knox's dream that a school should be established in every parish in Scotland (again a surprising discovery, in view of the popular impression of him), but it was long after his death before his dream was realised. Still, by 1633 parliament was decreeing that taxes should be paid for the 'maintenance of parish schools' and the Synod of Argyll set sums aside for a similar purpose in the mid 1600s. The chief reason for the Kirk's support for schools was one that would have far-reaching and somewhat unforeseen effects. It is worth quoting the original motion placed before the Synod in 1650.

> Because the knowledge of the English language is so necessary for the weall of the Gospell, the scriptures not being translated in Irish (i.e. Gaelic) and seeing the country cannot have schools in every church for learning English, that therefore use be made of poor boys that can read and write English to teach the young and others that may be willing in the Parish to read and understand the English in the interim till schools may be erected and the ministers to oversee and make report of their diligence and of the fruit of it to their several presbyteries and to the next synod.

Thus, for reasons that must have seemed entirely praiseworthy at the time, began a long process of attrition for the Gaelic language on Kintyre and islands such as Gigha. The process was by no means inevitable, and by the end of the century, the psalms and shorter catechism had in fact been translated into Gaelic, but nevertheless it was the start of a process that is sadly almost complete on this island at least, although not elsewhere in the Highlands and Hebrides. There are only a handful of people alive on Gigha for whom Gaelic was their first language as young children and since the language varies so much between islands we are losing something precious in the process, although I believe that recordings have been made for the School of Scottish Studies of Seamus and Willie McSporran talking about the Gigha landscape in their mother tongue.

As we have seen from the Synod motion above, the kirk may well have been overseeing a certain amount of education on the island, but the employment of the first proper schoolmaster seems to have been the work of John McNeill of Colonsay, who was always very concerned for the well-being of the island and islanders. A schoolmaster named John Galbraith was appointed by the laird in the early 1780s. As well as employing this schoolmaster, John McNeill was the laird who encouraged the enclosure of land in order to improve farming methods and assist over-wintering of animals for the benefit of all concerned. He built some good new houses and prompted the building of the road from the harbour at Gigalum and 'half way to the north end of the island to the great convenience of the inhabitants.' Fraser points out that although parliament had allotted money for roadmaking, most of it went on the more important mainland roads, so the Gigha road had been built entirely at Mr McNeill's expense.

Galbraith, the Gigha schoolmaster in the late 1700s was able to teach bookkeeping, navigation (a useful skill for boys who were likely to go to sea), reading and writing, English and Gaelic, arithmetic and church music. In those days communities were expected to contribute towards the schooling of their own children, just as they were expected to contribute towards the upkeep of the kirk and the minister, but this could be a real burden on families for whom earnings were very low, and payment was often in kind, i.e. goods or services.

From the existence of old schoolmaster's 'commonplace books' throughout Scotland – though not, alas, Gigha – we can see that children were generally expected to pay a little for their learning, although sums seem very variable and don't always depend upon size of family or age of child, so ability to pay must have been taken into account. They were also expected to contribute fuel for the school fire, although on Gigha as elsewhere, it was common knowledge that a couple of peats might be filched by the poorer boys on the way to school.

In 1784 we find John McNeill petitioning the Synod of Argyll for a contribution of £15 or £20 towards school funds, and to help with the building of a new schoolhouse. McNeill seems to be worried that there are thirty-five widows in the parish, most of whom have children at the school. We must assume that they would not have been able to pay much towards the education of their children. McNeill also points out that at least some of the children have sailor fathers who have been pressed by the Royal Navy, thus depriving them of the support that might have been expected. We also have the name of the man who may have been Galbraith's successor on one of the stones in Kilchattan churchyard: 'Donald McFarlane, Schoolman, Gigha, died at Woodend on 17th November 1792.'

We know from Mr Fraser's account of this time that there were fifty-five boys and ten girls attending the school. Education was not thought to be as important for girls as for boys, even though the Iona statutes had, so much earlier, suggested the substituting of daughters, in the absence of sons, to be sent to the mainland to learn English. But on the whole, it was thought that learning was a male rather than a female province.

Of those who went to school in Mr Fraser's day, i.e. between 1794 and 1802, eight were learning arithmetic and thirty-two were also learning English, bearing in mind that their mother tongue and everyday spoken language at this point would have been Gaelic. The rest of them were described as 'beginners', although how old these beginners would have been is not stated. The population seems to have been reasonably healthy, notwithstanding the great number of widows, but at least one of the reasons for early widowhood becomes all too painfully obvious from Rona Allan's list of inscriptions from Kilchattan, which contains a large number of young men 'lost at sea' or 'drowned.'[9] Fishing has always been a dangerous occupation, but we forget the hazards of living on an island at a time when open rowing or sailing boats were the norm. The Sound of Gigha may be narrow, but it is also dangerous. Willie McSporran's own grandfather, Alexander Graham, was, tragically, drowned off Cara and the body was washed up on Rathlin Island six weeks later. When the laird himself points out that men from the island were 'pressed' or conscripted into the navy against their will, we can also assume that some of them would have died in battle, again, most likely at sea.

Finally, one other sad reminder of the difficulties of island life in the past is also contained in the Kilchattan inscriptions. Time and again we are reminded of the deaths of a disproportionate number of children from infancy to early teens. Childhood was a dangerous time. Common childhood ailments could be deadly, while occasionally, infectious diseases would be brought from the mainland, ferried across with visitors. They must have spread through this small community like wildfire. With little contact off the island, and therefore little natural immunity, the children would surely be most susceptible of all. However, if you made it into young adulthood, and the sea didn't take you, you stood a fair chance of living to a reasonable old age.

13

Achamore

For much of its history, Gigha was a treeless island, albeit a southerly one which has always benefited from the Gulf Stream, resulting in a mild climate with winter storms but few frosts and very little snow. Visitors arrive at the ferry terminal, from which their first sight of Gigha is of a typically Hebridean island. But following the signposts through the village of Ardminish, and along the road to Achamore Gardens, they will be surprised to discover themselves encountering a paradise garden at the very heart of the island. The way lies to the right where a small lane slices uphill towards the old church of Kilchattan, the graveyard, the Ogham stone, and eventually over the hill to Keil, and beyond that to Ardlamey. But before that, at the village hall, there is a left turn along a little track through tall bird-haunted woodlands into a place that – quite literally – seems like another world, acres of incomparable beauty and richness.

These gardens are colourful at any time of year, but especially in spring when rhododendrons, camellias and azaleas are in full bloom. At times there is an almost bizarre quality about the sheer exoticism of the shrubs and climbing plants. It is easy to forget that you are on an island, let alone a Hebridean island. The garden is a refuge and an anomaly, and it is hardly surprising that it attracts so many visitors, and that it is also the pride of the islanders themselves, who appreciate the contrast it provides with the rest of their equally lovely, but utterly different landscape.

At some point on the well-signposted walk, the visitor will also be confronted by the island's 'big house' in the shape of a large and rather ornate mansion, which is Achamore House. As we have seen from preceding chapters, the sites of the various laird's houses seem to have changed several times over the centuries and it is now difficult, even on such a small island, not only to piece together their exact history but also to ascertain just how big these main dwellings were, and who lived in them at any one time.

As Blaeu's map tells us, there was once a very large house or settlement named Balmoir, up at the north end of the island. Pont, who surveyed these islands originally and upon whose plans Blaeu's maps are based, drew a fine big house with what look like three distinctive chimneys up there, although now little remains of that old building. This was probably inhabited by the old McNeill lairds as well as – depending upon its age at the time that Pont was recording its existence – being the site of a house of even more ancient origin. Balmoir or whatever settlement once stood there (the name actually means 'large township' but Willie McSporran calls the place Tigh Mor or 'large house'), may have been the seat of those Gallgael lords of the island who lived and ruled here before the McNeills. We have seen too that Leim has a long and distinguished history in the south of the island, and was probably the seat of the Galbraiths, another ancient family of importance, poets and harpists who owed their allegiance to the McNeills or to their Macdonald overlords.

In 1673, one branch of the McNeills gave part of Gigha to another branch of the family, the McNeills of Loch

Sweyn. Roger McNeill of Taynish granted the lands of Leim, Drumachro, Drumyeonbeg and Gigalum to Donald McNeill of Loch Sweyn. That particular branch of the McNeills of Gigha is believed to have made their home at what is now Gallochoille, where tradition has it that a substantial house once stood down on the seashore, a place which was said to have been involved in the early seventeenth-century skirmishes between McNeills and Macdonalds. It seems likely, however, that the Gallochoille name itself only came to be used with the accession of this same Donald McNeill in the late 1600s, as this branch of the McNeill family was in possession of a similarly named house on Loch Sweyn and perhaps brought the name with them to Gigha, in memory of that place.

The name doesn't figure on the Blaeu Map at all, although a large house is marked at a place named as 'Tremyeawin' which seems to be a variant of Drumyeon, but which also looks suspiciously like a remnant of a British 'tre' placename, where the 'tre' element means house, i.e. Ewen or Owen's house. It's worth remarking again that in King Haakon's time, Ewen of Lorne is known to have visited Haakon at Gigha, and to have been held prisoner on the island.[1] The present Drumyeonmore and Drumyeonbeg houses are much further north, but the position of Tremyeawin, relative to Kilchattan and Gigalum, as it is marked on Blaeu's map, is about right for the present-day Gallochoille. On the other hand, the Blaeu maps are not always accurate with regard to siting of particular places.

Estate records tell us that the Gallochoille/Loch Sweyn McNeills owned approximately a sixth of the land of Gigha, which was still the case when the Reverend Fraser was writing about the state of the island in his statistical account in 1791.

In searching for a connection between these McNeills, and later owners of these lands, Kathleen Philip discovered that a daughter of the house, Jane McNeill of Gallochoille, married Alexander Macdonald of Largie and Carnwath. Their son inherited his mother's share of Gigha, among other properties and it was duly left to his daughters Mary Jane and Emilia Olivia, who both predeceased their mother, dying childless in 1850 and 1851 respectively.[2]

Meanwhile, the lion's share of the island was still in the possession of the McNeills of Taynish until the 1780s when one John McNeill of Colonsay bought the larger part of Gigha, including Tarbert, Kinererach, Ardailly, Ardlamey, Chantereoch, Ardminish, Kilchattan, Drumyeonmore and South Drumachro. This purchase did not, however, come out of the blue and he seems to have had an interest in Gigha for many years previously, since his name crops up from time to time in connection with various purchases of land on the island. He had already bought the mill lands at Ardailly on the west coast, and this holding included the right to quarry the big quernstones needed for the milling process, from the rocks below Ardlamey. Thereafter, the miller held his mill as a tenancy from this same John McNeill. As we have already seen from the statistical account of his time, John became a very active laird and was instrumental in bringing a full-time minister to the island as well as improving the housing stock, introducing new and more productive methods of agriculture, procuring a proper schoolmaster for the island children, causing a 'carriage road' to be built on the island for the first time and making various other general improvements. The artificial mill lochs were, according to folk memory, dug at the beginning of the nineteenth century, which would also date them to John McNeill's time, but Anderson takes issue with this. He points out that the mill loch has often been drained to allow peat cutting from the sediment, because the island has so little peat for fuel and it may be one of these periodic drainings or perhaps an extension of an existing loch that is remembered. Anderson says that on the occasion of one of these periodic drainings, the foundations of an ancient crannog or lake dwelling were found and suggests that the lochs in their original form may have been created many years previously, for the purposes of defence.[3]

When this philanthropic John McNeill died in 1818, he was succeeded by his son, also called John, who inherited the estate exactly as it had been purchased by his father. Like other landlords of the island, before and since, John had severe financial problems, which Kathleen Philip speculates may have been connected with a mainland banking failure at the time although I could find no record of the particular financial disaster which she suggests. The younger John's financial difficulties may have been part of an overall picture of economic woes. The early to mid 1800s were a difficult time for islanders and landlords alike, mostly because of epidemic disease and its effects on the precarious economy of these places. Between 1831 and 1833 influenza and Asiatic cholera came to Scotland, followed, from 1836 to 1842, with more influenza, cholera and a virulent form of typhus known as Irish fever, because it was thought to have come with Irish potato harvesters

All of these had disastrous effects on poor families, not just in the industrial centres, but in the Highlands and Islands as well. People who travelled to cities such as Glasgow, or to lowland farms, in search of work might well bring disease back with them when they returned home and those who had lived all their lives on a small island would have little or no natural immunity. Edwin Chadwick, reported that in 1839, of every person who died of old age, another eight would die of specific diseases.[4] Many of these would be succumbing in youth or the prime of life, and the overall effect on trade between the islands and the mainland would have been disastrous.

During the 1830s and 1840s, trade was in a bad state and food prices were high. Cattle prices were falling and the kelp industries were in decline. Rent arrears were therefore commonplace, since tenants on small islands such as Gigha were struggling with impossible conditions. Added to that, the first half of the nineteenth century saw a period of prolonged droughts, followed by heavy rains. All told then – and although Gigha may have been in a slightly better situation than most, having had a caring landlord in the shape of the elder John McNeill, for a number of years – these were miserable times for the islanders.

Whatever the reason, perhaps a combination of unwise speculation on the mainland and falling revenues from his property on the island, the younger John McNeill seems to have incurred such debts that he was forced to mortgage Gigha, and when he went bankrupt in 1832 Gigha had to be sold. The total value of the island at that time was assessed as being 39,263 pounds, 6 shillings and 6 pence, with Ardlamey assessed as being the most valuable of all the farms along with Achamore and Kinererach. John Carstairs bought the island, or such of it as was for sale, in 1836. This purchase, however, seems to have been a family affair and there is a question mark over the nature of the 'purchase'.

Carstairs' own daughter Elizabeth was married to John McNeill's son, Alexander. In the documents outlining the transfer, it was written that it was 'for the love, favour and affection I have and bear to Alexander McNeill, son of John McNeill Esq of Colonsay and Gigha, and Elizabeth Carstairs his spouse, my own fourth daughter.' The rent on the island was to go to Carstairs during his life, while after his death, it would be inherited by Alexander, Elizabeth and their children. 'Love, favour and affection' is the conventional term which is still used today when property is gifted from one family member to another, and can be found even now on many property valuation websites describing a transfer of property between close relations. Carstairs' purchase of the island, and gifting of it to his daughter and son-in-law after his death may have been a way of the family avoiding any claims that McNeill's creditors may have had on the estate, if his son were to inherit it – as in fact happened. But all the same, things did not go according to plan.

Sadly, Alexander McNeill and three of his younger sons were drowned off Wigtownshire in 1850 but the bodies were brought back to Gigha, where they are buried at Kilchattan. In 1865 Alexander's eldest surviving son John Carstairs McNeill sold the island to James Williams Scarlett. Meanwhile, the surviving widowed mother of the two childless sisters who had owned Gallochoille, also sold him the remaining part of the island so for the first time in many years, Gigha was again owned by one laird.

The mid 1800s saw a time of migration from the island, and a corresponding drop in population, which had, in any case, been gradually reducing from its 1791 high. Between 1851 and 1861 numbers fell from 547 to 460 and from 1861 to 1871 another 70 people left, leaving the population at 390. This cannot be attributed to anything as drastic or intentional as 'clearances' but, nevertheless, the effects were much the same. Even allowing for temporary absences at the fishing or in service, it still seems that the trend was downwards. As Philip points out, 'the decline was largely due to the departure of youngish parents and their young families.' Perhaps the McNeill bankruptcy had acted as a wake-up call to some of the islanders who would have been children when it happened, and would have grown up with all the uncertainties of ownership, as well as the drowning of the new laird. Life was hard for these people, and the times were uncertain. The islands were periodically smitten with epidemic disease, and the first half of the nineteenth century had seen successive potato blights decimate the crop. Certain traditional industries, such as kelp, were in decline. The lairds were struggling financially, and their mainland-based trustees, the men with control of the money, had little feeling for the ordinary people of these islands. Gigha would have been no exception.

Couple these events with the attractions of swiftly developing mainland industries – the Glasgow shipyards, the mills of Paisley and Lanarkshire to name but a few – as well as the enticements of publicity agents coming from Canada, offering free passage to would-be migrants, with the promise of an acreage of their own land, in a new country, at the other side, and one can well understand how many couples with young families might have been tempted to seek a new and more secure life elsewhere. This steady drain on the island's young population has gone on from that time until the present, and only now seems on the verge of being halted and hopefully reversed.

But let us return briefly to the earlier laird, philanthropic

John McNeill of Colonsay and the relationship between his house and Achamore. According to Kathleen Philip the name Achamore (which means Big Field) appears for the first time in the 1836 McNeill bankruptcy papers, with regard to legal property at least, although it may well have existed as a place name, simply describing the field, long before that. Before that too, there are many references to the old manse at Kilchattan, which – since, as we have already seen, a new manse had been built elsewhere on the island – John McNeill of Colonsay had appropriated for his own use when he first bought the island in the late 1700s.

When John McNeill was living in the old manse at Kilchattan, Achamore was described as the site of his 'store', and we know that as a man who was interested in new agricultural developments, he had been experimenting with growing hay for winter feed for the island cattle. By 1841, Achamore suddenly appears on census records as a farm with four cottages, while Chantereoch has become Shensrioch – as we have already seen, the two names seem to be variant spellings of the same old Gaelic name – and appears as a large house with a cottage next to it. Twenty years later, it has gone altogether from official records, although it and its whereabouts are both remembered in island tradition.

Kathleen Philip suggests that when John McNeill came to live at the old manse of Kilchattan, his nearest *clachan* would have been Chantereoch or Shensrioch towards the western side of the island. But she suggests with some justification that the establishment of Achamore instead, as a kind of home farm, and the gradual desertion of Chantereoch, to the west, seems to date from this time as well and that the two events are connected. The timber skeletons of older cottages were discovered incorporated into the stables and byres of Achamore Farm when they were being renovated, so it is possible that John McNeill of Colonsay – who when he undertook his 'improvements' seems to have always been inclined to move activity on the island towards the more sheltered eastern side – set up his experimental home farm on the site of the present-day Achamore Farm, close to available arable land and not too far from the site of his house, the 'old manse of Kilchattan'. But where exactly was that 'old manse' and could it have stood on the site of the present-day Achamore House?

In 1865 James Williams Scarlett of Thrybergh Park in Yorkshire purchased the estate from John Carstairs McNeill, who seems to have had little interest in retaining a place that had been so unlucky for his father and brothers. In 1880, William James Scarlett, the third Lord Abinger, succeeded to his father and in 1884, the new big house on the Achamore Estate was built in its present sheltered situation. We can assume that the earlier Scarletts must have lived somewhere and that somewhere seems to have been a renovated version of the old Kilchattan manse, which had been inhabited by the Colonsay McNeills. On Blaeu's map, there is a house situated not far from the church, and both it and the church seem to be labelled Kilchattan. It seems fairly certain, therefore, that John McNeill's 'old manse' so often reported as being not far from Kilchattan, was on the site of the present Achamore House, since this sheltered hollow, to the south of the windy height where the old church sits, would also have seemed the obvious choice for a manse and glebe.

The new house was built to the design of one John Honeyman, at whose Glasgow company Charles Rennie Mackintosh trained and it is thought that this young and talented designer worked on some of the interiors of Achamore House. In support of the theory that the last McNeill lairds had also lived on this sheltered site is the fact that some of the trees in the grounds are thought to pre-date the accession of the Scarletts, so perhaps planting had begun much earlier to shelter the old manse, which once stood there and which the laird had appropriated for his own use.

As it happened, William Scarlett's wife had almost no time to enjoy her new house. Her grave is to be found up at Kilchattan, with the inscription 'Sacred to the memory of Henrietta Katherine, the beloved wife of Lieutenant Colonel W J Scarlett who died at Limecraig, Campbeltown, on the 10th February 1885 in her 37th Year and is buried here.' Her husband only survived her for a few more years, for his stone, a large horizontal slab placed next to hers, reads 'Sacred to the memory of Lieutenant Colonel William James Scarlett of Gigha and 6th Brigade Scottish Division, Royal Artillery, died 31st day of July, 1888 in his 49th year, and is buried here.'

The new house was remodelled in 1900 following a disastrous fire, which destroyed the topmost storey and which is described in Sandy Orr's ballad 'Flames at Achamore'. This was also recited for me by Willie McSporran MBE, the first chairman of the Gigha Heritage Trust.

I lowsed the horse out o' the cart
I galloped to the shore
I cried out to the golfers
There's fire at Achamore!

I jumped into the passages
So loudly did I roar

There's flames at Achamore boys
There's flames at Achamore!

The family were away from the island at the time, and the servants were playing golf down on the island's little golf course so the blaze was well under way by the time it was spotted. The furniture and the silver were saved by the servants and other islanders who rushed to help, although there is an account of a 'zealous housemaid' deciding to throw the family china out of the upper windows in an effort to preserve it. At that time, the house, which was to be extensively remodelled after the fire, was owned by William James Yorke Scarlett, who had succeeded to his father in 1893.

The Scarletts, who had bought the island mainly as a sporting estate, seem to have been as charmed by it as almost everyone who comes here. William James Yorke Scarlett planted areas of woodland to the north and south of the house with the main aim of providing shelter from the winds and salt spray and to give cover for the game that he wished to raise for shooting parties. The big house and estate surrounding it was, for a long time, an important source of employment on the island. These large houses were run on lavish lines. Many servants would have been needed to maintain such an establishment, and numbers of gardeners would have been employed, as well as agricultural workers, men and maids, up at the home farm.

After the Scarletts there came another period of great uncertainty on the island, which was finally sold in 1920 to Major John Allen. Allen's son, also called John, inherited it but after his death it was again sold to R.J.A. Hamer, who then sold it to a man who rejoiced in the name of Somerset de Chair. He must have been a relation by marriage, since his wife was a Hamer. Such a swift and seemingly uncaring turnover of landowners who considered their Scottish properties as no more than an addition to a portfolio of assets did little for the benefit of the islanders but in the mid 1900s, things were set to improve greatly when Sir James Horlick, the son of a family that had made a fortune in bedtime drinks, notably malted milk, bought the island and set about making changes to the gardens at Achamore.

Horlicks, the drink, was invented in 1873 in the USA by two brothers, James and William Horlick. In 1890 James left to set up a London branch of the business. In 1914 he became a baronet but with his death in 1921 there seems to have been a split in the business. It was in 1931 that the famous 'Night Starvation' campaign first began and in 1945 the US company was acquired by the British side of the business. Colonel Sir James Nockells Horlick was born in 1886 and bought Gigha in 1944. He is still remembered with a great deal of affection on the island as an autocratic, but very caring proprietor (one of the few) who loved the island for its own sake, and wasn't simply trying to 'make it pay'.

He had been exploring the West of Scotland in search of a suitable estate where he could indulge his great love of plants and establish an exotic garden, when he heard that Gigha was for sale. He came to view the house and the estate, and stayed to organise the planting of a garden which is a fitting memorial not just to his skills as a plantsman but to the many island gardeners who have laboured in it over the years, not least Malcolm McNeill, who retired in 2006. Sir James spent much of his time in residence at Achamore and took a keen interest in the island and islanders as well as in his beloved gardens, working with Malcolm Allan who was head gardener from 1918 to 1970.

Horlick was passionately interested in rhododendrons, the very mention of which tends to cause present-day conservationists to throw up their hands in horror. This is because according to the changing environmental fashions of the time, the common rhododendron is now viewed as a foreign intruder, a menace, inimical to wildlife and hugely invasive. However, it has to be said that the 'Horlick hybrids' of Achamore are a noble exception.

When Sir James took over, the gardens at Achamore consisted of some fifty acres of woodland, old mixed woodlands of sycamore, beech, ash and pine, which had been planted mostly for pheasant cover. He planted sitka spruce for all-year-round cover, and then created a network of windbreaks. He, or rather his gardener managed to create a unique environment in the already sheltered gardens, by cutting small clearings among the established ponticum and tree cover, where he could establish unique and tender species of rhododendron as well as camellias, azaleas and other sub-tropical shrubs and hybrids which seem to thrive here. In the gardens are, for example, masses of *Gunnera manicata* from Brazil, like enormous clumps of rhubarb beneath which not just children, but adults too can shelter and a *Rhododendron macabeanum* wood, where larger, heavier rhododendrons assume a faintly menacing air. The more tender shrubs were planted on small mounds with drainage channels that would guarantee some dry root run for the young plants.[5]

Sir James Horlick is buried in the new cemetery above Kilchattan and he has a commemorative window in the church. On his death he left some of his collection of rare plants to The National Trust for Scotland, and the gardens were – more or less – supported by successive owners thereafter, including Sir David Landale in the 1970s, and the Holt family, more recently.

The situation was, however, somewhat anomalous, with the plants being owned by the Trust, but the land upon which they thrived remaining in private hands. The brochure written by Savills, for the very last sale of the island in 2001, acknowledges the status of the gardens at Achamore by describing Gigha as 'Your very own Paradise Isle – one of the finest Scottish islands in private ownership, set in the outstanding scenery of Scotland and including the world-renowned rhododendron gardens.' Ominously, however, it goes on to state that 'The National Trust for Scotland does not have any right to or own any land in the gardens and the arrangement is not formal.'[6] Had the island been sold yet again to a private consortium, the new owner would have been within his rights, as John Martin so eloquently puts it, 'to padlock the gates of Achamore' and effectively cut off one of the island's biggest tourist attractions. Fortunately that was not allowed to happen.

After a string of more or less satisfactory landlords, some of whom paid rather more attention to their plants than to the people of the island, Gigha became the subject of the largest community buyout in British history in March 2002. Not long afterwards, Achamore House, one of the major assets of the Gigha Heritage Trust in assisting them to repay the loan which had allowed them to buy the rest of the island, was sold to Don Dennis, a Californian, who currently uses it as headquarters for his flower essences business and who also operates it as a comfortable bed and breakfast establishment. The house is now on the market again, although Mr Dennis plans to stay on Gigha and to continue to run his business from the island. The Gigha Heritage Trust, meanwhile, have kept the gardens, to be owned and managed for the benefit of the whole island, apart from a small private area around the house, which was reserved for the use of the new owner.

And so the Achamore estate became what it is today: a rather splendid country house, complete with library, large kitchen, many bedrooms and bathrooms, and a billiard room with particularly beautiful woodwork, including an extraordinary vaulted wooden ceiling, some fine woodcarving and oak panelling. The house has an imported sixteenth-century stone fireplace. There is a central tower with an open turret, which is where a boy piper used to stand to pipe the family to dinner on special occasions. The house once had a laundry block, a game larder and stables. It would also have had a tennis court, a generator and kennels for the inevitable dogs.

The public have access to a huge acreage of gardens and woodlands, laboriously reclaimed and planted with exotic specimens over many years. There are still peacocks in the gardens, although the outgoing laird took most of them with him in what John Martin, with a little grin, calls the 'double decker peacock carrier', which he was asked to construct for the purpose. The escapees sit high in the trees, and call to each other in their peculiar echoing howl. When they decide that the time has come to fly down, they edge their way into a suitable position, and glide elegantly onto the grass.

To explore these gardens is akin to walking through a series of outdoor rooms, which change with the passing seasons. One of them is named for Malcolm Allan himself. There are, besides, walled gardens that are planted with varied and lovely herbaceous borders as well as rare specimen conifers. It is fascinating to note that many of the stones in the gardens are ancient pieces of masonry, which look as though they belong to some much older building, now long gone. I noticed one such stone being used to hold down layers of rhododendrons, which were being rooted to form new plants. Meanwhile, the Gigha Heritage Trust has instituted a Garden Restoration Project to try to redress the balance after so many years during which funding for major infrastructure work was lacking, and work is under way to try to restore and maintain the gardens for the benefit of islanders, visitors, and interested plantsmen and women worldwide. The association with the National Trust for Scotland continues. Sir Peter Cox is the Trust's advisor to the garden, and there is an exchange of plants with other gardens.

Part of the charm of these gardens at Achamore is their unexpectedness. It is strange to find such exoticism, complete with peacocks, nestling at the heart of a Hebridean island and yet it is also at one with these people, seafarers who so often brought the weird and wonderful back with them from their voyaging. Nevertheless, the effect of the gardens is to shield the big house from all perception of its surroundings. It is quite possible to imagine yourself in some sheltered mainland valley with camellias in bright, exotic bloom, vibrant rhododendrons, towering and spectacular trees. But, strangely for one with an island setting, this is not a garden that celebrates the sea. For the most part, that is achieved elsewhere on the island, in a dozen cottage gardens where fuchsia hedges and hebes vie with wild whins, thyme and thrift for pre-eminence.

To appreciate the exotic planting in the gardens of Achamore is not to denigrate the wild flowers that grow in great profusion everywhere else on the island. Gigha is warmed by the Gulf Stream, winters are mild, and there are long hours of sunlight. The air is clean and clear. The whole island is a wild flower garden, rich with rare specimens, the blossoms of heath and moorland and the sea-coasts. The late Vie Tulloch, the woodcarver who used to live at Gallochoille, and who spent many years working on Gigha and documenting its flora and fauna in words, artworks and sculptures, also wrote a booklet on the wild flowers, birds and mammals of Gigha.[7]

Vie listed a wealth of flowers that thrive in the mild climate of the island. Flag irises, marsh marigolds and celandine are commonplace. Even on the exposed hillsides a mass of buttery primroses are interwoven with banks of wild violets. Late spring brings 'soldierly foxgloves', dog roses and that most Scottish of roses, the 'burnet', which is so fond of the sea. In 1846 Samuel Lewis in his *Topographical Dictionary of Scotland*, is to be found writing about the wild 'musk roses' of Gigha, which grew on the island in profusion. This rose, incidentally, was the flower most associated with Epona, the goddess of horses, the goddess too of those ancient Epidii inhabitants of the island.

The hedgerows are home to bluebells, campion and ragged robin. Common spotted orchid grows over the whole island, as well as marsh and fragrant orchids. Then comes honeysuckle, which threads through the hedges all summer long, like clotted cream. Gentians are to be found on the short coastal grass. There are clumps of thrift, threading the shoreline like a natural rockery, with wild thyme enlivening every outcrop.

In high summer, there are harebells, with the rare 'grass of Parnassus' and meadowsweet, which was once used to strew on floors, to sweeten them. Purple loosestrife grows in profusion, as do thistles and ragwort, which is poisonous to horses and farm animals. The island is rich in brambles, first with their white flowers in summer, and then glistening with plentiful berries in the autumn.

Brambles and blueberries would have been a useful addition to the diet of the islanders in the past, and they are still picked and made into pies, jams and jellies. Vie named other plants, such as wild carrot and angelica, which would have had culinary uses in the old days. Carrots were particularly prized, to the extent that songs were written about them. The afternoon of the Sunday preceding St Michael's Day (another patron of horses and horsemen) on 29 September was once known as *Domhnach Curran* (Carrot Sunday) and marked the harvesting of the carrots for winter storage.[8]

As you walk around the gardens at Achamore, there is only one spot from which you suddenly become aware of exactly where you are, of the contrast between the sheltered and exotic gardens below you, and the rest of this sunny flower-strewn island. This is a part of the garden called the Spring Bank. From the back of the walled gardens, there is a steep path that zigzags up the hill only to burst suddenly through the trees where the visitors will be confronted with the long slope to the rocky western coastline of Gigha, with misty Islay and the mountains of Jura, floating in a sunlit sea.

This separation between Achamore and the rest of Gigha seems intentional, and the development of this garden also seems to mark a change in the attitudes of successive lairds and landlords to the island and, more importantly, the islanders themselves. Many of the old lords of this isle were difficult men, quarrelsome and mercurial, to be sure, but they were also, at root, men of this place, and this culture. True, many of them would have been absentees, but there is a sense in which the islanders would have been kin, members of the family, living and working, farming or fishing on the island. There were many ordinary people, men and women who bore the clan name, whether it was McNeill or Macdonald, and who owed allegiance to their chief.

But with Scarlett, or perhaps even earlier, with Carstairs, there seemed to come a profound change. Where before, loyalty to the rightful laird had been a question of emotional allegiance, long memories and blood ties, the relationship between the islanders and these new owners had shifted. And (with the possible exception of Horlick) these new men had a quite different relationship with the islanders. A succession of owners saw the place either as a business opportunity or a retreat, or a combination of both. For these people, financial expediency would generally override the social welfare of the islanders. This goes some way towards explaining why the community buyout – precarious as the decision may have seemed to many – happened exactly when it did. Or, as John Martin put it, 'I thought, here we are in the new millennium, and we're still living under a feudal system. Something has to change. It's time.'

14

The Keeper of the Purse

The Sound of Gigha is littered with submerged rocks, and is something of a hazard to visiting yachtsmen although the local fishermen and ferrymen know the place well enough to avoid them.

'Do you know where *all* the rocks are?' asked a deeply impressed visitor, of Willie McSporran.

'No,' he said, 'but I know where they aren't and that's good enough for me.'

The formidable Willie McSporran, MBE was the first chairman of the Gigha Heritage Trust and played his part in the successful community buyout. At the time of the sale, he was quoted by the BBC as saying, 'This is a historic and wonderful day for the islanders – it marks a new chapter in our story and I'm sure the celebrations will be remembered for a long, long time.' But it was when questioned about the islanders' ability to pay back the million pound tranche of the loan within the given time that he made the most telling statement. 'Of course it will be done,' he said, simply. 'A Highlander always keeps his word.'

A new chapter it most certainly was, but it was also the culmination of an old struggle, and one with which Willie's own family, the McSporrans of Kintyre, had been involved down the centuries. Arguably, and although very many members of the community, as well as the local MSP George Lyon, were involved with the buyout in many positive ways, Willie himself played a historic role in the persuasions and negotiations that went on beforehand. Cometh the hour, cometh the man, and there is a sense that Willie was there at exactly the right time, to tip the balance in favour of the buyout, when fears of the huge financial responsibility involved might have seemed very daunting. I suspect that for Willie, along with other more senior residents, it was a 'now or never' moment; they believed that it was time for the islanders themselves to seize the initiative, after so many years of being at the mercy of successive owners, or at the mercy of those who saw fit to lay claim to the island and were prepared to fight to get it. His wisdom and experience must have been invaluable.

On first meeting Willie McSporran I felt a bit like David Balfour in *Kidnapped*, when he first encounters Alan Breck, another engaging but alarming Highlander: 'Altogether I thought of him, at the first sight, that here was a man I would rather call my friend than my enemy.'

McSporran is an old and venerable surname, and one with particular Kintyre associations. The surname McSporran means 'Son of the Purse' and traditionally the family were the keepers of the purse or treasurers to the Lords of the Isles. When Donald, first Lord of the Isles, appointed sixteen office bearers, one of them was given the title of *sporan*, or purseholder. This was a recognised office, much like an official treasurer and with the same functions – i.e. looking after the family or in this case clan finances. In view of this, there is a certain satisfactory symmetry about Willie's role as first chairman of the Gigha Heritage Trust.

It is possible to trace the history of the McSporrans over

many hundreds of years. There is some evidence of the existence of one Paul O'Duibhne, or Paul O'Duin of Loch Awe, also known as Paul of the Sporran because he was nominated as treasurer to the Lord of the Isles. Martin Martin describes him as being buried on Iona. It was his daughter, Eva, who married Gillespie Cambel and from them the great Clan Campbell would spring. Paul's father was believed to be Arthur Armdhearg, Arthur of the Red Armour, who in turn claimed to be descended from the warrior kings of Dalriada.

The gravestone of *Paul An Sporain* is supposed to lie in the north-east corner of St Oran's chapel on Iona although the stone has since been moved.[1] The slab is said to be carved with a serpent around a column of eleven discs, which are thought to be silver coins, a fitting memorial to a treasurer, although since there is no name on the stone, we can't be sure whether that, or some other meaning, was intended and a serpent with eleven coils is a sacred symbol that pre-dates even the Celts. Once again, we have lost the language of these stones, which must once have been quite clear to those who carved them.

Much later, in 1541 we find one Duncan Roy MacSpairand renting land in Kintyre, while it is on record that two brothers (and perhaps many more of the same name) left Kintyre for Ireland in the troubled early 1600s, and settled there. Certainly, there is an example of the McSporran or McSparran coat of arms in Dungiven Priory in Northern Ireland and the name in one form or another, occurs throughout Ireland, but with a concentration still on the Kintyre peninsula and evidence of many McSporrans having lived on the Isle of Gigha.

When I first visited Gigha we always seemed to meet Willie down at the south end of the island. He was always at work on a boat or tinkering with an engine. Back then, I found him slightly alarming, a feeling which has persisted, although it is now overlain with affection and admiration. He has a fine line in irony and suffers no fools gladly. Over several sessions, I recorded Willie talking about the old days on the island, and at the end of that time, a vivid and enchanting picture emerged, of a way of life which is very much within living memory, but which is sliding away from us with every year that passes, with every loss of one of the senior islanders.[2]

Willie's grandfather for whom Willie himself was named, was a stonemason on the estate. Willie tells how a young and very religious boy was set to labouring for his grandfather on a building project. Every now and then, he would offer him a particular stone, which was always thrown down unceremoniously. Eventually, this older Willie McSporran exclaimed, 'Don't put that bastard up to me again!' whereupon the young man expressed shock at being sworn at by one of his elders and betters. There was, however, a form of stone, very unsuitable for building, which was known as the 'bastard whin', so poor Willie had been innocently giving the stone its traditional name, with no thought of upsetting the younger man's religious sensibilities.

For the first eight years of his life, Willie himself and his brothers spoke Gaelic:

> The whole island was Gaelic except for the few that were incomers and in fact some of them would have Gaelic parents but they didn't use it in the homes, so it wouldn't have come to the children. But at New Quay, uncles and grand uncles and mother and father, until he died, all had Gaelic so it was a commonly

> used language. It was an everyday language. At one time you'd have to think in Gaelic and translate into English before you could speak which sounds daft, to somebody that never had too much of it, but that was the way it was.

Although Gaelic is no longer spoken on Gigha as a matter of course, there is a sense in which the language still flows beneath English, like an underground stream. The place names are mostly Gaelic, and there are many words of the old language still in common usage on the island. Many parents are keen for their children to have some knowledge of the language, and there is a possibility that it may yet re-emerge in its living form, in the future.

Willie McSporran was born in New Quay Houses at the far south end of the island in May 1936. The family moved to Brae House where his brother Seamus was born, and then moved back to the New Quays a little later.

> We had to walk from New Quays to the school, which would be near enough a couple of miles' walk, and back on an afternoon, through rain or snow. The worst year I can remember was the heavy snow of '47. We had the short trousers, and the snow was sticking to you, and we were freezing so we turned back.

When Willie was a boy, he remembers that there were still some thirteen working farms on the island. 'Leim would have had the farmer and his wife, Macdonalds by name, as well as two men and a maid at least.' His own mother would go up to Leim to milk the cows, before the advent of the milking machine. 'She went away from New Quay about four o'clock in the morning. Each person had to milk eight cows by hand, no easy feat though it was alright when you were used to it.'

South Drumachro was a family farm, where a 'fair-sized family' would have worked it themselves. Achamore was what Willie called a 'bachelor farm' then farmed by one Seamus McSporran. 'I don't think a relation of mine, or if he was, very far out.' There was a great deal of work at Achamore because it was the biggest farm on the island, and we have seen something of its history as the experimental home farm of the McNeill lairds.

Ardlamey, on the western side, had a farmer who was, at that time, almost a bachelor, because his family didn't live with him, but he had five men and a maid working for him. North Drumachro was one of the smaller farms with another bachelor owner, also a Macdonald, who shared his land with his brother at Leim. South Ardminish, where the Gigha Hotel stands now, was a farm and small hotel combined and was run by the MacPhersons who employed two men and two or three maids for all that they had a big family. The farm was 'immaculately run, a showpiece of a farm, the stacks were beautiful. It was tidy, and you wouldn't see roots and gorse growing where it shouldn't be'.

North Ardminish had a hill farmer, Neil McKinnon, and his wife, and 'it was a well run place too'. Achamhinish Farm was rented by the Wilkiesons who had the shop, and their nephew was a working manager who bred show Clydesdales. The wife of the Drumyeonbeg farmer was a district nurse, who cycled about the island, although Willie remembers that you had to go to her most of the time. Kinererach and Tarbert were worked together, and the farmer there bred Shetland ponies for the pits.

There was no single creamery on Gigha. As Willie puts it 'each and every one made their own milk, cheese and butter' along with all the other jobs of the farm, and some were more successful than others, but the flowery grasslands of Gigha seem to produce a particularly good milk, which in turn goes to make an especially tasty cheese. It was mostly mixed farming in those days. The cattle were shorthorn crosses and were often referred to as 'liquorice allsorts'. The impression gained is that everyone was connected, if not by marriage then by the need to help each other out in a small community. They were 'hard times and happy times'.

With Sir James Horlick, however, came a big change in cheese production with the construction of a proper creamery at Achamore, which saw the beginning of the characteristic 'Gigha cheese' as a commercial venture. Horlick set up a company, through which the farmers would bring their milk to the Achamore creamery. Some of the farms drove their own milk to the creamery while the smaller farms had the milk collected, first in a couple of carts and then in a bigger four-wheeled horse lorry. The finished cheese went by horse and cart to the wooden pier, where it was laid on straw to await the ferry. From the island, it was sent to the old and distinguished cheesemaking company of McLellands in Glasgow (which had been founded in 1849) for packaging and distribution.

The increasing demands of the creamery saw a corresponding demand for milk, so that within a few years of Willie leaving school everyone had a milking machine, a novelty in those days. Although Horlick had been instrumental in bringing the farms up to scratch, the creamery itself proved problematic.

There was some form of bacterial contamination in the water or in the building, and it was decided to close the creamery down for a time to try to address the problem. The milk began to be sent to Campbeltown instead, and it was eventually decided to abandon the creamery altogether, which seemed to signal the end of traditional cheesemaking on the island. As we have already seen, a creamery was reinstated at Leim Farm for a brief spell, but once the indigenous knowledge of such a craft has gone it is very hard to reintroduce. The Gigha brand of cheese, which is now sold on the island as well as in specialist food shops throughout the UK, is still made in Campbeltown, although it would be better perhaps if it could actually be made on the island.

Willie's father died when the boys were very young – he himself was only six – and his mother was left a widow with three sons. At that time, it was the custom for children to stay at the Gigha school from the age of five to fifteen. They would sit a qualifying exam, which meant that a handful of them would be able to go away to schools on the mainland, but for the most part, the older children stayed on the island.

'Education came from Dunoon and it was in the form of assignments, posted to Dunoon for marking.' There were two classrooms in the school and Willie remembers that at the time when he left, in 1951, there were thirty-two pupils. At the time when I first recorded several conversations with Willie, back in 2003, there were only seven children in the island school but with new houses being built, and new people arriving or in some cases returning to the island, there would be as many as twenty children in the school in 2006–7. Willie tells of pastimes such as 'going for nuts and taking an hour and a half to do what should have been done in half an hour, smoking when you shouldn't have been smoking and so on', but there were other, now redundant, occupations: 'Many a trampling we did to the blankets as boys and hung them out on the top of gorse bushes and then you got into bed and got a jag on the rear.'

Getting and eating gulls' eggs was another useful pastime for the island children, especially the boys. 'I've eaten dozens of them in the past, and still would, except that it's now against the law to eat them!' said Willie, with a grin. 'Gigalum, Cara, Garbh, are loaded with gulls' eggs. You used to fry them, boil them, make pancakes with them. Terns' eggs were very very red. But they were all good eating, better than any caviare.' The eggs are now safe, and the island gull population, common, herring and great black-backed gulls are breeding in profusion all round the island. Terns are, as Vie Tulloch says, 'temperamental' and try out many sites before settling, but if you are walking the island, their screaming will alert you to their colonies, as it must have alerted those young egg collectors, so many years ago.

Other pastimes were equally uncomplicated. 'You had to make your own entertainment. There was no provision. No radios. Two or three people had a radio and you would go in and listen to the news or the McFlannels.'[3] Dances were held on one of the farms, before the village hall was built, or perhaps at the school. There were a couple of fiddlers, one of whom was Angus McVean, who also made fiddles himself, and who died only recently, as well as a man who played the melodeon, so the music for the dancing was all home-made. The new village hall was built near Kilchattan, at some distance from Ardminish, in case the noise of merrymaking should disturb the neighbours (presumably the inhabitants of the old graveyard don't mind). It was well used for draughts, badminton, concerts, and various other gatherings and meetings and is still considered a great asset to the island. New entertainments were not neglected. The Highlands and Islands Film Guild brought a film in once a fortnight and a generator at the hall drove the big projector.

When Willie was a boy, there were few tractors on the island, which was still largely farmed using horse power, although things were already changing. 'Vehicles were a thing that was unknown, apart from the one at the shop. An old Ford van it was. The ploughing in those days was done using horses. Most of the larger farms, Leim for example, would have six working horses. There would be three pairs, and then there would be young horses, one- and two-year-old foals. There would be a pair ploughing, a pair carting, and whatever.' The farm would employ a ploughman, a byreman and an 'orraman' who, as his name suggests, would do everything else, including carting which would involve moving turnips, potatoes, oats and hay.

If you had a big field it would take three horses to pull six harrows while ploughing was mostly done with a pair. However, three horses might also pull one big plough. The horses were Clydesdales by that time, and as Willie says 'some of them could be very big'. He says that within his memory, at least on Gigha, it was rare to see four used together, although his uncle in Kintyre certainly did. The norm on the smaller farms was to have a pair, with a younger horse 'coming up.' The last foal was born in early summer, as Willie remembers it, and the mares didn't work when they were in foal. June, July and August were hay time and harvest time.

> It was [says Willie] a real art to get the beasts to pull together, and a real art to train them for the job in the first place. You had to break a young horse, and it wasn't the easiest job to start them from scratch. It took a lot of hard work and determination to break a young horse, but a good horse was worth another human being. You would speak to the horse constantly. Some of the old horsemen would shout 'whoa' to their tractors when they first came in and of course the bloody thing would carry on!

It was especially tricky working with a three-horse yoke, especially when some horses were better than others, but they had to be coaxed into pulling evenly. When the horses were put out to grass they 'tended to get soft and stubborn' so much so that by harvest time, it might be hard to get a beast to move. The sound of the machinery would scare a young horse, and it was customary to block the animal's ears with cotton wool, to deaden the frightening sound of the machinery coming behind. (In Islay, some of the ploughmen would put butter in the horse's ears for similar reasons.) One big problem Willie remembers with the horses was the horseflies or 'clegs' which would bother not just the horses 'who got spooked and went daft with them' but were equally difficult for the men who were just as likely to be bitten as the beasts. Cleg bites are extremely painful and prone to becoming infected afterwards.

As we have seen in preceding chapters, there is a long tradition in the Hebrides of moving beasts between the islands and the mainland, or from island to island, and Gigha is no exception. Willie remembers his mother telling him about a man who used to ferry his horses over to the island of Gigalum, for the summer grazing there. Each horse would know its name, and although he would have to ferry them out, he would simply stand on the Gigha shore and shout for them when he wanted them, and they would swim back to him, over the narrow sound of Gigalum. This same man retired to the island of Cara, and would take his stirks out there in a small boat. Willie relates how one of them was tethered to the inside of the boat but took sudden fright, jumped over the side and almost capsized the boat.

There was, of course, no such thing as artificial insemination, so 'you had to travel the beast' and if this involved cattle, rather than horses, there might be problems. 'Some of the bulls weren't very friendly. Mind you, I was never attacked, though I was charged by a cow, once. When cattle were going to the market, they would all be going on the steamer to Tarbert and would have to be loaded onto the boat. If it was a bull, you had to travel with it, and the same went for a horse. You got free on the steamer, but you had to pay for the horse or bull.'

Willie tells one story of taking a bull down to the pier on Gigha. They had blindfolded him, to keep him calm, but

> he was choking with the ropes, so we let him out onto the pier, when he took a notion he would argue with us, and went over the side of the bloody pier. This blindfolded bull went over the pier, but there was a pole jammed up between his horns and that made him keep his nose up out of the water. The boat was coming. We ran and got the nearest dinghy, rowed it round, and, with a combination of youth and determination, got hold of the bull, towed the bull behind

> the dinghy, got him in a horse box and he went on the ferry that day!

'The first tractor only came to the island in the very late 1940s and that was on one of the Horlicks farms.' Willie remembers that 'nobody thought a tractor was capable of doing what the horses could do'. The tractor was used for harvest, hay and so on, but you wouldn't use a tractor for too much on the land. Meanwhile, necessities such as fertiliser and cattle cake all came to the island by puffer. Instead of it being delivered, somebody had to go to the pier with a horse and cart, or later on with tractor, to collect it and the sacks were heavy.

Bags of grain also had to be carried to the granary and fed down to the bruisers to make feed for cattle. First thing in the morning, the areas where the cattle lay had to be scraped out by hand.

> You mucked out the byres, eight big barrowloads of cow manure. There were pigs to muck out, and the horses as well, of course, when they were still worked and all before you started your day's work in the fields. Ploughing was done at the back end of the year. You ploughed the lea in the back end so that it had all winter and the frost to break it down. There was stubble land and red land. You would plough the red land a couple of days before you sowed it so that the weeds didn't have time to come up.

All jobs were done by hand. Then as now, lambing was one of the first signs of spring but lambs had to be castrated and their tails cut, all by hand. Sheep too had to be clipped by hand. The wool would be spun and woven and there are still a few original Gigha spinning wheels in island homes. One in particular used to belong to woodcarver Vie Tulloch, and was a thing of great beauty. Calving happened in the summertime and cattle had to be dehorned using caustic soda. In June, turnips, which had been sowed in the spring, would be thinned. Harvest time involved cutting corn and stooking it, when there was no combine harvester. 'Corn' went to the mill at Ardailly, where it was ground to meal for porridge. Willie describes how the mill wheel there, one of the biggest in the area, was 'brought in by sea', which was much easier than trying to fetch it overland to the remote west side of the island.

Meanwhile, home-grown fertilisers were also used on the land, in the shape of lime. There was a lime kiln next to Gigalum cottages at the south end of the island and the stone was burned using a particular method: hawthorn branches were laid at the base of it, then a thin coating of limestone, then more branches and more lime, until the kiln was full. The stone was burnt to a powder and then taken out and spread on the fields. 'Everything about the farm', as Willie observed, 'was labour intensive and hard work.'

There weren't, Willie told me, so many potatoes grown when he was young, but he knew that his ancestors at Achamore had 'exported the tatties to Ireland, as ballast in sailing ships.' There were few Irish 'tattie howkers' on the island in Willie's day. Instead the fishermen would come and give a hand to gather them, if need be, especially the lobster fishermen who would help with the potatoes in the afternoons, after they had lifted their creels. Similarly, 'if you were finished your harvest or whatever, on a good day, you would take a horse and cart and give someone a day, and it was the same with the potatoes.' Stories were told of skippers who were so impressed with the Gigha potatoes that they paid for them on the spot, and Willie too reiterated the story of the Irish merchants who put the potatoes on top of bags of their own merchandise to make them look better.

Willie himself left school when he was fifteen, and was immediately employed on one of the island farms. 'The day I left school in June of 1951 I ran down the road and within a quarter of an hour I was working for the handsome sum of thirty shillings a week and that was from a quarter to seven in the morning to six o'clock at night.' He remembers that the farm was a good place for food. The men were well fed and when so much of the work was so physically demanding, this was important. Stories are told of places where you had 'salt herring and potatoes coming out your ears.' Willie relates how on one Kintyre farm the wife asked how the men were getting on with their herring. The reply was to quote the number of a Bible verse. Curious, she looked it up to find that it read 'Jesus Christ, the same today, tomorrow and for ever after.'

On the farm where Willie worked first, they had a tractor, but there were still horses on the farm, which were used for carting turnips and ploughing the softer land. He tells how the men would all help to cut the harvest and bind it. 'By then you had the binders but you still had to stook the corn. If it was wet weather you'd maybe to change the stooks, turn them around and change them about.' He remembers how mechanisation was already beginning to take some of the hard physical graft out of farming but also meant a corresponding cut in the numbers of men and maids employed on the farms.

Mains electricity came to Gigha in 1955, via an underwater cable from the mainland, but many of the farms were already installing generators for themselves. Before that, paraffin lamps were used and carried about from place to place – a distinct fire hazard when there was so much straw and other flammable material about. When electricity first came to the island most people would have just one socket installed in a room. They couldn't conceive of needing more, but this was to prove a boon to Willie who – working with Neil Bannatyne who had done a correspondence course in engineering – spent some time extending electricity supplies, adding extra wall sockets for people who had underestimated their requirements. One big knock-on effect of the electricity was that electric motors could now be used to pump water into the houses. Before that, the farms had all used spring water, but now it is only Achamore House that still uses 'fine water' from its own spring.

In the mid 1950s Willie began working in the shop, when his younger brother Seamus, who had been working there, left to do his national service. The job also demanded an oilskin and wellies, because so much was transported to the island in bulk, aboard the puffers that were then commonplace on the Scottish west coat and which were immortalised by Neil Munro in his tales of *The Vital Spark*, and her crew.[4] The puffers, which came in to the wooden pier at the south end of the island, brought gravel, slate, sand, cement, tiles, coal and chips for the road. 'The hold was deep and you had to dig from the top down to unload the cargo.' Fertilisers and cattle cake came once a week and had to be unloaded by sling, manhandled and taken to the shop. Groceries came in by boat, as well as lobster pots. All of this meant an early start, going down to the pier at 3 or 4 o'clock in the morning, but you 'worked when work was there'. For all this Willie was paid £5 a week.

He remarked that because cartwheels had a steel tread at that time, the track along the pier was wooden with steel rails for the wheels. The estate built the first pier, but when it wore out, Argyll and Islands Council took the pier over. In '1952 or thereabouts' Willie remembers that they started bringing in materials to build a concrete pier, all of which were brought in on puffers. He carried on working in the shop when his brother came back from his national service, but also turned his hand to 'fencing, ditching, draining, storm dyking and anything that turned a pound'. When the tractors started coming in, there was work to be done with them too, servicing them, changing oils and so on. I find it fascinating to note how Willie's working life had encompassed the change from horse to plough. People adapted to this new way of working, and if that involved learning a whole new set of skills, then that was what they did. If they regretted the passing of the horse, they also welcomed the benefits of mechanisation in easing at least some of that 'hard physical graft' to which they had become accustomed.

Prior to the advent of the car ferry *Bruernish*, and then the roll-on roll-off ferry, Willie remembers how a couple of small launches were used as passenger ferries to and from the island. One, the *Shuna*, belonged to the council, and the other, a small launch, belonged to Ian McKechnie. It was called the *Cara Lass* and he had built it himself. These boats had twenty-horsepower Kelvin diesel engines and as Willie says it was 'bad enough when the passengers were able to walk aboard. The crossing took twenty-five to thirty minutes and on a bad day you would be soaking wet before you got to Tayinloan.'

The biggest problem, though, was when somebody who had been taken ill had to be transferred to the mainland by boat. Then, day or night, a stretcher had to be carried down to the catwalk in Ardminish Bay, which was where the small ferry came in. Because of its narrowness, it would only take two men, one each at head and foot. Willie, who was a big strong young man in those days, would go at the front, carrying the invalid down the catwalk to where the small ferry boat was bobbing about. Getting the patient aboard meant lowering the stretcher, complete with occupant, head-first into the bottom of the boat, tilting it at a dangerous angle, to negotiate the solid shelter on the bow of the boat. 'It must have been worrying for them because I know it was worrying for me, though we had no disasters that I can remember,' says Willie. 'Many a soaking we would get, but we're still here to tell the tale.'

Sometimes the trip had to be made to the mainland to fetch a coffin for somebody who had died. Willie remembers that the first 'tractor funeral' was in 1957, because they had had snow and a hard frost on the island, and the ground was too hard for the horse and cart to carry the coffin.

After his time in the post office, Willie went back to farming for a while, but when the chance came to work on Archie McAlister's fishing boat, he leapt at it. When Willie was a boy, it was his relatives, the Graham family, down at New Quay, who were the fishermen, as traditionally they had been for many hundreds of years. The McNeills were a big fishing family too, as were the McAlisters. Cod fishing was done with long, baited lines although Willie remembers that there came a time when French trawlers fished the waters and were accused of ripping away the local lines. Gigha fishermen would still go away to the herring fishery, as we have seen that they did for many generations, no doubt still coming back with too much money in their pockets for the minister's taste, and too little to spend it on. When marine engines first came in, few people had any experience of them, and Willie tells how the fishermen would only use the engine to get to and from their creels. 'After that, the engine was stopped and they rowed from then on. They had to have the sweeps crossed because the boat was narrow and that meant rowing with your arms crossed. It was fantastic to see these old men, you would hardly think they were putting any effort in and yet it was fantastic to see the boat cutting through the water.'

Fishing superstitions were rife. A little red-headed child, encountered each morning by a fisherman on his way to his boat, could cause consternation, to the extent that a letter was sent to the parents, asking if she could leave a little earlier or later for school!

'Salmon was a very bad word to say on a boat, the red fish, you couldn't take salmon on a boat, even tinned,' says Willie. 'You couldn't mention a rat, it was a long tail. I know one yet who doesn't mention a rat. And you had to wait for the fisherman to speak first, if you met one on the road.' Swans were unlucky at sea, and a certain brand of matches with a swan on the box would never be taken on board. Pigs were anathema, and even the minister was not very welcome on board. Boats were never, and still are not, turned against the sun, i.e. anticlockwise either in the water, or out of it. Anything anomalous was seen as unlucky, in the precarious environment of the sea.[5]

It was at this point in his long and varied career, that Willie McSporran was responsible for repairing the six-cylinder

Perkins belonging to a certain diving and clam fishing boat named *Striker*, which had arrived in the Sound of Gigha with my husband aboard, and promptly broken down. 'There was an old lorry lying up at the north end with a similar engine, air cooled while of course *Striker* was seawater cooled. With the help of a case of beer and some whisky, we got the cylinder head off the lorry, installed it in the Striker and, with a bit of technology and a bit of luck, it worked.'

After a spell at the fishing, Willie then worked as handyman on the estate for a number of years, which meant a 'sure wage, paid at the end of the week.' By that stage Willie was married to Ann, from England, and they had had two daughters. For the estate he worked on silage pits, shed building, cottage renovation and, as he said to me in 2003, 'a hell of a lot of things that are now needed done again.' Fortunately much of that necessary renovation and restoration work has either been completed or is at least well under way. While he was working on the estate, Willie sustained an eye injury, which was greatly helped by a corneal graft. When Archie McAlister's mother had a stroke, however, and his father Angus came ashore to look after her, Willie went aboard with Archie as a 'permanent man' and fished with him for five or six more years, clam fishing and trawling for prawns.

Having applied to Caledonian MacBrayne some time before, he was asked to work as relief man aboard the small roll-on roll-off CalMac ferry, which by this time was sailing directly to the new slip at Ardminish Bay from Tayinloan on the mainland. Having been asked to work for a couple of days a week, he was soon working full time, and spent five or six years on the ferry as full-time crewman. This was, so he says, the only job he had ever applied for in his whole life, although he had never been without work. When he was sixty-four he had a lung operation and has been 'retired' ever since, although he says that since his retirement, he has been busier than ever, with the advent of the community buyout.

15

Faith, Hope, Charity . . . and Harmony

For all that Gigha has received publicity, local and national, I am constantly surprised by just how few people even here in Scotland know exactly where it is and what went on there only a few years ago. A little while before the community buyout which sparked so much media interest, the population of Gigha had fallen to an all-time low, from a probable high in 1791. We have no way of knowing just how many people lived here in prehistoric times, but it was almost certainly fewer than the 614 of the 1791 census. The population at the time of the buyout had fallen to fewer than a hundred people, but perhaps more significantly, some eighty people had left during the preceding twenty years, which meant that the very viability of the island as a community was seriously under threat.

Anyone who has ever made it as far as St Kilda, as I myself did some years ago, courtesy of an army helicopter, when I was commissioned to write an article about the island for *The Scotsman*, will know just how sad it is when a once-thriving community becomes – effectively – a museum. The remote island of St Kilda and its deserted village is now a World Heritage Site, but lovely as the landscape is, and fascinating with regard to its flora and fauna, it still seems to me that without the human inhabitants who gave life and meaning to the place, it is as empty and poignant as any other long-abandoned home. It is essentially a fossil: interesting, informative and beautiful, but frozen in time. The military, stationed at the missile-tracking station, the National Trust and their willing 'conservation volunteers' who pay for the privilege of shoring up the sad walls of the old houses are a less than satisfactory substitute for the ordinary St Kildans who once called this place home.

At some points during the last thirty or forty years, it seemed as though Gigha too was heading for non-viability as a community. Our small islands are fragile places, and their human populations are as much under threat as any other endangered species. If such people were puffins, measures would have been put in place for their protection long ago. Nesting birds and bats are protected under pain of heavy penalties, but what of that other indigenous threatened species, the Hebridean islander? At the end of the twentieth century, the people of Gigha were leaving their island, trickling away, driven not just by the lack of housing and the lack of work, but – or so it seemed to me at the time – by their lack of autonomy. Psychological studies of workplace conditions have shown that lack of control over one's environment lies at the root of workplace stress. We are all circumscribed by rules and regulations. Many of our jobs are unsatisfactory. But most of us have the illusion, at least, of autonomy in our everyday life. The Gigha islanders, living and working under what was essentially a feudal system, did not.

Most mainland farms and even villages these days remain viable only because of their value-added businesses: bed and breakfast and self-catering establishments, cafes, farm and craft shops, cheese or ice cream making ventures and so on. Planning regulations must be obeyed, but within certain parameters a great deal is possible and there is always the right of appeal. But for many years, none of this was an option for the tenants of Gigha, since all such ventures had to be referred to the landowner of the time, who may or may not have approved. His word was final. There was no right of appeal and no democratic redress. And whatever landowners may claim about their good intentions, such a situation inevitably infantilises those who must live under its yoke. It is a situation that exists on many similarly 'owned' estates throughout the north and west of Scotland, although arguably, much of this land has little in common with the smaller communities where buyouts have at least been feasible. Those planning land reform in Scotland should be aware of risks as well as opportunities. Perhaps there too, Gigha has something to teach us.

The modern-day depopulation of Gigha could be compared with that which took place in the early to mid 1800s. This was nothing so savage as a clearance, nor was it wholly a drift towards the mainland and even further afield in search of financial security, although that too must have played its part. But then, as now, the main factors seem to have been a general disillusionment with the feudal way of life on the island, the way in which people were governed and circumscribed, coupled with the perception of greater freedoms to be had elsewhere.

In modern times, the problems for many young people began with their education, which all too often took them away from the island and – before a regular daily ferry brought them home again at night – started the process of alienation much too early. By the time they were in their teens they had already, mentally at any rate, abandoned the island. But there were those with the foresight to perceive that this gradual drift to the mainland was neither inevitable nor unstoppable. Times and work were changing and in this age of small businesses so many of which rely on new technologies to sustain them, there began to be no real reason why – with a certain amount of help, enthusiasm and a decent broadband connection – our smaller, remoter communities should not remain as viable as the conurbations of the central belt of Scotland.

At the time of the community buyout, in 2002, there were a number of media references to the cost to the taxpayer of the whole enterprise and it would be fair to say that there have been plenty of 'teething troubles' since, not least press reports of debt and discontent in 2014. But it has always seemed to me that communities such as Gigha, while relatively expensive in terms of provisions such as medical services and education, are also extremely cost effective in terms of what central government doesn't have to provide for them, namely, extensive policing, widespread road repairs and the countless other services that have to be addressed for more needy and less caring communities.

The islanders are taxpayers too, and have had precious little return for their contributions over the years. It is the contention of writers such as Andy Wightman, who researches land issues, that the state has abdicated its responsibilities towards people such as the Gigha islanders, leaving them with stark choices: submit to the vagaries of a new landowner, or go for the buyout option.[2] The loans and grants that helped the islanders to buy their own island included a great many back payments. In 2003, when the new Scottish Land Reform Bill was in the offing, the *Sunday Times* ran several articles lamenting the demise of the traditional rural estate and the threat to the investments of landowning 'A List' celebrities in the Scottish Highlands. The transition has been far from easy, but the doom-laden predictions of the right-wing media have, so far at any rate, fallen just a little short of the mark. Besides, we should perhaps face the fact that the alternatives were untenable.

Although the population was undeniably ageing (some 70 per cent were of pensionable age at the time of the buy-out), although people were draining away from the island in what must have seemed an unstoppable tide, it was clear that there were young people who wanted to stay on Gigha. There were also those who wished to move back, providing that they could be suitably housed, people with family connections on the island. And there was a third group of people who were keen to move to Gigha from the mainland, anxious for a different (although by no means easier) way of life. Even allowing for the supposed disadvantages of composite classes, many parents will understand the attraction of small rural schools for those with young families. Just as there are no paradise islands, there are no perfect schools, but parents can surely be forgiven the urge to slow down the gallop of their children towards premature adolescence in a reasonably stress-free environment.

Most of these would-be islanders must have felt that there was no way for them to make a living on Gigha, even if they were prepared to set up small enterprises, and certainly no decent homes to live in when they got there. During the years before the buyout, when we were visiting the island most frequently, a large number of the cottages and houses which might have been most suitable for families were already let out as self-catering holiday homes. These may have been reasonably productive for the estate, struggling to 'make the place pay' but did nothing whatsoever to add to the residential housing stock on the island. 'Business is business' said William Howden, who was managing the place for his father-in-law Derek Holt at the time.[3] Several of the island farms were empty, little if any new building was permitted and at the point where the island was last put up for sale, it seemed as though it was in danger of becoming yet another temporary hideaway for some new celebrity owner with only the faintest idea of the responsibility of, literally, owning the livelihoods of a hundred people.

Even the Horlick family, philanthropists as they undoubtedly were, would move their tenants about on a whim, or more paternally on the grounds of what they believed might be good for them. The days of the clan chief being responsible for the well-being of his extended family were long gone, if they had ever really existed. As we have seen in the preceding pages, there is a huge gap between the theory and its practical application in a hundred skirmishes over who owns what. But the situation is little better nowadays and those who can afford to buy such remote islands, or large chunks of the wilderness, are almost never truly philanthropic in their intentions – or even realistic in their perceptions – although those who depend upon them for their homes and livelihoods can find themselves on a carousel of hoping for 'better luck next time.' They are all too often absentee entrepreneurs making an investment, or foreign celebrities with a dream of bonnie Scotland that bears little relation to reality. They soon become disillusioned.

Looking at the history of Gigha, for so long held hostage to the fortunes and dispositions of successive owners, one is tempted to reiterate the old Scots saying that you can 'tell what the Good Lord thinks of money by the folk he gives it to.' With a few notable exceptions, Gigha has had its fair share of less than satisfactory landowners, from the days of the feuding McNeills and Allan nan Sop to more recent times. There can be few experiences more distressing than coming home to find an eviction notice chalked onto the door of your house because the landowner of the day has neglected to pay his debts.

The story of what was then the largest community buyout in British history came about because Derek Holt, of Holt Leisure, who had owned the island for eleven years, decided that the time had come for him to leave Gigha and put the place on the market in August 2001. The real beginning of the buyout, however, probably came much earlier than that, with the accession of a Scottish parliament in 1999, and a corresponding sea change in the political will. The status quo was no longer seen to be satisfactory. Small communities, which until this time had been the passive recipients of the goodwill or otherwise of successive landowners, suddenly began to perceive that they might – with a certain amount of outside help and expertise – take control of their own destinies. Other communities, notably the Isle of Eigg, were already succeeding. The political will to support such buyouts was there, not least because the idea of a land reform bill, one which would give crofters the right to compulsorily purchase the land upon which they lived and worked, was already in the offing, and would become law in 2003.

By the turn of the new millennium, with all its accompanying sense of new beginnings, the island had been under feudal control for some 600 years, so any change was always going to be of monumental – and monumentally challenging – proportions. The whole place, with the exception of a few council-owned homes and one or two private houses, was part of the 'estate' and was let out to tenants. When the island was advertised for sale for the last time, there were, apart from Achamore House, the hotel and six holiday cottages, thirty estate cottages, the post office, five let/partnership farms and two registered crofts. Some of these were 'retirement tenancies', many were 'short' (i.e. with security of tenure limited only to a period specified in the agreement), some were 'assured' and some few were 'protected'.[4]

This in turn gave the landowner a large amount of freedom as to how he organised these various tenancies, how much he spent on maintenance of housing stock and how much leeway each individual tenant had to develop his or her property. In any case, there was little incentive for tenants to improve their houses for themselves, since many of them could be (and sometimes were) moved around the island on the whim of the landowner. It was this state of affairs that – with the accession of the new Scottish parliament – began to seem less and less tolerable to modern sensibilities.

There was much debate in the community, and a great deal of support by local MSP George Lyon. Willie McSporran, an islander born and bred, charismatic, occasionally brusque but widely respected and authoritative, was vocal in supporting the community buyout. When the islanders first met to discuss the possibility, there were only fourteen people in favour, but that was soon to change. Willie saw it not just as an opportunity but perhaps also as a last chance, while the island was still viable in terms of population numbers. But interest, casual or otherwise, was being shown in the island by the usual celebrity dreamers and investors, so time was of the essence. There was a referendum and some dissenting voices, but the upshot was that the islanders agreed to launch a bid to buy the island for themselves, and a steering committee of seven trusted members of the community was set up with Willie McSporran as chairman. This was the foundation of the Isle of Gigha Heritage Trust.

In 2002, Derek Holt sold the island to his tenants, in spite, so it was reported in the press, of a higher bid from some unknown source, for just over £4 million. The Scottish Land Fund (formed with £10 million from the New Opportunities Fund, part of the National Lottery) had offered the Trust £3.525 million, which with a grant of £500,000 from Highlands and Island Enterprise, was enough to allow the community buyout to go ahead, on condition that £1 million of the money from the Scottish Land Fund would be treated as a loan and would be paid back by March 2004, in just two years' time. The Trust was confident that the sale of Achamore House (although not the gardens, which were reserved to the Trust) as well as some other small pieces of land, would account for a large percentage of the sum, but it still left some £200,000, which would have to be raised by a hundred islanders. It must have seemed a tall order, but there is a diaspora of those for whom Gigha was once home, as well as all those people who have visited and fallen in love with the place over the years.

On 15 March 2002, in a ceremony that was televised all over Britain to the accompaniment of media emotions that ranged from unbounded joy, through caution to downright criticism, the island was handed over to the Trust. Stone and earth of the land of Gigha, the traditional symbols of a change of ownership, were given to Willie McSporran, representing the people of the island. The 'New Dawn' had come for Gigha. A nominated director from Highlands and Islands Enterprise joined the seven directors of the Trust. One of their first tasks, quite apart from the momentous undertaking of repaying the debt, was to ensure a smooth transition for the hotel and its accompanying holiday cottages, which were booked up well in advance. Improvements would have to be made, but initially at any rate, it must have been a case of making assessments and making sure that nothing went too disastrously wrong in the transitional period. Those who expected a sudden and complete change overnight would be doomed to disappointment. Nothing so momentous is ever quite so easy. Once the islanders had bought their island, a powerful will to make things work was born, but all the same there were destined to be challenges along the way. It was never going to be easy.

At the time, there was, as Dr James Hunter of Highlands and Islands Enterprise termed it, the sense of Gigha as 'a kind of microcosm for Scotland as a whole'. Once again, God's island seemed to be showing the rest of the nation just what might be possible. Kenny Farquharson called the buyout 'a fable for our times', but added a prophetic caveat about Scottish insecurities and the difference between aspiration and reality.[5] As it turned out, his warnings about the possible difficulty of finding a buyer for the big house proved to be unfounded, and the house was sold within a reasonable time. That, combined with a superhuman effort of fundraising, and perhaps also with the help of a large diaspora of McNeills, McAlisters, McSporrans, Allans, Martins, Grahams and Galbraiths, to name but a few of the many families long associated with the island, meant that the islanders managed to repay the £1 million within the requisite two years. There were ceilidhs and music festivals, all kinds of sponsored events and auctions. Everyone participated

One of the knock-on effects of this relative success is that the project that helped the islanders to buy back their own island has been extended and enlarged. In November 2005 *The Scotsman* was reporting that the scheme was already changing the pattern of land ownership throughout Scotland. Jim Hunter, former chairman of Highlands and Islands Enterprise, and a supporter of the Gigha islanders in their bid for a measure of freedom said, 'Community ownership has been a roaring success.' At this point we might ask ourselves if he was right. There have certainly been many challenges and Gigha is not out of the woods yet. Perhaps it would be more accurate, with all the benefit of a few more years of hindsight, to call it a 'qualified success' but infinitely better than the alternative. Immediately following the buyout, the islanders were involved in many projects aimed at attracting visitors, from establishing a proper network of pathways, to setting up a website and, more recently, an attractive Facebook page. The pathway booklet was an inspirational little venture undertaken by the minister at that time, Rosemary Legge, with her husband Bill, John Martin, the estate joiner, who complemented the walks with some nicely designed gates and stiles, the late Vie Tulloch, who walked the island for years, and her daughter Catriona Scott, as well as Christine Mineham, Rab Didham, Simon Munro and Lorna Andrew.[6]

The most important initiative of all, however, and the single issue which probably swayed most of those who had voted in favour of the community buyout, concerned the extremely poor, and deteriorating, state of housing on the island. Little had been done over the years since Horlick to maintain the housing stock and almost no new building had been permitted. A survey of island properties in 2003 found that three-quarters of housing stock were 'below tolerable' while most of the remaining quarter were 'in serious disrepair' – a very moot distinction! The bill to upgrade the housing stock and infrastructure to acceptable levels was estimated at a further £2.9 million.

Previous lairds may have managed to make the island profitable, as an estate, but such solvency had come at a price for those who called the place home, never mind those who might wish to live and work there. On the other hand, there was a sense that in the rush to build new houses, and accommodate necessary small businesses, care must be taken not to destroy the very qualities that brought so many visitors to Gigha, and it was acknowledged that tourism will always remain a major factor in the life of the island.

Central to this problem is the premium which outsiders are prepared to pay for properties on Gigha, and the struggle which the Trust had, and will continue to have, to establish some kind of equilibrium between the desire of people to own their own houses (which can then, of course, be sold on as second homes), the need to provide accommodation for visitors, and the need to build and retain affordable properties, domestic and commercial, for people who wish to live and work on the island, as well as the need to encourage people to build for themselves.

If the Trust is too prescriptive, it seems little better than all those generations of feudal landlords. Too easygoing and the island could become, like parts of Devon, Cornwall and the Lake District, a holiday hideaway for a whole host of absentees, with expensive houses which lie empty for most of the year. It seems to call for an unenviable balancing act, needing wisdom and goodwill on all sides.

It was quickly recognised that people would not move to the island unless they had somewhere to live. A significant number of Housing Association homes have been built by Fyne Homes in the village of Ardminish, not far from the hotel. The houses are simple and traditional enough in style to blend in with older island houses, but with all the benefits of contemporary construction. Their superb insulation and the use of solar panels on this sunny island means that they are some of the warmest and most energy-efficient houses on the island, if not the entire peninsula.

Small business units have been built, and an art gallery and craft business has been established. Various new enterprises are up and running and some older businesses, such as the island shop and the Boathouse restaurant seem to have been given a new lease of life. Gigha Halibut, producing award-winning, sustainable and delicious halibut, is an example of the kind of small industry that can thrive here, given the required will and energy. I myself saw what a roaring success Gigha Halibut was at the BBC's Good Food Show in Glasgow in 2014.

In tandem with this, and perhaps most vital for the future of the community, most of the Trust properties have been refurbished and many islanders, old and new, have built or are in the process of building houses for themselves.

Younger settlers who bring practical skills (and children) are being encouraged to come to the island, not just those who might want to retire there. The school roll still fluctuates but this is normal for a rural area and there are babies on the island and infants attending pre-school.

A member of the board told me some time ago that a

number of applications had come in to build houses in the wild and wonderful north of the island, but if all of them had gone ahead it would no longer be so wild and wonderful. On the other hand, as we have seen in preceding chapters, the north was once quite a populous place, so there would, in future years, be a case to be made for a certain amount of controlled development there. But for the moment, the plan is to keep the north as unspoiled as possible.

The various self-catering cottages have been renovated to a high standard, more have been converted from disused farm buildings, and excellent private bed-and-breakfast accommodation is available. The island shop seems to be thriving under new management. The hotel continues to attract visitors; refurbishment is imminent and plans are already well under way to attract more business. The island has a website and a good presence on social media.

But it is the wind turbines that seem to be one of the biggest symbols of the changes that have taken place, and so are their names – Faith, Hope, Charity and Harmony. There have been one or two disapproving comments, usually from outsiders, about the Gigha turbines, but this is a small wind farm, built with community support.

In sharp contrast to so many of the massive new wind farms planned for mainland Scotland, the Gigha wind farm is, much like the buyout itself, a model of the way these things might be managed. This was Scotland's first community-owned wind farm. It is making excellent use of a natural local resource with the democratic agreement of the community, it is financially viable, nobody else is getting rich on the back of it and it seems to be a model project which could usefully be replicated throughout the rest of Scotland.

An article in *The Scotsman*, in 2003, described Gigha as a 'work in progress' and cheerfully analysed the island as if it were a company that had undergone a management buyout with the help of a number of investors, and which was now looking to renew and diversify its business interests. Viewed in this unsentimental light, the community buyout of Gigha made complete sense.

A very great deal has been achieved over the past twelve or so years, but much more remains to be done. The whole venture has not been without a certain amount of trouble and strife. But then, realistically speaking, whoever expected otherwise? A wise commenter, in one of the many press articles about Gigha, positive and negative, remarked that for incomers to an island such as this, the experience ought perhaps to be viewed very much like joining a large, loving but occasionally quarrelsome family. People may be needed and welcomed but if they are wise, they will tread carefully and ask what they can do for the community rather than wondering what the community can do for them. This is an island that has survived for hundreds if not thousands of years on hard work and self-sufficiency. Anyone seeking to fit in will surely have to do the same.

Where next for the Gigha islanders? Well, lairds have come and gone, but the relationship between the people, the land and the sea endures here, even into modern times. With it comes a consciousness of history, and a sense of stewardship which survives to this day, a combination of wisdom and emotion that is part of the true magic of Gigha. A great venture still lies ahead for the islanders, those who live there now, and others still to come. But it is one in which we should all be interested. On their continued commitment to succeed rests our conviction of our own capacity for change and growth, our belief in the worth and value of small communities, and their survival, through good times and bad, no less than the large conurbations.

It seems to me that the windmills are in many ways symbolic of the whole history of Gigha, of the new dawn of the community buyout, and hopes for a bright future, come what may, alongside all the problems and challenges of the years since. When I visited the island in May 2006, I walked down to look at the windmills – only three of them at that time – and was presented with the striking image of a tractor, trailed by dozens of gulls, busy with the worms and grubs that were being turned up in its wake. Perched on the hill just behind it were the windmills, their white wings swooping over the island in a mirror image of the swooping gulls.

The history of this island is one of Gigha's own renewable energy, in all senses. Just when things might have seemed to be at their darkest, some sense of the worth of the place, some quality in the island itself, but no less in the islanders who live here, some sense of faith in the future, hope for better things, and charity to their neighbours, invariably brought out the best in people. Gigha's renewable energy is not just the wind that blows across the island from the west. It is also the spirit of the islanders themselves, islanders new and old, who down all the years have invested this place with a significance over and above its size.. Perhaps – like the fourth turbine – a little more harmony is needed. Surely, then, we should wish all love and luck to the Gigha islanders as they move forward with the required blend of caution, optimism and enthusiasm. The way forward may be tricky, as the Sound of Gigha may be rocky. But it's knowing where the rocks aren't that really matters. And the islanders are as well qualified as any to navigate these perilous waters.

16

Postscript: A Pilgrimage Rewarded

Ever since I first visited the Isle of Gigha, some twenty-one years ago, and as well as exploring the many other sites of interest offered by a place so rich in prehistoric remains, I had been hunting for the Great Well which lies in the north of the island, on the slopes of Cnoc Largie. It had played such an important part in the lives of the people of Gigha, and I knew that many islanders must have resorted to it over the years, not just as a 'catholicon for diseases' but also in an effort to work the kind of weather magic that would be invaluable for island dwellers. I was determined that I was going to find it before completing this history of the island, but I seemed to be stymied at every turn. The well is marked on the Ordnance Survey map, but the terrain of Cnoc Largie was difficult to negotiate, and besides, I had begun to wonder if anything at all recognisable might be left on the ground.

To make one more effort to find it, and to check how the Gigha Heritage Trust was progressing with all its new ventures, we arranged another trip to the island in May 2006. Enquiries to the ever-helpful Rona Allan who worked for the Heritage Trust at that time, elicited the information that John Martin, the estate joiner thought that he knew where the well was, although he said it was twenty years since he had been there, and the place would be very overgrown by now.

Nevertheless, he thought that if we were prepared to ferret about a bit we might just find it. 'There's so much *seileach* growing there,' he told me, 'that it might be difficult. But we'll see what we can do.'

John was in his sixties back then, a very pleasant, knowledgeable man, who has lived on the island for many years and who featured in 'Buying our Island', the BBC's film about Gigha, which sympathetically followed the progress of the first year or so after the community buyout. It was John Martin who, only a few years previously, had come home to find an eviction notice posted on his cottage, after one of the landowners went bankrupt. That, I think, had been something of a turning point for him. He tells the story simply and movingly, but it is obvious that the enormity of such a thing – the fact that it could happen, as a matter completely outside his control, in late twentieth-century Scotland – still shocks him beyond belief.

Now, here he was, a species of Gandalf, brandishing a long walking stick like a wizard's wand, and talking about the *seileach* making the going difficult. I saw what he meant, but still wasn't completely sure what these small dense trees were, although they cover the lower slopes of so many of the island hills with a tangle of branches. My excuse was that they were not yet in leaf, but they were still impenetrable and occasionally John would prune the odd branch away with a saw, which he had brought along for the purpose. I looked the word up later in my Gaelic dictionary and, of course, they are willows.

We had parked at East Tarbert Bay, where the island narrows to a small isthmus, where the Vikings once dragged their boats across, and walked back along the beach, south towards the lower slopes of Cnoc Largie, negotiating a fence and a semi-flooded field in the process.

'This is an interesting place,' said John, as we walked. 'You know it was quite near here that they found the Viking scales when they were storing their potatoes. There was an old burial ground around here as well. And of course there used to be a chapel in that field up there – you can see the remains of the stone cross still.'

We came at last to the precipitous drainage ditch that separates cultivated land from the rocky hillside. My family and I had encountered this on a previous visit during the summer months, but on that occasion the ditch had looked too deep to cross and the vegetation beyond had seemed utterly impenetrable. This time, however, in early May, it looked manageable and I was properly shod, and besides we had the long walking stick as well as the small saw, and John knew what he was doing. He led us unerringly to the one place where the ditch wasn't so dauntingly deep. We jumped over, and then climbed the tussocky slopes of Cnoc Largie with John casting about him, trying to remember the exact whereabouts of the holy well that had once been one of the wonders of the Kingdom of Dalriada. It felt a little like the search for the Well at the End of the World. Would we find it? Would there be a salmon of knowledge? And magical hazelnuts? Had I spent just too long reading folk tales of the ancient Celts?

The lower slopes of the hill were hard going, threaded with whins and willow scrub and brambles, just coming into leaf but still armed with a million thorns. The spaces between the taller undergrowth, though, were beautiful, scattered with celandines and bluebells and with more primroses and violets than I have ever seen in one place before, not just clumps of them, but large patches, drifts, hillocks. We were drowning in yellow and purple flowers.

'Look for stones and damp places,' said John, but the whole place was stony and damp, especially since the week before had seen heavy rains. It seemed an impossible search. We peered among dense willows and found plenty of stones and damp places, but nothing that looked like a spring. The flag irises, not yet in flower, marched here and there in vertical bright green spikes, like newly painted fence posts. Afterwards, I thought that, had I been alone up there, I could have searched until Christmas and still not found the place. I think we would have gone on looking, even if it had taken hours. But perhaps some magic came to our assistance. If so, I like to think that it was wrought by our combined determination. Quite suddenly I found myself glancing upwards, noticing a patch of hillside where the random willows seemed to be growing less randomly – in a circle, in fact. Even then, I probably wouldn't have seen it because it was so well camouflaged by time and vegetation.

'Look,' I said all the same. 'There's a big stone. And it looks wet.' John, who had noticed the place at exactly the same moment, was already fighting his way into the middle of the willows and I followed him. It was quiet in there, and peaceful, a sheltered space among the trees, the mossy stones and the flowers, with the late afternoon sunlight slanting down into it. It was a golden place, with an air of calm watchfulness about it. And I would have sworn that like so many sites on Gigha it felt numinous, a 'thin' place where the boundaries between this world and another seem somehow to be worn away. There was a boulder, a very big one, moss-covered, fringed by willows and lush grasses, with a cascade of muddy patches among the green. In the silence, we heard running water. John scrambled down into the space beneath the stone and began guddling about, first with his walking stick and then with his hands. I don't know which of us was more excited. 'It's fresh water,' he said. 'Fresh running water. And look. It has been capped at some time. There's the capstone.'

Sure enough, there was a flat stone, at the base of the boulder, which looked as though its placing was deliberate. And there was a trickle of water bubbling out from beneath it. Even as he cleared the accumulation of leaves and moss away, you could see a small pool forming miraculously under his hands. He scooped a handful up, and it was cold, clean and clear, so he drank some of it and so did I. We had found the ancient Well of the Winds, its water still fresh and sweet and with its capstone firmly in place, lest it should flood the whole world.

As we turned to leave, I thought I caught a glimpse of somebody dressed in white, a vague figure among the trees. But perhaps it was only a trick of the light. We realised that we had found the well at exactly 5 p.m. on 5 May. Neither of us had any idea what that might mean, but it felt significant. And I think we understood that if this had been a place sacred to some goddess for who knows how many years before even the Epidii came to Gigha, then we had just been given a little moment of revelation.

From the well, it seemed right to go in search of the associated Holy Stone, so we retraced our steps along the beach. If we had been lucky enough to rediscover *Tobar a Bheathaig*, the gods, or more likely the goddess, might smile on us enough to allow us to find the stone as well.

'You know, I've always wondered about *that* stone' said John Martin, in passing, gesturing at a long, smooth finger of rock which lay along the tideline, nothing like the rest of the stones or boulders hereabouts, but – once it was pointed out to you – exactly like a large central section of a standing stone. Gigha is full of such unexpected and serendipitous discoveries.

From Tarbert, we moved a little further south and, following the line of an old drystane dyke, began another difficult search, again casting about the overgrown slopes of Cnoc Largie for a long-forgotten sacred site. Moving higher up the hill, just to get our bearings, we emerged from the willows onto open moorland where heaps of boulders marked the site of three old burial cairns, an unexpected bonus. John explained how twenty years ago he had brought visitors, a married couple, to visit the Holy Stone and very soon after, the woman had fallen pregnant! Some time later, and when I was beginning to wonder if we were going to be disappointed in this second search, John called out from a little way in front. He was standing beside a flat slab of schist, like an altar, although – as when Anderson first claimed to rediscover it in the 1930s – half of it was hidden by the earth that had slipped down from the hill above. We had passed a few yards from it earlier on, but hadn't noticed the size of it from where we were standing. Suddenly, it seemed huge. Like Anderson, we too spotted the cup mark immediately but the other symbols carved into the stone are very hard to see, so worn and weathered has it become over time. But you can feel them very clearly if you run your fingers over the surface, particularly the incised linear cross in the centre.

As we walked back to the car, with that sense of elation that comes after a kind of pilgrimage, John Martin observed, 'It's not the same if you just drive to a place is it? You have to walk a bit. You have to make the effort to find things.' Afterwards, I thought about this remark and realised that, not only is he exactly right, but he was expressing the precise charm of this island. You have to find things, and leave them intact and undisturbed when you go away again. The beauties and mysteries of this place are subtle and some of them are pretty much hidden. But that is as it should be. You can't simply drive about in your car and expect to have these places presented to you all wrapped up in somebody else's interpretation.

New houses and new businesses will never – as some outsiders feared – 'spoil' the island. Instead, they will be the lifeblood of Gigha. With a little forethought, such developments, like the windmills, will only enhance the beauty of the place, which is again in the process of becoming a thriving community. But one of the challenges for future islanders will be to care for these magical remnants of previous civilisations, in which the place is so rich, without over-interpreting or commercialising them. If that ever happens, the island surely will lose some of its magic. But, given the common sense and sensitivity of the islanders, I believe that it never will happen. Instead, the interested visitor will be helped as far as possible, to make his or her own pilgrimage. The island sits there, like a beautiful and mysterious woman who reveals her secrets only slowly, and only to those who are prepared to make a modicum of effort on her behalf.

Meanwhile, it occurred to me when I got back to the cottage where I was staying, that we had left the well just a little revealed. The capstone was firmly in place, but still the waters were trickling. It had been a calm day, but as I lay in bed that night, I heard a sudden wind, which seemed to have sprung up out of nowhere, howling around the old building. And I must admit – before I fell fast asleep, exhausted with the day's discoveries – I did wonder . . .

Appendix 1

From *The Book of the Dean of Lismore*

believed to be a poem about Lachlan Galbraith of Leim

Who is now chief of the beggars
Since the famous man is dead?
Tears flow fast for the man
For beggary has lost its strength.
The orphan is in a piteous case.
Beggary's gone since Lachlan's death.
In every homestead this is sad
That beggary should want for knowledge.
If he be dead I've never heard
Of one that could compare with Lachlan
Since God created man at first;
It is a source of bitter grief
That without mother or a father
Poor beggary should be so weak.
Since that Bretin's son is dead,
Why should I not mourn his loss?
There is no man now on earth
Who can beg as he could do.
Since Lachlan the importunate's dead
Great's the grief that is in Erin.
Who will now beg a little purse?

Who will even beg a needle?
Who will beg a worthless coin?
Since that rough palmed Lachlan's dead.
Who will beg a pair of brogues
And then will beg a pair of buckles?
Who will beg a shoulder plaid?
Whose begging now will give us sport?
Who will beg soles for his shoes?
Who will beg a peacock's feather?
Who will beg an eye for his belt?
Who will mix in any mischief?
Who will beg an old felt hat?
Who will beg a book to read?
Who will beg an early meal?
Who is it wears arms with his dress?
Who will beg for boots and spurs?
Who is it will beg for bristles?
Who will beg for sids[1] and meal?
Who will beg a sheaf of rye?
Who will ask a sporran spoon?
Who will gather without shame
Since Lachlan the hero is dead?
Who will now afford us sport?
Who will beg for maidens' shifts?
Since old shoe'd Lachlan is dead.
Sad the fate that he should die.
Who will ask men for a rullion?[2]
Who will steal the servant's feather?
And who is it can't tell the truth?
Who likes to travel in a boat
And likes his old friends to visit?

Who will beg the hen with her eggs?
Who will beg a brood of chickens
And ask the hen's overplus
After a handful of money?
Who will beg a headless pin?
Who can read as he can do?
That Lachlan should leave no heir
Is that which mournful makes his death.
Who will beg for a hook and line?
Who will seek for open doors?
Who will beg for unboiled rennet?
Who will beg for anything?
Who won't give a penny to the poor
And yet even from the naked begs?
Who could oppress the very child
And is cruel to the infant?
Who would beg for wool and batter
That they may have it after Lachlan?
Who would beg a woman's collar?
Who is it likes a dirty heap?
Who would beg from young women?
From little dogs and weasels?
Who would take the fire from an infant?
Who would steal e'en the dead?
Who is sick when he is well?
Who on his gruel begs for butter?
More sad for me than this man's death
Is that he has left no heir
For fear that beggary should die
And none be found to keep it up,
Do not ye forget the man.

Men of the earth do ye
Each of you for himself make rhymes.
My malison on him that won't.
If Lachlan died on Monday last
Every man will joyful be,
Sad it is that for his death
None there is who will lament.

The author of this extraordinary piece is one Duncan MacCailein, known as the Good Knight of Glenurchy. The Dean of Lismore's book is a volume of ancient Gaelic poetry transcribed phonetically, as early as 1512 and now in the Advocates' Library, Edinburgh. This translation is by Thomas MacLauchlan and was published with an introduction by W.F. Skene, by Edmonston and Douglas, Edinburgh, 1862. The poem is an entertaining satire on a fellow poet whose miserly tendencies seem to have reached epic proportions. It is in the tradition of a 'flyting', i.e. a battle in verse, albeit a one-sided one, since the other protagonist is dead. It is interesting for the (sometimes bizarre) picture it paints of everyday life, as well as Lachlan himself, for its illustration of the connections between Ireland and Scotland and for the fact that the poet seems to be encouraging other poets to join in this haranguing of the dead Lachlan under pain of his 'malison' or curse.

Appendix 2

Eighteenth- and Nineteenth-century Population Returns for Gigha and Cara

Year	Population
1755	514
1764	461
1771	550
1791	614
1801	556
1811	550
1821	574
1831	534
1841	550
1851	547
1861	460
1871	390
1881	382
1891	401

Appendix 3

The Road to the Isles

(Written for the lads in France, during the Great War)

It's a far croonin' that is pullin' me away,
As take I wi' my cromach to the road,
It's the far Coolins that are puttin' love on me
As step I wi' the sunlight for my load.
Sure by Tummel an' Loch Rannoch an' Lochaber I will go
By heather tracks wi' heaven in their wiles,
If you're thinkin' in your inner heart braggart's in my step,
You've never smelt the tangle o' the Isles.
It's the far Coolins that are puttin' love on me
As step I wi' my cromach to the Isles.
It's by Shiel Water that the track is to the West,
By Aillort and by Morar to the sea,
It's the cool cresses I am thinkin' o' for spunk,
An' bracken for a wink on Mother's knee.
Sure by Tummel etc.
It's the blue islands that are pullin' me away
Their laughter puts the leap upon the lame,
It's the blue islands from the Skerries to the Lews
Wi' heather honey taste upon each name.
Sure by Tummel etc.

From *The Road to the Isles* (1927) by Kenneth MacLeod, Minister of Gigha and Cara from 1923 to 1948

Appendix 4

Selected transcriptions from a series of conversations during April and July 2003 between the author and Willie McSporran, MBE

WM: I was born in New Quay houses . . . and then we moved up to Brae House and my brother James was born there, and not long after that we moved back to New Quay. The school was where it is, but we were . . . then we were back in New Quays so we had to walk from New Quays to the school. Right down by the pier almost, by the main pier at the South End. Which would be near enough a couple of mile walk, on an afternoon, through rain or snow, and the worst year I can remember coming up was the heavy snow of '47. Short trousers. The snow was sticking to you and we were freezing so we turned back. A couple of days and the road cleared.

Our father died when we were very young. I was only six year old and Seamus five or thereabout. So my mother was a widow and she had a son prior to that which made no difference, he was always known as our brother and the three of us are still living. One next door to me and the other in Ardrishaig. And he (Seamus) had the shop here for many years.

At that time you didn't need to go to secondary school, you stayed in the Gigha school from five to fifteen. When you were twelve year old, you sat what you called then a qualifying exam, unless you passed it, you could go away or you could stay on, which we chose to do and education came from Dunoon and it was in the form of assignments: Algebra, History . . . and it was posted off to Dunoon for marking. There were two classrooms working when I went at the start. I left in 1951. You had none of these computers and all.

CC: Did you speak Gaelic?

WM: Yes, from infancy. The whole island was Gaelic except for the few that were incomers, and in fact, some of them would have Gaelic parents. But they didn't use it in the homes so it wouldn't have come to the children. But at New Quay uncles and grand-uncles and mother and father, until he died, all had Gaelic, so it was a commonly used language. It was an everyday language. In fact I think now we're losing a bit of . . . but at one time you'd have to think in Gaelic and translate into English before you could speak it, which sounds daft to somebody that never had too much of it but that was the way it was.

But these are the changes as far as school days go, now you've got school cars and if there's a shower of rain, everybody's in a car, just to take their children to school, even a hundred yards. We had a lot of fun in walking, going for nuts and taking an hour an a half to do what we should have done in half an hour, smoking when you shouldn't have been smoking and things like that.

At that time, there were no tractors at all hardly and vehicles were a thing that was unknown, apart from that there was always one at the shop. An old Ford van it was, I remember it well. We used to run up and down the road in it. It was a great thrill to get a lift in the car, nowadays you get fed up looking at them, but these are the changes we have and instead of jumping on the back of a tractor as a boy it was a horse and cart . . . we lived quite happily.

CC: So there'd be a lot of horses on the island?

WM: Oh yes, lot of horses. There'd be at least . . . most places would have six working horses which would be three pair and then there would be young horses, one- and two-year-old foals . . . and that was how the system worked. I left school in 1951 but before that it would be, you were working back and forward on farms since thirteen and there were a lot more horses then, but by the time I left school officially, tractors had begun to come in. There was a tractor in Leim and a tractor in Tarbert but nobody thought a tractor was capable of doing what the horses could do, the result being that in Leim farm, for instance, there was still a pair of working horses and you had the tractor, and the tractor was mainly used for road work. You wouldn't use a tractor for too much on red land which tended to be soft and the horse was used there. In its heyday, prior to any tractor, there would be six working horses in Leim itself, so that was three pair: a pair ploughing, a pair carting and whatever. Normally what you had was a ploughman, a byreman and an orraman. So the ploughman would be mostly ploughing, which was the title of his job, while the orraman would be the man that was used for anything which would include carting and carting included at that time a hell of a lot of work. The horses were Clydesdales by then, very big. Not as big as a Shire, but heavy. Some of them could be big. There was a big mare in Leim, a big heavy beast.

You grew turnips, potatoes, oats, hay. And some other things. And then also there were roads to repair and the only thing that was available was a horse to do it. Achamore farm was a bigger farm and you would have at least that amount plus young horses, two-year-olds, one-year-olds and probably mares with foals and when the mare was in foal she wasn't working, and foals were normally born about June, the result being June, July, August, you were coming into hay time and harvest time.

So you'd maybe a pair of horse, at least, would be going on a reaper, another horse on a hayrake maybe, another horse on a tumblin tom. Horses were heavily relied on and so you went on through the island, and no matter where you went, there was a pair at least, even on the smaller farms and probably younger horses up and coming, but there was always horses and a lot of good horses were on the island and a lot of bad ones too! As I said, by the time I started there wasn't so many horses being used. It took a lot of hard work and determination to break a young horse but once you got that past, it was no problem.

To have a good horse was as worth as much as another human being. You were constantly speaking to it, not just to give it any order, you just spoke to it and in fact I knew some of the old horsemen when they started working with tractors, and they would want it to stop, and they would shout 'whoa!' and the bloody thing would carry on.

They weren't used to the situation, nobody was. People who had never worked much with engines had to come into this. The horses were wonderful to watch. You'd always three on a binder, a three-horse yoke and you had to pull it evenly, to turn it. Some were good, some were bad. The problem with a horse in summer time when got out to grass, it tended to get soft and stubborn, so when it came to harvest time or hay time, what was a good horse when you put it out in the spring of the year, you found it wouldn't put its weight to the collar and sometimes the cure was hard to watch, because you had to get the beast to move. Some of them even plugged their ears with cotton wool because it was the noise of the machinery that scared them at first. They could go daft with the noise but if they didn't hear, they went on alright. So these were the things that had to be tried, and the other thing was the clegs (I got the first one just there the other day) and you can imagine working with horses, they would get spooked with them, go daft with them.

The hayrake was seven or eight foot wide. You had to rake the whole field with this. It was no joke because the seats were hard and the heat was hellish and sweat and flies and all that but there was a lot of work and friendship attached to the work and people helped each other a lot more than they do now, and if you were finished first and there was somebody away behind, you were told you'd better take a horse and cart and give so-and-so a hand and that was what you did.

On the fields of hay and at harvest time, a refreshing drink was a handful of oatmeal in a can of water. That was what you got to drink. It was interesting work. Many a time you would be working till eight or nine o'clock at night. You would have three or four carts carting into the stack-yard. After all the harvest was in you'd to thatch the stack and then in the winter time you'd to put that into the barn, feed it through a thrashing mill. There was a hell of a lot of work compared to now. There's not the same labour and there's not the horses to do it now. You had to look after your horses. The horses needed the smithy. And that was another job that the youngest one got, going to the smithy with a pair of horses. It wasn't at all easy for the smith and by God he was hardy too. Many a bad smack the blacksmith got, but they were hardy old men. The whole secret is getting as close to the horse as you possibly can.

At that time, all the fertiliser, cattle cake and any other farming needs, all came by cargo boat or by puffer, which meant that instead of being delivered to the door, you had to go to the pier yourself, or as a farm labourer, with a horse and cart or, as it progressed, with the tractor.

At that time, the bags didn't weigh 25 kilos – they weighed 112 or 224 pounds. The same with grain, when it was stashed, it was put in bags and you had to carry it up thirteen steps of a ladder and put it in the granary. From there it was fed down to the bruisers to make feed for the cattle. Also, first thing in morning, when you went to work, areas where the cattle lay had to be put out with a graip, by hand. When I went there first, you mucked the byres, eight big heaped barrow-loads of the best of cow manure, you had probably some pigs to muck out and the old horse as well, that was before you started your day's work in the fields.

The seasons of the year. You start off at the back end of year, you start ploughing, there's hardly such a thing done now. You ploughed the lea in the back end of the year so that it had all winter and the frost to break the ground, then stubble land was ploughed and the red land. The stubble land was where corn was grown the previous year. The red land, as we knew it, was where the green crop was, turnips, kale, maybe a bit of vegetables for the house, and two or three acres of potatoes. You tried to plough the red land just a couple of days before you sowed it so that the weeds didn't have time to come up and it kept the ground much cleaner. You sowed a mother crop, which was oats, and then you sowed it out with grass seed and clover, which then, two years later, was the hayfield.

So that was the sowing past and before that you had lambing, but the calving was mostly in the summer time, because they didn't produce so much milk in the winter time. So it was more economical to have grass milk while the cows were out grazing. So you progressed on to the autumn, harvest time – when the benefit of all your spring labours came to being. The first thing you had to do in June was thin the turnips you'd sowed in spring. At hay time you cut the hay and stacked it, I could do it yet. Then you had the harvest, cutting the corn, stooking it. Before you ploughed the stubble, you'd the midden of dung to empty. You took your barrows out to the byre, it was loaded by hand into a trailer or cart and then put it out to the coops. That had all to be spread by hand, and it was all labour intensive and heavy work.

And then you came to the harvest of potatoes, which was dug with what you called a digger, it was just a shovel that went below the drill that the potatoes were planted in, and a spinner went round at the rear of that, that scattered the potatoes, shook it up, shook the earth off and hopefully with a bit of digging with your feet and hands you got the main bulk of potatoes out.

There weren't so many potatoes grown when I started, but ancestors at Achamore exported tatties to Ireland, and the big sailing ships would come up from Ireland and the captain was the man in charge. Aboard the vessels to keep them in ballast, coming up, was what they called hot lime.

It came ashore down there by the pier. Next to Gigalum cottages, up from the shore a bit, is what they called the lime kiln. The lime kiln was used to burn lime before it was spread on the fields as a fertiliser. How the kiln worked was, you put a layer of hawthorn or some tree branches at the base of it, then spread a thin coating of lime or limestone, then another layer of branches, then another layer of lime and so on, till the kiln was full. There's three domed shapes on the exterior of that building and if you look closely enough you'll see that they are open to the inside of the kiln, which was to facilitate the burning. You could go in there, put your hand in with a match or whatever and light it up and it burnt the stone, which then turned to powder, and you could take it out and spread it on the fields as a form of fertiliser.

The skipper of the ship, he went up and looked at the potatoes and offered the farmer. If they both agreed, the captain paid for the lot of potatoes on the spot. And because of the quality of them, some were put on top of bags of loads of Irish potatoes to make the quality of their own potatoes look better. That is a bit of history that was well-remembered, in my young day.

CC: What about you? Where did you start work?

WM: The day I was fifteen. I'd been playing around in this farm for a few years before it. But when I left school I was asked if I wanted a job, which I did take because the job was what I needed to have, because you had not as much aid and anything else, and my mother needed money and everybody needed money. So the day I left school in June of '51, I ran down the road and within a quarter of an hour I was working for the handsome sum of 30 shillings a week which in today's money is £1.50. That was from a quarter to seven in the morning to six o'clock at night and by that I mean that . . . it wasn't you . . . left the house at a quarter to seven, no, you started work at a quarter to seven and you stopped work at six. And certainly with the food then it was a good place. So that was the first job had a tractor . . . a grey Ferguson by then, so I started young enough to be able to start working on them but they weren't used for anything. There was still a fair work on horses.

So that started it. By then you had the binders but you had still to stook the corn. If it was wet weather you'd maybe to change the stooks, turn them around, and change them about and then when it came to the time . . . into the stack. Pull them out, open them out, get them dried, and if it rained you had to re-stook them again. There was an awful lot of work in it but mechanisation took a lot of it out of it. And then . . . hay time it was cut with what was known as a reaper or a mower. But if there was no hay turner in the barn you were in, you had to turn it by fork and a rake. It was all manual. When all that was completed it was left there to mature. Then you'd to fork it onto a cart and fork it off the cart onto a stack which was built. The stack was then thatched. It was all a . . . a different kettle of fish to what it is today.

And of course at that time all the farms were as working farms. There were thirteen. If we go through them, as you would start at the south end, you would have Leim Farm which would have the farmer and his wife, two men working and probably a maid at least. You had South Drumachro farm which was a family farm even then, the Allans had it as far back as I can remember and they had a fair family. But they would have worked it themselves. There was two sons at home, a daughter, man and wife and they would have been able to work it themselves, but it wasn't just the man and wife as the boss, they all had to work. Achamore Farm, it was a bachelor farm, Seumas McSporran, I don't think a relation of mine, or if he was, very far out. He would have at least three men and two maids and himself all year round and there was a lot of work on that, because it was the biggest farm on the island.

Ardlamey Farm, I wasn't very well acquainted with it, but I went to work on it in the1960s, I think it was, and there were five men working on it and the farmer himself and he had a maid in but he was almost a bachelor – his wife and the family didn't live with him. When I went, there were five men working there and by the time I finished working, it was three. But that's Ardlamey, and you come across to North Drumachro Farm, which was one of the smaller farms. I remember a bachelor farmer, old John Macdonald, and he had a man working for him all the time, but he shared his land with his brother, who was on Leim Farm and the two of them worked hand in hand and it was sort of a shared working business.

So then you come up to the South Ardminish Farm which was then South Ardminish Farm and Hotel. The hotel and the farm were combined and it was run by a family, the McPhersons, but they employed two men. Besides they had quite a big family themselves, they had two or three women worked on there and a man, but that was run on the hotel which was only small. I can't remember, they had two or three bedrooms. The bar was there and the farm and it was an immaculately-run farm, it was a showpiece of a farm, the stacks were beautiful as you see in the photographs I showed you, the roadside down the fields were all trimmed and sheared with a scythe, so hence the reason they had the men, to do the work. It was tidy, you wouldn't see roots and gorse growing where it shouldn't be and that takes you up as far as North Ardminish.

That had a hill farmer and his wife, Neil McKinnon, and he always had a man and it was a well-run place too and it was all horse work in these days. That was prior to the tractor coming and Neil didn't change any, even if he was there, but I don't think he was, when tractors came. Achamhinish Farm at that time was owned by the Wilkiesons or at least rented, they were all rented farms, as they still are. Achamhinish was rented by the Wilkiesons that had the shop and he had a nephew in it, as a working manager. He bred show mares, show Clydesdales. He was known throughout the horse fraternity for that. Then his nephew Archie took it over himself and he employed a man. Drumyeonbeg was owned by a brother of Archie that owned, well, rented, you should never say owned because there was no such thing, he had the farm of Drumyeonbeg rented, and he and his wife that was a nurse at the time, she was the district nurse, or whatever they were called then, she used to go about on a bicycle and if you were ill you had to go to her. But they employed a man and a maid.

Drumyeonmore, you'd the same there, it was old John Andrew and his wife, and they employed at least one, if not sometimes two and themselves and I'm talking about themselves as if they were . . . but they were working, they were all working farmers, there was no, none of those soft hearts sit back. Highfield it was the McVeans that were in it, as far back as I can remember. Old Angus is still in life, and they're all in life, the three of them, the two brothers and a sister, the sister lives in the village here, a brother in Sandbank and Angus beside the post office up there and Angus, and he also, his father, not that I can remember it, he did the ferry up the North End, but we'll come to it later on. So that covers Highfield. And you go up, the next one, and you get Tarbert Farm. Now Tarbert farm. I can maybe just remember when the Gillies had it, but then there was Archie Bannatyne and his wife, and they took it over from his wife's mother. I think it would be the mother because the father had died prior to that, he would employ two men, and at least the daughters themselves all worked, but Kinererach and Tarbert were together, and Archie ran the lot. But Kinererach farm there was also a man John Covetes, and he bred at the time Shetland ponies for the pits, but they were known as pit ponies, and it was a great day for us the day that the stallion came, for you went down to the . . . that came into the pier from Glasgow and everyone was on his back . . . before he got to Kinererach to do his duty!

They were hard times, very hard times . . . you must remember that there was no creamery, as such, on Gigha back then. The creamery, the way it was then was each and every one made their own milk into cheese, and made their own butter. If they were successful . . .

CC: Was it mixed farming?

WM: A lot of mixed farming. There wouldn't be many pure Ayrshires at that time. They'd be running shorthorn crosses, I suppose the best description would be more or less liquorice allsorts. As one farmer said once upon a time about potatoes, when asked what kind had he got, he said they were liquorice allsorts. The other farmer said 'I've never heard of them,' he said, 'but were they good?'

My own forebears came to farm at Achamore farm and there was a big family of them. And my grandfather, who I'm called after, one of the sons of I think, Donald was my great grandfather, William, he went away to sea, and was working on some sort of cargo boats and was travelling up as far as the Shetlands. Anyway, he married one of the Grahams of Gigha and they settled in Keil cottages. And he finished up being the estate mason, so maybe it's there I get the few skills I have to throw some stones, or had because I can't throw stones any more, but that's how the island becomes connected to each other, the McSporran married a Graham, that was the grandfather married a Graham. Then my father married a Graham, so you've got the connection with everybody on the island if you look closely. Hard times and happy times.

Old Archie Bannatyne, he farmed in Tarbert. And there was another man Angus McNeill. One morning, Angus arrived at Tarbert looking very very down.

Mrs Bannatyne says 'What's wrong?' and he says 'I'm not feeling too good', so she suggested maybe a hair of the dog that bit him would do him some good, and gave him a half of whisky. While Angus was drinking his whisky, she turns to him and says, 'I don't know what beggar was in here last night and ate all the beetroot I had in jars!'

'Ah to hell,' he says,' I feel better now, I was worried this morning, when I went to the toilet, I thought I was bleeding!'

The man that Angus had working for him was the same age as myself, and he used to travel to and from on a motorbike and Angus had some message to be delivered to his family, at

Keil so Angus said to him would he take this message, and he said yes.

'Will I put it on a piece of paper or will you take it by word of mouth?'

'Oh,' he says, 'You'd better put it on paper, because my mouth won't hold it!'

CC: What about when Horlicks bought the island?

WM: I think what helped the farming here was when Horlicks bought the island. There were the Hamers and then the de Chairs ran it for a couple of years after that, and they sold it and it was Horlicks that bought it. So Horlicks of course ran on to complete what Scarlett had started, as far as the gardens were concerned, but it was Scarlett that I suppose put the first spade into what is now the well known Achamore gardens, but it was Horlicks that had such a love for the island, a love for plants and a love for the people.

He had the money, but it didn't bother him if it didn't make a profit, so long as it sort of washed its face he was happy, and he was happy among the plants and he employed about, I think there must have been about fourteen gardeners worked there at the start of it, and what you've got to remember is there was no chain saws then, there was no tractor, no heavy machinery to lift things. There was what we called a monkey wrench to pull out the roots so as he went on, he pulled out roots and set up a shelter belt . . . then planted inside that what are now hedges and the one thing came from that and then he grew his plants in that. But I think the biggest thing that developed the gardens also was there was a lot of gales, heavy storms, when he came and of course the woodland there was fairly old and it was tearing down, and as it was taken down, it was ploughed by horse and so it could be developed into the gardens.

CC: No wonder you needed so many gardeners!

WM: That's right, because there were no motorised mowers, it was all push mowers or an old horse-drawn mower and when the horse was going along she had big boots that were put on it so the shoes wouldn't mark the lawn. Leather boots from Kintyre, to spread the load!

CC: Was the house like it is now?

WM: Well I don't remember too much, I remember being at a sale before the Horlicks took over. The only thing I can remember about that was the billiard table was there and it was set up and there was an old chap taking aim at a cue ball in the centre, and us young 'uns running past and scatching the balls to hell and him chasing us through the corridor with the cue. My mother bought two or three bits of trinkets and she was holding up sheets and she says, 'There's holes in the sheets,' and, 'Aye missus,' he says, 'there's ones in yourself too and you'd be pretty poor wi'oot them.'

Anyway, Horlicks did a big pick of renovation on the house. What we've got to remember was there was no electricity on the island at that time. No water mains as we've got now, so he put in big Lister generators to give himself electricity. He renovated the house, and they were working there for a long time, men between it and Ardailly. But that's when the big transformation came to Gigha, as regards Horlicks starting gardens and then he formed a company with the farmers, to produce the cheese, a cheese factory, but prior to that certain farms made their own cheese and others didn't. But the cheese was very well known.

The farms on the South End: Leim, Ardlamey, Achamore and South Drumachro, drove their own milk to the creamery in churns and cans, I suppose eight gallon cans it would be at the time. With a horse and cart, you put the cans on the cart. The milk from the other farms was taken by an old chap that was in the smithy, and I call him old but he wouldn't be as old as myself now, and he had a couple of carts at the start and then he got what was known as a four-wheeled horse-lorry that was able to carry more, and that was how the milk was taken to the creamery

Achamore farm was where the creamery was. The cheese was made in the creamery and it went from there to McLellands in Glasgow and how it got there was it was taken by horse and cart to the pier, and at that time the pier was wooden and they put straw on the pier first thing in the morning and laid the cheese on top of that and they covered it with a tarpaulin and the old ferry came in, loaded the cheese, with all the other stuff that was shipped. None of this roll on, roll off . . . it was all shipped.

When a house was being built, it was puffers, they were known as lighters latterly, but they're still puffers to me, and they came in with gravel, slate, sand, cement, tiles, fuels of all sorts, chips for the roads. Coal was another thing – the hold in the puffer would be deep, so you had to dig from the top of that, down to the ceiling which strangely enough, was at the bottom of the boat. If she hit the pier with too much of a bang when you had reached the bottom, the whole lot fell down and you had to start digging again, for about a shilling a ton, and that was how cargo was handled. But things have changed a lot since then. I think we were happier then, though we had less money.

CC: Where did the ferry and the puffers come in?

WM: The ferry and the puffers, it was the first pier that we had, at the south pier was a wooden pier and going down the gangway there were two steel rails about nine to ten inches wide, with a slight lip on the inside edge and in between those rails, there were pieces of wood laid, about an inch thick by nine inches wide, the reason for that was the rails took the cartwheels, which were all steel tread. The first pier was built by the estate, which I can't remember, but that's who owned the pier even when I was young. Eventually the council took over the pier, and of course, like everything else, it wore out, maybe 1951 or thereabouts. In 1952 they started bringing in materials to build the concrete pier, all that was brought in on puffers and we carted the stuff with three tractors, everything was made here.

So anyway, we're coming on now to once the creamery came, the next thing that was required was the farms needed a bit of renovation, for the capability of increased milk production. When I left school everywhere had a milking machine, but I can remember when I was a good bit younger everyone had not got a milking machine, there were people went to milk the cows morning and night by hand, and my mother was one of these went to Leim farm. The reason I'm involving myself is that I can remember these things. My mother would go away about four o'clock in the morning from New Quay, to Leim farm. It was her cousin who had the farm, they were getting paid for this, although it was only a few pennies, but what each person had to milk was eight cows by hand. Now I can tell you, it was no easy feat, it was maybe alright if you were used to it, but you had muscles where you didn't know muscles existed . . .

Then of course, the farmers put in milking machines but the byres at the time were not up to what the standard should be. Byres had to be widened so this Horlicks did on most of the farms, albeit that they weren't all done at the one time. You didn't have bulk tanks, it was eight-gallon tanks. At that time there was no electricity, it was all engine-driven pumps. You'd an engine for every job on the farm, if you were lucky. So that was how your farms were altered and brought up to scratch.

But the creamery eventually came to having a problem. By then we had advanced to the roll-on roll-off ferry. And it was decided to close the creamery for a time and sort out the problem that seemed to be, there seemed to be cracks in the floor, cracks in the walls that were full of bugs.

I was working on the estate at that time, as a handyman. The milk started going to Campbeltown and it was far too easy to travel the tanker back and forward on the boat, the result being that the creamery was no longer needed, and it closed. And that is how these things happen. And sometimes progress is not the best in the end. It seems to be at the time that it is a lot easier, a lot more convenient, but the knock-on effect is not good for the island.

CC: What about fishing?

WM: Well, the fishing again when I was a young boy, not a youth, but a boy; the Grahams that were in my family tree, my history, the Grahams at New Quay were fishermen and they used to go out the banks, my uncle that had launched the netter and she hadn't a lot of freeboard but they would be travelling out about three miles, down to the cod banks to shoot their lines and they found the boat was a bit wet on a stormy day, so they put an extra six-inch plank on there. But that was fine, until the French trawlers came along and they were ripping away the lines, and of course it wasn't viable. They stopped that and of course they went to the lobster fishing. Prior to that, the Gigha cod was caught, salted and when they went away to God knows where and sold to Jura, Islay, that was long lines.

But there was no trawlers as such then, cod-fishing was lines. The McNeills of course were fishermen of Gigha and then a lot of them went away to the herring fishing, away as far as Skye, with fairly big what was known as the Loch Fyne skiff, that type of boat, and mostly sail, and of course when the engines started nobody had that kind of experience, for instance when they started creel fishing they stopped the engine and somebody rowed the boat, and the other one picked up the pots like that and set the engine in motion, and a lot of them didn't have a reverse gear and it was a case of you'd hear the old boys, chugging along to the pier and somebody was down at the engine on his knees and all you would hear was 'Stop her!' and the engine would suddenly stop and he would spring up and grab what it took to stop the boat.

And then of course they started potting and going away up to Eilean Mor on the west coast, bigger boats with sort of forecastles on, and coal fires, and God knows what. I remember as boys going down and eating half their stores before they would leave, God knows how they survived, but most of them at that time had a gun aboard and they were shooting cormorants and rabbits. The McNeills were a big family and they all had a boat. The Gigha McNeills.

And then there was cousins of theirs, James and John and Dougie and Donnie. Most of these boats had just two in them, they just went away, it would be like a convoy, the big skiff would be towing a wee skiff and the wee skiff would be towing a punt. So the three were in line and off to work.

CC: What about seabirds' eggs?

WM: Seabirds', gulls' eggs, we used to eat dozens of them. Plenty of them, Gigalum is loaded with gulls' eggs, Cara is loaded with them, Garbh Eilean up in the north west corner, it's loaded with gulls' eggs. (*Author's note: there is an interesting correspondence between Willie's 'Garbh Eilean' and Blaeu's 'Garuellen'.*)

CC: What are they like?

WM: Beautiful, better than any caviare. Fry them, boil them, make pancakes with them, lovely big pancakes – you never saw a better coloured pancake in your life. Also vividly red, the tern's eggs are very very red, but it's now against the law to eat them; everything's against the law now.

I spoke there about the thirteen farms, but now we are down to three, with the hope of putting a fourth one back on the map, but this happens all over, it's not only on Gigha it happens. I said there were a lot of small farms here, well, two of them started going into one, three into one, now there's two and three and maybe four into one to make it viable, but the only unfortunate thing about that is it's only one family is getting the work out of it. There's so much machinery now that machines have taken over from man, so you don't need the labour. A tractor could plough in a day what the horses would take three days. You've got the minus side of it always: with the population, there's not so much work. I never looked for work in my life.

CC: What about entertainment?

WM: The village hall only came to being about '48, '50. Prior to that there was a place called the Iron House. It was a house on a farm where the dances were held and it's now flat. I think there are people going to build a house in the same area. Before the hall was completed, it was in the school; there was a couple of fiddlers on the island, old Donald Macdonald and Angus McVean who's still in life, and now makes fiddles himself or has done in the past, and very successfully too.

There was always the odd person with a melodeon or an accordion at the time, but then, when the hall was built, it was a place where people could meet in the evenings for draughts, they started badminton, there was various things like that went on. Concerts went on. There were people pretty good at acting, as there still are, myself included. You had to make your own entertainment; there were no televisions, next to no radios. Two or three people had a radio, where we lived at New Quay, there was a couple of radios. My uncle had one and you went in there and listened to the news and you were told to give it a slap and switch it off. My grandmother bought a wireless for us and it was the Ever Ready with one dry battery, and it was a great thing because as you'll recollect I said, prior to that, there was no electricity. So you had to send the accumulators, as they were called, to Tarbert, to a man called McKay, to have them recharged. On a Saturday night there was a programme on the radio, the McFlannels, an old Glasgow family, some people maybe still remember them. And that was about it.

Christmas trees when I was young were a rarity. At school you'd a wee party. Mrs Wilkieson The Shop, as we called her, would maybe give you a wee bar of chocolate, an orange or an apple. The teacher's uncle who was Donald Macdonald, as I mentioned with the fiddle, would come up, you would do 'Strip the Willow', have a jump around the school and that was your Christmas. You went home and maybe got a bit of coal and a sixpence in your sock or stocking. That's the way that has changed considerably, and now we've got a very good hall with all the modern things in it. The reason the hall was built where it was, outside the village, was that the older generation thought it would be too noisy, and I'm glad it was built there, because now that I live in the village myself, I would be one of the old ones grumbling about it!

The hall now belongs to the island, not the Trust. The hall is a separate thing from the Trust. We've all got to work together to make it function no matter what it is. The Highlands and Island Film Guild, we used to get a film in once a fortnight, the late Neil Bannatyne ran the films at a loss to himself, many a time. We'd a petrol-driven generator which then drove the big projector, and that was another part of the entertainment. That was when we started getting motorbikes instead of push-bikes and half-killing each other going up and down the road at thirty mile an hour instead of five.

Before electricity it was paraffin lamps a lot of the farms used. You'd a lantern and you had to take it with you from place to place, and God only knows how there was no fires, because you had to take it with you through barns and byres, through stables full of straw. But latterly some of them were putting in generators themselves. Macdonald of Achamore, Macdonald of Leim for his time was somebody that wanted to see things moving – he got a car for himself, a wee Morris A8 – he then bought a lorry, a Morris Commercial, one and a half ton which we then thought was huge. Nowadays it would sit in the back of one and you'd never notice it.

He put in a sort of generator system at Leim, for light only, and he had the same system in Achamore, he got a generator, and was able to put the electricity through the farmstead which was a lot better than carrying lamps. The light itself came on in 1955, the mains electricity, the hydro-electric, came across in 1955, from the point of Rhunahaorine, in Kintyre, to the point over there, and then was put into all the houses, but what happened at the time it was put in, people had no experience of it, so they were only putting in one light, one socket in a room, which today we find hard to believe.

But that was in 1955 that was switched on, so that was a very big thing because then we could go to electric motors, electric pumps for water. Now it comes from the main at the mill dam. All farms have mains water and electricity but Achamore House still has its own water supply from a spring in the woods. Most places have their own septic tanks. It was Horlicks put in the sanitation into the houses and that wasn't so terribly long ago.

I went to the army which was in 1954, I did my two years National Service as many others had to do, got demobbed in July of 1956. My older brother was getting married and Seumas was going to the Air Force.

So the shop people, who Seumas was working for then, asked me if I would take employment with them, when Seumas left. Which I did. That was for 5 pounds per week plus a drop of petrol, a set of waders, an oilskin coat and a sou'wester, which in the course of time you'll find out the reason why.

That was 1954, so I started work in the shop then. There was no such thing as roll-on roll-off. We'd the mail steamer, as we called it, and the Islay steamer came from West Loch Tarbert on a Tuesday afternoon, called at Gigha pier, and went on to Islay, Port Ellen. Wednesday morning it came on the return trip and came to Gigha pier, Port Ellen to Gigha pier, and Gigha Pier to West Loch Tarbert. It discharged what it had there, reloaded again, and then sailed out, via Gigha north end; Craighouse, Jura; Port Askaig on Islay; Colonsay. Came back in from Colonsay and lay at Port Askaig overnight. So that on the Thursday morning, it did the cross in reverse.

The part now where the wellingtons and the oilskin coat came in was because at Gigha north end, there was no pier. It was a small, well, what was supposed to be a fairly large, and well-built sixteen-foot clinker-built boat. By the time I was there it was an outboard motor, no reverse gear, no clutch, no nothing. Your timing had to be absolutely correct to get in alongside the boat, it was only for mails but I can assure you it was many more than mails came and went – many a calf travelled that way. Rabbits, eggs, potatoes, and things like that that were exported from Gigha at the time which are now all imported.

Now we were speaking about the shipping coming from West Loch Tarbert. What I did forget was, prior to the roll-on roll-off ferry, there was also a small launch. In fact, there were two of them. Ian McKechnie had one of them, one belonged to the council. The name of that vessel was the *Shuna*. The other was Ian's own, he had her built himself, he had her built up in Crinan, and she was the *Cara Lass*. They were very similar in build, they were fairly open launches. I think it was twenty-horsepower Kelvin diesels. This is not so long ago, 1970–75. The result of all that was that it was bad enough with passengers who were able to walk aboard. On a bad day, you were soaking wet before you reached Tayinloan. The crossing in these boats took about twenty-five to thirty minutes depending on the weather.

The biggest problem was with a patient or somebody who was taken ill at night, that had to be travelled out on a stretcher, you had to physically carry that stretcher down the catwalk. After getting there, you'd to carry them down and because of the narrowness of the catwalk, two men was all you could do, so if you'd a heavy guy, it was usually myself that was put at the front, because at that time I was reasonably strong, and you carried the patient down like that to the ferry. Now you can see this small boat bobbing about beside the catwalk. You can imagine it dark. But the big problem was when you were lowering that stretcher into the boat, there was solid shelter on the bow of the boat, which was only about three feet from the stern one, with the result you had to lower the head first, right down into bottom of boat, which must have been very worrying for them. I know it was worrying for me when you would be doing it but it must have been even more worrying for them wondering if they would be let go, slide off, or what would happen. No disasters that I can remember. We always got them safely across. But many a dark, stormy night we had to go across. Many a soaking we would get, but we're still here to tell the tale.

Sometimes you had to go across on sad occasions to get coffins for people that were deceased. Nowadays it's all done by undertakers, but when I was younger it was part of the job of the Post Office.

CC: Was there more than one graveyard?

WM: To my knowledge there was. And when I was young, in the new part of the graveyard, there was only three graves occupied. Now there is hardly a space left. When my brother was doing undertaking, you had to lay the body out yourself. We had to coffin our own mother. It was just one of those things that had to be done. People on the mainland, you take all this for granted. But it is much simpler now with the roll-on roll-off. Now we have an ambulance to use on the island, where before it would be a pony and trap. I can remember when they used the horse and cart for the funeral – a grand-uncle of mine that died. It was the first tractor funeral on Gigha, because the snow and frost was so bad, in January '57, and there was a hell of a frost and snow, and the tractor was used as a hearse because it was too cold.

When you were working at the shop, at that time, it wasn't always what it is today, pre-packed. It all came in bulk, it was brought up in bulk from the pier, unloaded by sling onto the pier, manhandled into the van, taken up to the shop, and unloaded there, into the shop. The feeding stuff for the cattle was put . . . there was a small store at the end, which has now been added onto the shop, broken through into it. On the top of having to do all this, you'd the cargo boat came once a week, with fertilisers for the farms, cattle cake, various grocer-ies, sundries of all descriptions, empty lobster boxes that were coming for the fishermen that were sending their lobsters to Billingsgate at the time, all sorts of things like that.

You had to be up at four o'clock in the morning, three o'clock in the morning, it didn't matter when. You'd to work when work was there and you didn't look at time, because you couldn't. And that was all inclusive for 5 pounds. So I worked in the shop when my brother was away, about three years or something like that and when he came back, they kept me on. By then they were getting older themselves and were glad of the hand. You must remember at that time we'd to do all our own maintenance. It wasn't convenient to send your vehicle to the mainland as it is now and apart from that nobody had any money to do these things.

So when I left the shop, I was in various jobs. I worked with a cousin at fencing, ditching, draining, storm-dyking, digging and building septic tanks, anything that turned a pound. That was what you had to do, and again that was what you call piece work, so much per job. If you didn't work you didn't make money.

When tractors started coming in, I went in with Neil Bannatyne and we were servicing them, changing oils, taking them to bits, there was nothing too big or too wee, and it was nothing to be working till midnight, maybe three or four in the morning to keep farmers of the time functioning.

People had electricity in and they discovered that they needed many more sockets, so Neil had qualified as an engineer on a correspondence course, and I was more than willing at the time to learn, and between us we were installing electricity, extending electricity supplies, putting in wall sockets, extra lights and in old houses it was no easy task because you had to channel down through stone or brick or whatever.

So I went from there and I was back at farming and this and that and time went on and the chance came available to go on a fishing boat. My second cousin Angus's son was skipper of it at the time. He'd only left school but he'd started lobster-fishing with it. So I went for a time with Archie at the lobster-fishing and also line-fishing for dogs, which I did with my uncle.

About that same time a boat by the name of the *Striker* appeared, round the Mull of Kinytre and believe you me, she was very well-named because where the rocks weren't, the *Striker* crew ably found them. And then we all knew where they were. But as luck would have it, the six-cylinder Perkins packed up, so they were tied up by the quay, they could do nothing but scratch the little hair that was on their chins for the lack of money to buy razor blades and things like that. As a bit of luck would have it, with a bit of practice over the years we had achieved a certain amount of mechanical skill.

There was an old lorry lying up the north end with a similar engine, the only thing being it was air-cooled and *Striker* was sea-water cooled. With the help of a case of beer, and some whisky, we got the cylinder head off the lorry and fitted it to the *Striker*. They looked at us in amazement and said, 'Do you think it'll start?'

'Of course it'll bloody start. What do you think we put it there for?'

Well, with a bit of technology and a bit of luck we got the boat in order and we've remained friends ever since.

From there, what did I do next? I was working on the estate for a good number of years as handyman. There again we found some skills were put to good use, and I was on a sure wage at the end of the week. We built silage pits, we built big sheds, we renovated cottages and did a hell of a lot of things that are now needing done again. And people look at me today and say, 'What the hell did you ever do?' when you tell them what they can do or what they shouldn't do. Little do they know how much we had to do, how much we did do, for a very little money and, a hell of a lot of the time, got nothing, for the sake of doing it and seeing the end result, and the movement forward.

So that covered a number of years on the estate, until I got an eye injury. And I was five years blind in the right eye, but with a bit of luck, and somebody else's misfortune, I got a corneal graft which restored enough, but not full, sight – enough that I can see. But that finished me with the estate.

So Archie McAlister's mother had a stroke, and his father, who was nineteen years older than I, decided to come ashore and look after the mother, and I told Archie it was time he was looking for a permanent man. And he turned to me and said, 'What about yourself becoming permanent? We'll try it for a wee while.'

The 'wee while' that I stayed with him was about five or six years. He changed from the *Vestra*, which was when I joined him, clams only, and we went from that to prawns and he sold her and he bought a boat called the *Mhairi d'Or*. We were clamming and again netting fish of all description out the west side of the island. But then I decided that I had had enough of the heavy work and I said to Archie that he should look for somebody else, because it was getting a bit too much for me and I was thinking of getting a small boat to start potting with on my own.

So that was fine, I bought a small boat, sixteen foot six, and I had acquired some creels – Archie and his father gave me some, and I was getting set up to go when a friend came to the pier and said MacBrayne had been phoning and I was asked if I wanted a part-time job. So I became relief man on the small roll-on roll-off ferry. He said it would only be a couple of days a week which would have suited with my lobster-fishing. I could have four days fishing and two working on the boat. Well, I went on to be relief man, but I hardly got a day off for a month. And I did between five and six years on the ferry as a full-time crew man. That was the only job I had ever applied for in my life. After the sixth year, I had to have a lung removed and was never fit to go back to the job again. I'm five years retired, and now I'm doing more than ever . . . and trying to make history with a book!

There was one story about an uncle of my own that was working on a farm on the mainland and the particular place, as in most cases then, you had nothing to eat much but salt herring and potatoes, coming out your ears. So this day the farmer's wife said to the maid, 'How are they getting on with the herring? Go and see if they're satisfied.' So she asked how was dinner. Oh, he quoted a chapter of the Bible. So the maid ran back through to the farmer's wife, and said 'He quoted me this chapter of the Bible.'

'You'd better have a look,' the wife said, so they found the Bible and opened it and the verse went, 'Jesus Christ, the same today, tomorrow and for ever after!'

CC: Tell me, was there any spinning done on the island?

WM: There would have been spinning and weaving, there are still a few spinning wheels, there was quite a bit of spinning over at the mill, I remember the lady there she did it. The mill now, they took the corn over to Ardailly and it was ground to meal for porridge. I don't know how they worked it, paid for it, but it was one of the biggest wheels around the area and it was taken in by sea and built up there – people may wonder at the size of it, but it was taken in by sea, it's only about fifty yards from the shore and you can get close. Each farmer had to put a load of gravel onto the mill road as well.

In these days, there was a lot more helping each other. The fishermen would come and give a hand to gather the potatoes. When they started lobster-fishing here, they were only working about forty-eight creels each so they could manage that in the forenoon, and in the afternoon they would dig potatoes, or do whatever else they could do. There was a shop down on the shore, just at Gigalum, where the Irish potato merchants came, and my uncle could remember buying sugar there.

Cattle when they were going to the market, they would all be going on the steamer, going to Tarbert, you had to load them onto the boat. If it was a bull, you had to travel with it on the boat. Also a horse you would have to go with it, you got free, though you paid for the horse or the bull, but you got free.

If a vehicle came on the boat, it was lifted by a derrick onto the pier with nets and spreaders and cushions, they lifted it onto the pier, that was how the vehicles came, and it was a heavy load.

They used to put horses onto the island of Gigalum, I remember my mother telling me about it, Angus McGougan was his name. He used to ferry horses over to Gigalum, for summer grazing, and when he needed one, he would go and shout the horse's name that he wanted and it would come to the water and swim back. He was the last person, he retired to

Cara and he used to put stirks to Cara. One time he had one tied to the inside of the boat and the beast jumped over and almost capsized the boat.

It was all done by hand. To clip sheep was all done by hand. You used to cut the cattle tails, there was a clipper for it. When you started dehorning at first, it was with caustic soda but you had to be very careful not to put too much on. You had lambs to castrate and cut their tails. When we knocked down the old village, that was all done by hand and loaded on a tractor, where the old gardens are. The smithy was there as well. These houses that we're in now were only finished in the seventies.

Gigalum belonged to Gigha, when Horlick died, a grandson of his and his wife kept Gigalum, and the grandson built a house and he ferried all the stuff across in a rubber dinghy. And the house is in the shape of a fifty-pence piece, but on each consecutive straight side there's a room and where there's not a room there's a window, four rooms and four big windows. The centre-piece is a big stove. You can sit round this and have a fantastic view. I was at the housewarming there. How I got home, I don't know!

Cara never belonged to Gigha, but it belonged and still does, to the Largie estate. It's a chap Teggin that has the house. Cara supposedly had a population of about sixteen. The man that had Cara in my mother's time he would come across once a fortnight for his provisions and on his way back to Cara, he would have a wee drink in him and he would sing 'To Australia We Will Go', in the boat! Rumour has it about the wee brownie, the wee brown man, you always doff your hat to the brownie when you go ashore. Oh, you've got to or else 'dire ill fortune soon began to visit the astounded man!'

Down at the south end you've got the Mull of Cara on the sou'-east corner of it, you've got the brownie's chair where you can sit and wish a wish that never comes true. Malcolm Macdonald that had Leim had the lease of it from Macdonald of Largie. It was off Cara my grandfather was drowned, my grandfather on the Graham side, and his body was found six weeks later on Rathlin. He was hoisting sail just off Cara and a squall come over the hill and capsized the boat. That must be coming close to about hundred years ago because his youngest son wasn't born then. He was born a few months later.

CC: Were there any fishing superstitions?

WM: You couldn't say the word salmon. Salmon was a very, very bad word to say on a boat. You could say the red fish or the red fellow. In fact they wouldn't take salmon as a fish aboard a boat, maybe unless it was secured in a tin.

You couldn't mention rat, it was a long tail. The same with the word rabbit, it was always bob-tail. I know one yet who doesn't mention rat. And a minister – you'd never see a bloody fish again! And if you met a fisherman on his way to the shore you had to wait till he spoke first. I knew an old man used to fish from the west side. There was a family, and they had a daughter, a nice wee ginger-haired girl. And the old man was meeting her on the road and because he was sure she was bringing despair and destruction, he got someone to write to the girl's mother would it not be possible to alter her time going to school.

Down at New Quay, my uncles were fishermen, cousins and so on. There was two old chaps, this night they set off and jumped aboard their dinghy, and they were only out about fifty yards and this almighty cursing and swearing started, and they had forgotten the rods, but no way could they come back for the rods and go out again, but my uncle by the tone of their voice could hear what had happened, so he ran down the hill, picked up the rods, launched another boat and took them out, and off they went but had that not happened, they would have come back in and not gone out again that night. You used to carry a horseshoe in the stern of the boat, open side up, so that it carried all the luck. I know one person who wouldn't go to sea with mince aboard!

Even when the engines started, in the launches and skiffs, they wouldn't lift the creels with them. What happened was there was always two on the boat, it was about forty-eight creels a man, the engine was stopped and one of them took the oars, and it was no mean feat, you would see them with their arms crossed. The boat, she was built for rowing, she narrowed in towards the bow, for easier cutting through the water. You had to have the sweeps crossed and just a wee pull and there was so much spring in the oars, a long slow stroke, different entirely to the oars now, a sweep oar, a long slow sweep and if you put your weight on, they would bend. It was fantastic to see these old men, you would hardly think they were putting any effort in and yet the boat would be cutting through the water and that was the way it was.

Notes

1 The Road to Gallochoile

1. Vie Tulloch, *The Isle of Gigha, Wild Flowers, Bird and Mammals*.

2 Sailing to an Island

1. Gee-a, with a hard 'g'.
2. Freddy Gillies, *Life on God's Island*, p. 19.
3. Kathleen Philip gives an excellent summary of the history of the estate in her *The Story of Gigha: The Flourishing Island*, self-published in 1979 and quoted here. Other material referred to is to be found in the *Origines Parochiales Scotiae*, published by the Bannatyne Club, 1851, in the parish records and in the old and new statistical accounts of the island, 1793 and 1845, written by the Revd William Fraser and the Revd James Curdie respectively.
4. *A Description of the Western Isles of Scotland circa 1695*.
5. Kintyre Antiquarian Society, *The Place Names of the Parish of Gigha and Cara and Willie McSporran, MBE.*
6. Curdie, *New Statistical Account of Argyleshire, the Parish of Gigha and Cara*.
7. Philip, *Gigha*, p. 80.

8. Estate papers.
9. See Chapter 14.
10. Yearling heifers, or bullocks.
11. Philip, *Gigha*.
12. R.S.G. Anderson, *The Antiquities of Gigha*, p. 35.
13. Neil Munro, *Para Handy and Other Tales*.

3 The Lost Language of Stones

1. Stuart Piggott, *Scotland Before History*, p. 23ff.
2. Anderson, *The Antiquities of Gigha*, p. 61.
3. Ibid., p. 25.
4. Alternatively, 'I am a nun from the Island of the Boar.'
5. Anderson, *The Antiquities of Gigha*, p. 38.
6. Sheet 426.
7. See Chapter 16.
8. Thomas Pennant, *A Tour in Scotland and a Voyage to the Hebrides*.
9. David MacRitchie, *Fians, Fairies and Picts*.
10. Betty McNeill of Keil, sister of Malcolm McNeill, head gardener at Achamore, walked the island for many years and made many observations as an amateur archaeologist and historian. She is mentioned extensively in Kathleen Philip's account, and was one of her main informants.
11. The author collected this same superstition from many Ayrshire fishermen, see *Fisherfolk of Carrick*, p. 44. John Martin repeated it to me as being common throughout the Western Isles.
12. Anderson, *The Antiquities of Gigha*, p. 132.
13. Anderson, *The Antiquities of Gigha*, p. 133.
14. Angus Martin, *Kintyre Country Life*, p. 34.
15. Piggott, *Scotland Before History*.

16. Anderson, *The Antiquities of Gigha*, p. 133.
17. *Exploring Historic Kintyre*, a pamphlet published in 1992 by the West Highlands and Islands of Argyll Tourist Board talks of the *Bodach* and the *Cailleach* 'gazing out across the tumbling terraces of old Cantereach and beautiful Ardlamey Bay.'
18. There is a great deal of contemporary written material about the *Sheela na Gig*, some more speculative than others, but one of the most interesting accounts is to be found at www.bandia.net, in an analysis called 'Sila na Geig – Sheela na Gig and Sacred Space' by Kathryn Price Theatana.

4 The People of the Horse

1. Piggott, *Scotland Before History*, p. 64.
2. Edmund Spenser, *A View of the Present State of Ireland*, 1596.
3. See Ronald Williams, *The Lords of the Isles*, for an excellent overview of the early Kingdom of the Scots.
4. Anderson, *The Antiquities of Gigha*, p. 122ff for a full account of this fort and others.
5. Anderson, *The Antiquities of Gigha*, p. 122.
6. Anderson, *The Antiquities of Gigha*, p. 123.
7. J.F. Campbell, *Popular Tales of the West Highlands, Orally Collected*, Volume 3.
8. Ibid., p. 51.
9. Anderson, *The Antiquities of Gigha*, p. 123.

5 The Well of the Winds

1. See T.W. Rolleston, *Celtic Myths and Legend.*

2. F. Marian McNeill, *The Silver Bough*, p. 62ff.
3. Pennant, *A Tour in Scotland.*
4. William Fraser, *Old Statistical Account of Scotland, Parish of Gigha and Cara.*
5. Anderson, *The Antiquities of Gigha*, p. 78.
6. Anderson, *The Antiquities of Gigha*, p. 60ff.
7. Adomnan, *Life of St Columba.* Translated by W. Reeves.
8. This early Welsh legend is to be found in many versions, including Rolleston's *Celtic Myths and Legends*, and in various orally collected stories.

6 Leim

1. Fraser, *Statistical Account of Scotland.*
2. Piggott, *Scotland Before History*, p. 67.
3. Anderson, *The Antiquities of Gigha*, p. 131ff.
4. Anderson, *The Antiquities of Gigha*, p. 32.
5. In *Grettir's Saga* the hero battles with the ghost of Glam, while in *Laxdaela Saga*, the restless ghost of an unpleasant individual called 'Killer Hrapp' is reported as having murdered most of his servants and plagued his neighbours, after his death.
6. Henry Foster McClintock, *Old Irish and Highland Dress*, 1943.
7. For more information about the ancient art of dyeing in Ireland, visit www.reconstructinghistory.com/irish/saffron.html.

7 The Magical Galbraiths

1. Anderson, *The Antiquities of Gigha*, p. 95ff.
2. Rolleston, *Celtic Myths and Legends.*

3. Ian Finlay, *Columba*, p. 155ff.
4. Skene, Introduction to *The Book of the Dean of Lismore.*
5. Spenser, *Present State of Ireland.*
6. An excellent local history resource, edited by Angus Martin and still available online at www.kintyremag.co.uk.
7. See Appendix 1 for a translation of this extraordinary poem.
8. A.B. Lord, *The Singer of Tales.*
9. There is a carving of an ancient clarsach thought to date from this period, on a stone at Knapdale on the Kintyre mainland.
10. Keith Sanger, 'The McShannons of Kintyre, Harpers to Tacksmen', www.kintyremag.co.uk, 1998.
11. See Appendix 2 for nineteenth-century population details.
12. Margaret Storrie, '"They Go from Home" – Nineteenth-century Islanders of Gigha, Scotland', *Scottish Economic and Social History* Vol. 16, 1996.
13. There are records at New Lanark of the Highlands and Islands being the main recruiting ground for Dale's model mill and industrial community, as early as 1785. Highlanders annually visited the lowlands in search of seasonal work, and were recruited to the new factories. For more information see *Historic New Lanark* by Ian Donnachie and George Hewitt.

8 Kilchattan

1. This is the only reference I have found to these 'caverns' and I am not sure what Martin meant by them.
2. Lloyd and Jenny Laing, *The Picts and the Scots*, p. 57ff.
3. Anderson, *The Antiquities of Gigha*, p. 42.

4. Captain T.P. White, *Archaeological Sketches in Scotland*, Chapter III Knapdale and Kintyre.
5. Anderson, *The Antiquities of Gigha*, p. 67ff.
6. A.L. Brown, 'The Cistercian Abbey of Saddell, Kintyre', reprinted at www.kintyremag.co.uk.
7. www.kintyremag.co.uk has published several interesting articles about Saddell, its stonecarvings, and related subjects, including 'A Cross Head from Saddell' by D. Rixon, 'Saddell Abbey' by Frances Hood and 'Campbeltown Cross' by A.I.B. Stewart as well as Professor Brown's article. Andrew McKerral also wrote 'A Chronology of the Abbey and Castle of Kintyre' published in the *Proceedings of the Society of Antiquarians of Scotland*, 86 (1951–2). Though beyond the scope of this book, interested readers should consult the Kintyre Antiquarian and Natural History Society for more information.

9 The Norseman's Scales

1. W.F. Skene, *The Highlanders of Scotland*, Chapter II.
2. John Martin repeated this story to me, saying that those who discovered it were 'looking for somewhere to store their potatoes'.
3. The scales can be seen at the Hunterian Museum, Glasgow University.
4. Kintyre Antiquarian Society, *The Place Names of the Parish of Gigha and Cara*.
5. See Ronald Williams, *The Lords of the Isles*, Chapter 11 for an extensive account of Somerled.
6. A full account of Haakon's campaign is to be found in Ronald Williams' *The Lords of the Isles*, as well as in *Haakon Haakonson's Saga*, translated by G.W. Dasent in

1894. The Vikingar Centre in Largs gives a useful overview of the period and the events that led up to the Battle of Largs.

10 The Lords of the Isle

1. I have pieced together the enormously complicated history of the McNeills and their relationship with their neighbours from various sources, including Kathleen Philip, R.S.G. Anderson and Ronald Williams with some reference to original documents, as well as oral traditions on the island.
2. Anderson, *The Antiquities of Gigha*, p. 114ff .
3. For more information on Cara, see Freddy Gillies, *Life on God's Island*, p. 65ff.

11 The Kirk and the People

1. Information about the early history of the Kirk on Gigha was pieced together from primary sources such as the Minutes of Synod of Argyll, 1639– 61, from the Kirk Session Records of 1791 onwards, from the statistical accounts of two ministers (see bibliography), from occasional references in Anderson's *Antiquities* as well as Kathleen Philip's later account.
2. Dictionary of the Scots Language (www.dsl.ac.uk). A unit corresponding to the number of grazing animals, usually cows or sheep, which a certain area of pasture can support.
3. See Appendix 2 for nineteenth-century population returns for Gigha and Cara.
4. Philip, *Gigha*, p. 64.

5. William Jardine Dobie, 'The Witch of Gigha', *Scottish Law Review*, 1939; reprinted in the *Kintyre Magazine*, no. 10, Oct 1997, p. 4.
6. Philip, *Gigha*, p. 66.
7. Sydney Smith, *Donald MacFarlane of Gigha and Cara*, p. 19.
8. Ibid., p. 31.
9. Ibid., p. 82.
10. Ibid., p. 84.
11. Ibid., p. 86.
12. Ibid., p. 100.
13. Ibid., p. 108.
14. Ibid., p. 109.
15. Ibid., p. 109.
16. Ibid., p. 132.
17. Kenneth MacLeod, 'The Road to the Isles'. See Appendix 3 for full version of this song.

12 Farmers and Fishermen

1. Pennant, *A Tour in Scotland.*
2. A. Martin, *Kintyre Country Life*, p. 98ff.
3. F. Marian McNeill, *The Scots Cellar*, p. 50.
4. Pennant, *A Tour in Scotland.*
5. I.F. Grant, *Highland Folk Ways*, p. 221.
6. A. Martin, *Kintyre Country Life*, p. 165.
7. Philip, *Gigha*, p. 49.
8. Andrew McKerral, *Kintyre in the Seventeenth Century*, p. 148f.
9. See the Gigha website (www.gigha.org) for a full account of the Kilchattan inscriptions as deciphered by Rona Allan.

13 Achamore

1. Williams, *The Lords of the Isles*, p. 138.
2. Simon Macdonald Lockhart, *Seven Centuries, A History of the Lockharts of Lee and Carnwath.*
3. Anderson, *The Antiquities of Gigha*, p. 13.
4. Edwin Chadwick, Report ... from the Poor Law Commissioners on an Inquiry into the Sanitary Conditions of the Labouring Population of Great Britain, London, 1842.
5. See www.gigha.org for more information about the history of the gardens.
6. The Isle of Gigha, sales brochure, F.P.D. Savills, 2001.
7. Tulloch, *The Isle of Gigha.*
8. Alexander Carmichael, *Carmina Gadelica.*

14 The Keeper of the Purse

1. Robert Graham, *Antiquities of Iona.*
2. See Appendix 4. I recorded Willie McSporran's memories over several sessions – 24 and 25 April 2003 and 4 July 2003. He spoke eloquently about his childhood on Gigha and his working life, as well as telling stories of island life, and confirming various island place names for me. I have quoted extensively from these sessions here.
3. A popular BBC radio serial based around a working-class Glasgow family, first broadcast in 1939.
4. Munro, *Para Handy.*
5. See Catherine Czerkawska, *Fisherfolk of Carrick*, Chapter 13 for more on superstitions among fisherfolk.

15 Faith, Hope, Charity . . . and Harmony

1. 'Gigha – Buying Our Island', Saltire Films for BBC 2, January 2003.
2. See www.andywightman.com.
3. 'Gigha – Buying Our Island', BBC2, January 2003.
4. Information from Savills brochure for the sale of the island, 2001.
5. *The Scotsman*, 5 January 2003.
6. *Walk Gigha Path Network*, published on the Isle of Gigha in 2005.
7. See www.gigha.org for more information about the Gigha windmills and the business model.

Appendix 1

1. Inner husks of oats.
2. Raw leather shoes, as worn in the Highlands.

Select Bibliography

Adomnan, St, *Life of St Columba*, ed. and trans. W. Reeves, Edinburgh, 1874. (Also translated by A.O. and M.O. Anderson, London, 1961.)

Anderson, Revd R.S.G., *The Antiquities of Gigha*, Newton Stewart, 1939.

Ashe G. (ed.), *The Quest for Arthur's Britain*, London, 1971.

Campbell, J.F., *Popular Tales of the West Highlands, Orally Collected*, Edinburgh, 1860.

Carmichael, Alexander, *Carmina Gadelica*, Edinburgh, 1994.

Chadwick, N., *The Celts*, Harmondsworth, 1970.

Curdie, James, *New Statistical Account of Argyleshire, the Parish of Gigha and Cara*, Edinburgh, 1845.

Czerkawska, C.L., *Fisherfolk of Carrick*, Glasgow, 1975.

Donnachie, Ian and Hewitt, George, *Historic New Lanark*, Edinburgh, 1993.

Finlay, Ian, *Columba*, London, 1979.

Fraser, William, *Old Statistical Account of Scotland, Parish of Gigha and Cara*, Edinburgh, 1793.

Ganz, J. (trans.), *The Mabinogion*, Harmondsworth, 1976.

Gillies, Freddy, *Life on God's Island*, Ellon, 1999.

Graham, R., *Antiquities of Iona*, London, 1850.

Grant, I.F., *Highland Folk Ways*, Edinburgh, 1961.

——, *The Lordship of the Isles*, Edinburgh, 1935.

Hjaltalin, J. and Goudie, G., *The Orkneyinga Saga* (1873), reprinted Edinburgh, 1973.

Jackson K., *The Gododdin: The Oldest Scottish Poem*, Edinburgh, 1969.

——, *The International Popular Tale and Early Welsh Tradition*, Cardiff, 1961.

Johnson and Boswell, *A Journey to the Western Isles of Scotland / The Journal of a Tour to the Hebrides*, Oxford, 1970.

Kintyre Antiquarian Society, *The Place Names of the Parish of Gigha and Cara*, Campbeltown, 1945.

Laing, L. and J., *The Picts and the Scots*, Stroud, 1997.

Lord, A.B., *The Singer of Tales*, Cambridge, Massachusetts, 1960.

Macdonald Lockhart, Simon, *Seven Centuries, A History of the Lockharts of Lee and Carnwath*, published by the author, Carnwath, 1977.

MacRitchie, David, *Fians Fairies and Picts*, London, 1893.

McKerral, Andrew, *Kintyre in the Seventeenth Century*, Edinburgh, 1948.

MacLauchlan T. (trans.), *The Book of the Dean of Lismore, a Selection of Ancient Gaelic Poetry*, Edinburgh, 1862.

MacLeod, Kenneth, *The Road to the Isles*, Edinburgh, 1927.

McClintock, Henry Foster, *Old Irish and Highland Dress*, Dundalk, 1943.

——, *The Scots Cellar*, Edinburgh, 1973.

McNeill, F. Marian, *The Silver Bough*, Edinburgh, 1989.

Martin, Angus, *Kintyre Country Life*, Edinburgh, 2005.

——, *The Ring Net Fishermen*, Edinburgh, 1981.

Martin, Martin, *A Description of the Western Isles of Scotland circa 1695*, reprinted Edinburgh, 1994.

Munro, Neil, *Para Handy and Other Tales*, Edinburgh, 1937.

Palsson, H. and Edwards P., *The Orkneyinga Saga*, Harmondsworth, 1981.

Pennant, Thomas, *A Tour in Scotland and a Voyage to the Hebrides*, London, 1772.

Pennick, Nigel, *Celtic Sacred Landscapes*, London, 2000.

Philip, Kathleen, *The Story of Gigha: The Flourishing Island*, published by the author, 1979.

Piggott, Stuart, *Scotland Before History*, Edinburgh, 1996.

Rolleston, T.W., *Celtic Myths and Legends*, London, 1994.

Scottish History Society, *Minutes of Synod of Argyll, 1639–1661*, Edinburgh, 1943–4.

Simpson, W. Douglas, *The Ancient Stones of Scotland*, London, 1973.

Skene, William F., *The Highlanders of Scotland*, Stirling, 1902.

——, Introduction to *The Book of the Dean of Lismore, a Selection of Ancient Gaelic Poetry*, Edinburgh, 1862.

Smith, Sydney *Donald MacFarlane of Gigha and Cara*, London, 1925.

Spenser, Edmund, *A View of the Present State of Ireland*, 1596, Corvallis, Oregon, 1997.

Tabraham, C. and Grove, D., *Fortress Scotland and the Jacobites*, London and Edinburgh, 1995.

Tulloch, Vie, *The Isle of Gigha, Wild Flowers, Birds and Mammals*, Gigha, 1988.

Watson, W.J., *The History of the Celtic Placenames of Scotland* (1926), Edinburgh, 1993.

White, T.P., *Archaeological Sketches in Scotland*, Edinburgh, 1873.

Williams, Ronald, *The Lords of the Isles*, Colonsay, 2000.

Index

Index Note: Names beginning in 'Mc' are sorted as if spelt 'Mac'. In a few cases '*fl.*' (flourished) or 'd.' (died) are used to distinguish persons of the same name. *Passim* after a page range shows scattered references to the subject rather than a continuous discussion.